SOFTLY ON THIS EARTH

BY
ETHAN SMITH

Thank you and best wishes
-Ethan ☺

© Copyright 2004 Ethan Smith.
All rights reserved. No part of this publication may be reproduced, stored in a retrieval system, or transmitted, in any form or by any means, electronic, mechanical, photocopying, recording, or otherwise, without the written prior permission of the author.

Note for Librarians: a cataloguing record for this book that includes Dewey Decimal Classification and US Library of Congress numbers is available from the Library and Archives of Canada. The complete cataloguing record can be obtained from their online database at:
www.collectionscanada.ca/amicus/index-e.html
ISBN 1-4120-4127-9
Printed in Victoria, BC, Canada

TRAFFORD

Offices in Canada, USA, Ireland, UK and Spain

This book was published *on-demand* in cooperation with Trafford Publishing. On-demand publishing is a unique process and service of making a book available for retail sale to the public taking advantage of on-demand manufacturing and Internet marketing. On-demand publishing includes promotions, retail sales, manufacturing, order fulfilment, accounting and collecting royalties on behalf of the author.

Book sales for North America and international:
Trafford Publishing, 6E–2333 Government St.,
Victoria, BC v8t 4p4 CANADA
phone 250 383 6864 (toll-free 1 888 232 4444)
fax 250 383 6804; email to orders@trafford.com

Book sales in Europe:
Trafford Publishing (UK) Ltd., Enterprise House, Wistaston Road Business Centre, Wistaston Road, Crewe, Cheshire cw2 7rp UNITED KINGDOM
phone 01270 251 396 (local rate 0845 230 9601)
facsimile 01270 254 983; orders.uk@trafford.com

Order online at:
www.trafford.com/robots/04-1934.html

10 9 8 7 6 5 4 3 2

For my parents:
Joan and Bob Walsh
Michael and Patricia Smith
Donna and Colin Honan

GRATITUDE

An enormous thank you to each of the contributors in Softly On This Earth. Your support and your confidence kept me going while your written words flowed together into this wonderful book. Thank you for the incredibly important work you do. You are healing our planet.

Thank you, Guy Dauncey, for your guidance and support during the early stages of this project. Your experience and enthusiasm were a great help.

Thank you, Julie Johnston, for your phenomenal editing touch. Your words, *Courage isn't feeling no fear – it's feeling the fear and doing it anyway,* brought this book home.

Thank you to the staff of Trafford Publishing. You are making it all possible.

Thank you, Barry and Clare Mathias of Talisman Books. Your support of this project is greatly appreciated.

Most of all, thank you, Tania. You are my beloved partner and my best friend. Your soft footsteps are my inspiration.

Many people helped with the creation of this book. Your ideas, suggestions, support and information were invaluable and I thank you all. Together, we can accomplish just about anything.

SOFTLY ON THIS EARTH
Joining Those Who Are Healing Our Planet
****
TABLE OF CONTENTS

AUTHOR	PAGE
Prelude	2
Lorri Bauston	16
Jessica Campanelli	27
Diana Saakian Bokhari	31
Keith McHenry	37
Elizabeth May	46
Bob Banner	52
Nancy Fresco	63
Caryn Hartglass	70
Teri Barnato	79
Catherine Carrigan	83
Mike Carriere	86
Dr. Marc Bekoff	88
Heidi Howe	108
Robert Bateman	114
Lynn Landes	123
Honey Novick	127
Sinikka Crossland	133
Dave Smith	137
Don Morrill	142
Dr. Kenneth Shapiro	145
Deborah Williams	149
Maggie Macro	157
Lynn Jacobs	162
Vivienne Verdon-Roe	178
Kay & Tom Seliskar	188
Briony Penn	195
K. Lauren de Boer	197
Craig Miller & Paul Moss	205
Nancy Callan	209
Dr. Stephen Linn	214
Soft Footsteps	228

2 Softly On This Earth

PRELUDE

A very long time ago in human years, yet only a heartbeat in the life of a sequoia or, say, a mountain, I stood shivering in a tiny clearing, gazing up at a carpet of blazing stars. An owl's voice had called to me from across the snow's frozen crust and I shuffled sleepily outside; a tiny, naked child embraced by an icy night. It called again and I awoke fully, glancing first down at my bare feet in the snow and then up into the dark silhouette of trees where the owl was perched. Behind me, in the comfort and silence of our house, my family breathed together in deep sleep. A sudden shiver pulsed through me and I peered up into the tree beseechingly, yearning for something from the owl, grasping for something I couldn't quite reach. And then the owl dropped from its perch and sailed out across the snow-lit field before me, vanishing into the blackness of the night, leaving me gifts it would take me years to comprehend. She left me with strength, courage and faith.

Drawing upon those very qualities, the opening pages of Softly On This Earth are now climbing out through my fingertips, emanating from somewhere much deeper inside. In my hands, and now in yours, I have a collection of essays written by extraordinary people. Introducing them and the pieces they have written for this book is both wonderfully humbling and terribly exciting. I've spent a great deal of time fumbling sporadically through life while many of my contributors were already deeply focused on the things they believed in. Sometimes what appears to be a complex burst of spastic motion up close reappears, when seen from a distance, as a beautiful mosaic. At least, I sure hope it does.

I was raised in a remote valley in southern British Columbia. We arrived there in 1971, as mutineers from a hippie commune, in an ancient pick-up truck with a cow, a toolbox and a few changes of clothes. My parents discovered a delightful clearing in the woods at the end of a winding, mountainous, dirt road and excitedly proclaimed it as our new home. I celebrated my fifth birthday right there in that clearing, staring in bewildered awe at the vast greenery of the forest around us.

We became scavengers that first summer; building a house and a barn with lumber we recycled from abandoned mine buildings nearby. While we were building our house and planting a garden to get ourselves started (and I use the term "we" rather loosely since I really wasn't much help), we slept in old canvas tents out in an overgrown fruit orchard. Before long, warmly embraced by Mother Nature, we had created ourselves a small, relatively self-sufficient farm.

I grew up there, secluded from civilization, with no electricity, television, advertisements, fast food, movies, peer pressure, or school for that matter. My sister and I did all of our elementary schooling through correspondence courses. And, while we were very much secluded from civilization, we were overwhelmingly included in everything the natural world had to offer. The forest and our farm were a veritable cornucopia of wildness. Hundreds of species of birds, furry forest creatures of all shapes and sizes, wildflowers, gigantic Douglas fir trees, honeysuckles, thick foliage everywhere, towering forest canopies sheltering entire wild villages of literally thousands of species of life. The sounds and the smells and the tastes of this vast forest world became deeply entrenched in my soul. Until years later, I knew no opposite to this. Nature was my reality.

This life was not entirely idyllic. It was hard work and, as I grew older, I was given more and more of the workload. My mother would read us stories at night, often about pioneering families who were living the same lives as ours, one hundred years earlier. We made everything from scratch, which was something I wouldn't appreciate until many years later. At times of feeling completely overwhelmed, Mother Nature was my solace. I would run lovingly into her embrace, feeling drawn into something so much larger than myself.

Possibly the most extraordinary experience of those developing years for me was raising an orphaned fawn. When I was eleven, Bucky came into my life early in the spring when we discovered him lying by himself beside the road. He lived with us until the autumn, when his instincts guided him to join the rest of the whitetail deer population wandering through the valley. In the time he was with us, Bucky brought so much joy into my life. He had a relentlessly playful character. He would sneak up behind our old black lab, pretending to be grazing on grass every time the dog glanced over at him. Then he would suddenly pounce on the dog, bounding away gleefully while his reluctant canine friend growled ferociously, forbidden by us to harm his attacker.

Bucky absolutely loved the taste of raspberries; a crop we had in abundance on our farm. We frequently had deliciously fresh raspberry jam on our morning pancakes, waffles or toast. Bucky didn't care what it was spread on…he just wanted it. He would gently stroll up to the kitchen table, rest his head affectionately on my lap and then…wham!…my pancakes would be on the floor and slurped clean with astonishing speed. He did it constantly and I could never resist.

He had character, he had feelings, he interacted with us on a level that I've never seen any dog or cat or other pet demonstrate. He taught me, through his incredible zest for life, that all beings are full of light and life and autonomy. All these years later, I still believe I carry around a little bit of Bucky's influence in me. I'll see a situation I absolutely yearn to dive into and play with and I think of him. More often than not, I've followed his example.

Gifted with a great deal of knowledge and experience from the natural world but disturbingly weak social skills, I left home and ventured out into civilization when I was eighteen. I had no idea how to cope with the harshness that much of society's excessive speed thrust at me, but if it became too much, I was well equipped to flee into the woods to survive on huckleberries and bark.

One might think I would have chosen a life that allowed me to spend most of my time out in nature. Say, a biologist or a naturalist or even a hermit. But, no, after all those years of manual labour, I had developed an unquenchable thirst for anything but. I got a taste of what civilization could be and dove in as deeply and completely as I could. There were women out there. And there was beer. Cold, sweet, delicious beer. Even when I was fumbling through social circles that would have otherwise left me completely out of the loop, beer was the great equalizer. I discovered I had much more in common with everyone when we were all drunk. And there were cars and concerts and lights and noises of every possible decibel. It was all so incredible to me…like a moth being drawn irresistibly into the fatal throbbing of a powerful strobe light.

Every morning at 6:30, and again at 6:30 pm, I thanked God that I didn't have to head to the barn in my gumboots and milk the cows. Every time I stumbled drowsily into the bathroom for my midnight pee, I thanked the heavens for indoor plumbing and flushing toilets. Never again, I said to myself, would I trudge up through a foot of fresh powder snow in the darkness of a minus-twenty-degree January night, to sit in the frigid chill of our outhouse, just waiting for a cougar to pounce on me from the blackness, devouring me where I sat so defenseless. No way… it was going to be luxury for me from that point onward.

But an odd thing happened. As the years went by, every time I approached any state of being that suggested luxury, I immediately hurled it away. It was as though I had been hardwired by my upbringing to resist any level of comfort (at least, comfort by generally accepted definitions). Deep inside of me, I felt a constant impulse to experience as much as possible and to be in contact with as many people as possible. I was driven by some kind of primal calling to spread my message far and wide. The only hitch was that I had no idea what message I was supposed to be spreading. So I just made as much noise as possible. I leapt into life, yelling all the way. I leapt from situation to situation, sometimes premeditated but often not. Bucky's playful spirit was alive and well in me as I leapt to and fro, usually plunging ahead with great enthusiasm, although the resultant landings were often quite rough on me. My soul was subjected to continuous growing pains.

Sound like an exaggeration? Well then, I have numbers for you. From the time I left home in 1984, over the next decade and a half, I had twenty-two mailing addresses spread across four Canadian provinces. I packed up and moved twenty-two times over seventeen years. I've worked (in no particular order) as a security guard, a disc jockey, an environmental technician, a gas jockey, a landscaper, a window cleaner, an actor for theatre and film, a test driver, a writer, a financial newsletter bureau chief, a courier, a cross-country ski instructor, a printing press operator, a barista, an editor, a hospital test patient, a bartender, a stable hand, a shuttle driver, a tour company supervisor and a hotel assistant manager. I've never been fired from a job and actually truly loved a lot of these roles…it was just time to leap into something new again. I had spread my message of spastic glee and had to move on. And those are just the activities I've been paid for. Along the way, I've also leapt into all kinds of other adventures because they seemed like a good idea at the time. A whole lot more, in fact, than I'm going to go into here.

    Gradually, in my late twenties, I began to remember my connection to Mother Nature. It was like a whole lot of little shifts of consciousness - gentle reminders that I was part of something so very much larger. A few events really brought that intrinsic connection home to me. The first happened one evening when I hiked up to watch the sun set from the top of a hill above the city of Calgary, my home at the time. I found a large, flat rock to lie on and stretched out on top of it, allowing my head to hang slightly backwards over the boulder's edge. From this spectacular vantage point, with a cool wind drifting across my face, tickling my senses with smells from the high prairie, I was able to see 360 degrees of the horizon. I couldn't remember ever having seen anything like that before. From the stark, blue outline of the jagged Rocky Mountains to the west, around the periphery of rolling foothills to the north, along the flatness of the prairie to the east, across the sunset's golden reflection in the city's glass towers to the south and back into the Rockies again, I could see a complete circle. It was as though my vision had suddenly slipped into focus. I lay there in beautiful bliss, absorbing the evening, while the colours of the horizon shifted through a prism of rainbow hues sliding into darkness. Lying there with the glow of the city below me and the black outline of the Rockies off in the distance, I felt the warmth of Nature's embrace around me. Her arms felt absolutely wonderful.

    Not long after that, I experienced something truly incredible. If my little evening lounging on the boulder had been a gentle reminder that I was part of Nature, this was me getting grabbed and shaken until I really got it. I was out for one of my many long walks through Weaselhead Park in Calgary. Life seemed to be ganging up on me that day. A broken heart. Money problems. Dreams unrealized. You know those days where you think you're the only one who has this crap to deal with? It was one of those days and, well, the circumstances aren't important to the story. The thick foliage and happy melodies of the songbirds were beckoning to me and I strolled farther and farther into the abundance of summer. I breathed deeply, allowing the cool air to fill my lungs with its freshness and send little tingling rivulets of energy dancing all the way out through my fingers and toes. Then a pang of remorse struck me and I asked for Bucky. I had never done that before. But I asked for him. I asked for Nature to send me my deer guide, my totem. My request felt sincere and definite and powerful, like no request I had ever made before. Almost instantly, a small crack in the bushes made me freeze and catch my breath. Out of the undergrowth stepped a mother deer and her two fawns and my heart leapt up into my throat. I felt tears well up in my eyes and I thought I might just explode with joy. "Hello, there," I managed softly and the doe glanced at me, unconcerned, flicking one ear in the way deer do when they're feigning indifference. The two fawns stared at me with great, soft eyes and sniffed the air carefully before crossing the path and following their mother into the bushes on the other side. And then they were gone. And I was very alive.

Another reminder of my connection to Nature happened very early on a bone-chilling January morning in the Rockies. I was headed up to Sunshine Village with a group of skiers, ready to plunge into the powdery aftermath of a snowstorm. In the just-light of a roadside clearing, four wolves appeared. Two were black and two were silver and they stood, attentive and beautiful, watching the noisy vehicular disturbance that was interrupting their morning journey. I made eye contact with a large, black male and his eyes filled me with a sensation that was somewhere well beyond description. This was not my space, the vehicle I was in was not welcome here, and we left them in peace, allowing them to watch the sunrise in the privacy of their winter silence. The wolf's eyes stayed with me all day and I skied with more strength and balance then I ever had. When I got home that evening, the wolf's eyes were still with me and I wrote an article to the Calgary Herald about our experience. The newspaper published my article and I was delighted for a couple reasons. First and foremost, it was my first published article, which filled me with pride and netted me a pair of ski passes. Second, I felt a great sense of satisfaction that I may have inspired others around me to remember that there is beauty and life in the woods beside every road they're on, if only they're aware of it.

I eventually moved to Banff, allowing me to have a mix of abundant wildlife, relatively undisturbed wild places and a thriving social atmosphere in the resort capital of the Canadian Rockies.

My second summer there, I was the musical lead in an outdoor eco-play called Nature Bats Last, run by Precipice Theatre. I portrayed a guitar-wielding naturalist, narrating the story of his childhood and raising awareness about the plight of migratory songbirds. It was ironically perfect, performing this play in and around Banff. Our audiences were people who had come from all over to visit the National Park. In a small town that becomes a shoulder-to-shoulder tourist scramble in the summer, the air thick with exhaust from far too many cars, we did our best to inspire our audience to look around them, to step off the pavement and stroll into the woods a little way, to gaze up into the trees and take the time to listen to a warbler.

I lived in Banff for five years, working for a tour company and spending much of my free time well off the beaten path. Banff is a wonderful example of humans and nature living together. And, as such an example, it is far from perfect. From my management seat where it was my job to get as many people as possible to take our bus tours, I continually questioned my role in this human/nature interaction. I wanted people to come and see the stunning, natural beauty of the Rockies. I wanted them to appreciate how vital it is that we protect our wild places. Then, when they all came and rode our buses, I could smell diesel fumes throughout the valley floor. But, I reasoned, far better for fifty of them to be on one bus than to be in the twenty-five cars they arrived in town with.

Although the Rockies hold a huge amount of energy in their mountainous grace and will likely always feel like a second home to me, I was being called away by a whole other kind of natural beauty. Vancouver Island, with its vast temperate rainforests and its shorelines exploding with waves of life, had been calling to me ever sense I first set foot on a moss-laden path on the West Coast Trail many years earlier. With Tania, whom I'd met and fallen in love with in Banff, I moved to Victoria in 2001. The Island quickly drew us into its incredibly beautiful embrace and we spent our first summer here exploring as many of its wild places as we could find time for.

Vancouver Island is rich with community, as are the many smaller islands along its East shore. This is a part of the world where people from all walks of life seem to merge and develop their own collective way of doing things. Artists, loggers, musicians, fishermen, naturalists and farmers, all living together in a region that thrives on its natural and cultural abundance and diversity.

Things began to click into place for me as I opened my mind and my heart to the newfound communities around me…things I'd been considering for a long time but hadn't acted on. I became more and more aware of the intrinsic connection between our environment, our health and the way we treat one another. And by one another, I mean all life forms on this beautiful planet of ours.

I'm going to back up the story a bit for a moment. A couple years previous to leaving Alberta, I befriended someone who once worked at, and still lived near, one of the largest cattle slaughtering plants in North America. From several kilometres away, I could smell the unbearable reek of this place. Far beyond the smell, though, was the overwhelming sense of sorrow around this huge processing plant. The people I encountered who worked there, the expressions in the wide eyes of the cattle aboard the huge trucks lumbering into the plant, and the stories my friend told me from the inside of this huge business, made me absolutely sick. I won't share any details here. If you want details, I can tell you where to get them. What I will tell you is that cows' eyes don't naturally have wild looks of terror in them. I know this from experience, having raised many of them. Cows, when allowed to graze in an open pasture and coexist peacefully with humans, have big, soft, expressive eyes. They openly show affection to each other and to people…if given the chance.

Let's back up even further. When I was a child, one of our cows, Clover, managed to get a piece of barbed-wire caught up under an eyelid while stretching through a fence to see if the grass was, in fact, greener on the other side. Knowing I was nearby, instead of panicking, Clover stood motionless until I saw her and came to her rescue. After I carefully lifted her eyelid off its painful barb, Clover raised her soft face to mine and began to lick my cheek warmly in appreciation. Now anyone who has had their face licked by a cow knows just how rough and smelly and generally unpleasant that sensation can be, but the gesture of her gentle gratitude was, nonetheless, very memorable.

Thinking back to Clover, it amazes me that I haven't been vegetarian since childhood. And it amazes me that I didn't choose to become one after encountering the processing plant (although I very nearly did). But, let's get back to Vancouver Island. Here it happened for me. One day Tania suggested to me that we become vegan. *Let's respond to the total disregard so many of us show for the other species on this Earth*, she suggested. *Let's respond to that by not using them as a commodity any longer.* I agreed and it felt wonderful to do so.

In choosing to become vegan, I was at first concerned about our health, since I had heard much propaganda about sickly, waif-like vegans wandering this land, staring blankly forward from sunken faces. I read a lot, asked a lot of questions and learned to eat in a vastly more health-conscious way than I ever had. Instead of feeling sickly, I felt healthier and lighter and more peaceful than I ever had. I lost twenty-five pounds, even though I thought I was fit and active enough that I wouldn't have any to lose. Out of curiosity, I asked my doctor to give me blood tests to monitor my iron and other essential nutrient levels. At six months after becoming vegan, and again at eighteen months afterward, the nutrient levels in my blood were excellent and unchanged. I had lost no strength, and was still able to lift weights, hike and bicycle with just as much strength as I ever had before. Today, three years after becoming vegan, I feel better than ever. And all that while consuming absolutely no animal products, or byproducts, whatsoever.

Feeling healthier and better about life than ever before, and having had every myth I'd ever heard about vegetarianism blown out of the water, I began to dig deeper. Who had been propagating those myths? Why had so many people adamantly told me that we need to eat meat to survive? Surely this information must have been coming from reliable sources.

Then one day I watched a TV program where an "expert" was pleading the case for everyone to consume more milk, saying that the current drop in Canadians' consumption of this essential product was of great concern to her. After listening to the whole program with considerable interest, the program's host told the audience that this health professional was employed by a national dairy advocacy group. What I already seriously suspected then made great sense. Suddenly I realized why everyone believes that we need milk and meat in our diets. These gigantic, multi-billion dollar industries had been training and employing PR people and advertisers and spin-doctors of every kind for decades. In no way could the comparatively miniscule budgets of most concerned health professionals possibly keep up with corporate wealth.

I saw a bumper sticker that read *Question the way things have always been done*. This, to me, was one of the most profoundly wise and simple messages I had ever seen. I realized that this is exactly why we harbour so many of our most stringent beliefs. Because it has always been done that way. And that sweeping generalization goes way beyond my little soapbox rant about vegetarianism. Well-intentioned people everywhere want to believe, and trust, what they're being told. So they watch TV programs and read newspapers and listen to the radio and surf the Internet and they want so badly to believe it all. But what I was quickly learning was just how much corporate money goes into most of what we see and just how much control sponsors have over broadcast information of all kinds.

As far as trusting the way things have always been done, it occurred to me to look at history. When we say always, we tend to be referring to the technical and scientific discoveries of the past hundred years or so. That makes sense…we've been keeping really good records over that period of time. Our history doesn't go back just hundreds of years, though. It goes back millions of years. If we could tap into the records of people all over the planet who lived for many thousands of years without all of our discoveries, we might gain a whole new understanding of ecology and time and be prompted to take a serious look at the way we're treating our planet today. Of course, many wonderful scientists have already been, and still are, exploring those societies. What they're finding out is truly illuminating and it's not something many of our modern corporations necessarily want us to find out. They'd much rather we just keep believing that we actually need all their stuff.

In March of 2002, Tania and I embarked on an extended holiday. We packed our camping gear into the back of our car and headed south into the States. The mission of our trip was simply to see a lot more of, and learn a lot more about, this incredible continent of ours. We visited many parks and wild places and met many diverse and wonderful people. Early on in our journey, the idea for Softly On This Earth was born. We kept encountering, or hearing of, people who were doing extraordinary things to help the people and the natural world around them. It seemed everywhere we went, we learned of people who cared so deeply for life that they'd begun doing something about it. Honestly, I had no idea there were so many brave souls out there. I had, for years, feared that those few who had the courage to speak out in favour of a healthier and more compassionate world would always be viewed as "the lunatic fringe." But now, on this journey of discovery, I was learning just how many compassionate people already exist. They aren't outsiders. They aren't the fringe. They are from all walks of society, all ages, all religions and all ethnicities. They are connected only by their commitment to a more peaceful world and they have been living their highest choices instead of just talking about them.

I want to join them, I told myself. But what could I do? What contribution did I have that could be most helpful to this collective conscience? I took stock. I knew a little bit about all kinds of topics but a lot about almost nothing. If I began running around preaching my opinions to everyone, what was the chance that anyone would really care? Who gets tuned out faster than the person who spews out his opinions without having actually acted upon them? Wallowing in my delusions of insignificance, I began to scribble my thoughts down in my journal and then it struck me. I knew about all these people and I loved to write. And from the deepest part of my heart, I wanted everyone else to learn about the work of these people. I wanted everyone else like me who believed their own actions to be insignificant, to question that belief. I wanted to tell everyone about these people I was meeting and the possibilities that their choices were creating. I wanted to inspire everyone to walk softly on this Earth. And there you have it.

I told Tania about my book idea and we began to keep our eyes open for inspiring people as we traveled. Both of us kept journals and kept writing down details as we went along. We visited information centres and bulletin boards as we arrived into each new community, finding out what activities were going on during our visit and gleaning more and more possible contacts for the book project. All of this discovery went way beyond just the book project, though. We learned so much about the many diverse cultures that exist right here on this continent. And we only scratched the surface. We visited 29 U.S. states and 9 Canadian provinces and we got just the briefest taste of this diversity. And it was great fun. We watched incredible sunrises in Yosemite, the Grand Canyon and the Gulf of Mexico. We went kayaking and hiking and dancing and ate in some amazing vegetarian restaurants. We saw alligators, sharks, jellyfish, whales, tarantulas, pelicans, moose and literally hundreds of other species who share our natural world. And they were all still living in the natural world, no less. We also saw many species, though, that were no longer wild.

About a third of the way up the I-95 freeway along the Atlantic coast, we decided that we'd give up our car once we got home. Interstate 95 is basically an endless, turbo-charged, high-speed auto marathon, where people pass on the shoulder at eighty miles per hour. True story…it happened to us a couple of times…just because we were only five miles per hour over the speed limit. I can still remember the angry glare and middle-finger salute of a semi driver as he rumbled past us, in an urgently frantic rush to get wherever he was going. Interesting, I thought, they only give you half a peace sign on this coast.

Of course, there are many peaceful, wonderful people on the Eastern Seaboard. Many of them drive along the I-95 every day. But somewhere along the road, with frayed nerves, high speed and car exhaust, the sense of peace seems to vanish. And when an accident happens, and they do happen regularly, the freeway becomes a vast, smoggy parking lot. So dense was the smog, we weren't even able to see the city skylines of Philadelphia and New York the day we drove through them. So we decided that, once we got home to Victoria and could get around easily enough by bicycle, foot and public transportation, we would do our part to rid the air of one more pair of drivers. A few months later, we did just that.

When we finally got home, spilling over with great memories of our journey across the States and Canada, I began sifting through all the notes we had collected. From that, I compiled a list of everyone we had encountered or learned of who might make a great contributor for my book. A bit overwhelmed but very happy to have such a wonderful dilemma, I chose a diverse group of people from my list and contacted each of them personally.

The response was absolutely wonderful. The great part of inviting courageous, inspiring people to write their thoughts for this project has been their willingness to work toward this common goal. The challenge wasn't in finding inspiring people interested in a project like this. In fact, many of them told me that this project needed to be created and thanked me for doing so. The challenge was having them find the time to write their contributions. All of the people I chose to participate in this project either run busy non-profit organizations, have speaking and touring schedules, or just have their time spread so thinly that taking the time to create something original for this book was very difficult to get to. So here I was, living off the remnants of my savings while putting together Softly On This Earth. This gave me lots of time to play with while all my contributors kept me nourished with phone calls and emails, promising that they would eventually get something written for me.

I used my time as wisely as I could, spending many hours pouring over library books, surfing the Internet, attending lectures and generally learning as much as I could. As long as I was creating a book on walking softly on this Earth, I thought I had better find out as much as possible about how one could go about doing that. And, with each new inspiring submission sent by one of my contributors, the more I wanted to learn. Tania joined me in this process. It was like the two of us enrolled ourselves in a self-guided university curriculum in Earth 101. And, from the look of things, this is a course we'll be learning from for a long time.

The learning continues every day for us. Whether it involves reading the wealth of thought-provoking books and articles available to us, or sitting in complete serenity beside a tranquil lake, we keep on learning. We humbly try to do our part to help the world around us by being vegan, eating as much organic and locally grown produce as possible, and leaving as soft a footprint as we can.

Each of the contributors to this book is unique. All have been guided by their own motivations for the work they've done. They are all individual souls, sharing something with those around them so that we might have a more compassionate, healthier world to live in. The results of their work, including their contributions to this book, demonstrate that the whole is greater than the sum of its parts.

Softly On This Earth has been simmering inside me for a long time. When I sit above a rocky shelf along the rugged shorelines of the West Coast, a paradise I'm fortunate enough to call home, I watch the waves swell and ebb, abundant with a vast array of ocean life, and the energy behind this book flows from my heart.

When I watch river otters roll and play in the cool evening waters of a serene lake, that same energy flows through me. Their grace, their simplicity, their beauty and the ease with which they move with the currents of life leaves me in awe. I crave that same connection. So much of the time, our human world seems far from anything resembling grace or connection.

You are now holding the result of a graceful process in your hands. I invite you to meet these people through their words and to listen to their thoughts. They have powerful messages for us. Messages of strength and courage and faith.

The people represented in this book are only a tiny fraction of a higher consciousness that is unfolding in our society. For one thing, it only includes those, and only a fraction of them, who live in the United States and Canada. There's a whole world out there and it includes a lot of people who are doing wonderful work with their lives.

So, let's begin now. I'd like to introduce you to some people.

LORRI BAUSTON

Lorri Bauston is Executive Director and Co-Founder of Farm Sanctuary.

Farm Sanctuary is America's largest nonprofit farm animal rescue and protection organization. The group works to end the exploitation of animals used for food production through its farm animal shelters in New York and California, and its investigative campaigns and media exposés of the meat, dairy and egg industries with legal action and legislative initiatives, public awareness and education projects. Farm Sanctuary's shelters welcome thousands of visitors every year. Visitors can stay at the farms' "Barn & Breakfast" cabins, volunteer for a few days or a month-long internship, or attend a variety of conferences and shelter special events.

VEGAN KINSHIP

In 1986, Gene and I decided we wanted to do something to help farm animals, but we didn't know what or how we would do it. So we started visiting factory farms, stockyards, and slaughterhouses to educate ourselves, and that's when we started rescuing animals like Hilda.

We were investigating a stockyard in Pennsylvania when we found her. Gene and I were walking through the auction pens and discovered the stockyard's "dead pile" in the back of one of the buildings. Mounds of dead and decaying animals were thrown onto a cement pad. Cows with ropes tied tightly around their necks. Pigs with large wounds. Goats with twisted legs.

The insistent buzzing of the maggots and nauseating smell wrenched my stomach, as did the lingering questions. How long had they suffered? How many days of agony and terror did they endure before dying alone and in pain? Gene took out the camera and we walked closer to the pile. The camera clicked, and one of the sheep on the pile lifted her head. Gene and I stared at each other, both not wanting to believe what we had just seen. I knelt down next to the animal, and Hilda looked back at me. She was just inches away from a rotting carcass, and flies and maggots were crawling over her body. I held her head in my hands whispering "poor baby, poor baby" to calm her, and to keep myself from screaming. Gene ran to get the van, and within ten minutes we were rushing to the nearest veterinarian. Hilda had collapsed because of the brutal transportation conditions. She was not suffering any other injuries or diseases. We learned that Hilda had been loaded onto a truck with hundreds of other sheep. Despite humid, near 100-degree temperatures, the sheep were severely overcrowded, a standard livestock marketing strategy to get more dollars per load, even when some sheep will die from the stress. Hilda was part of the meat industry's "economic loss" calculations. The meat, poultry, and dairy industries even have a name for animals like Hilda. They call them "downers."

We took Hilda home, and then we knew what we could do to help farm animals. We started a shelter for victims of "food animal" production so that we could care for Hilda and other suffering farm animals, and we started exposing the atrocities of the "food animal" industry. As we continued our investigations, Gene and I learned that Hilda's story was not unique. Every year, thousands of animals used for "food" production are abused and neglected because animal suffering is considered normal animal agricultural practice. Blatant animal cruelties, like severe confinement, overcrowding, and abandonment are deliberately done to increase profits, despite the tremendous cost to animals. We have found day-old chicks discarded in outdoor dumpsters, because they do not grow fast enough to be profitable for meat consumption. We have seen emaciated dairy cows dragged to slaughter with chains when they were too sick or weak to walk, because they can still be sold for human consumption. We have heard turkeys screaming in terror while they were hung upside down fully conscious and bled to death, because poultry are exempt from slaughter stunning requirements.

People often ask us how we cope with seeing so much suffering and death. Whenever I'm asked that question, I find myself thinking about what inspires me and gives me hope, and I think about a pig I dearly love, a pig named Hope.

Hope had been dumped at a livestock market because she had a crippled leg and was no longer "marketable." She was just a baby, barely two months old. I remember how frightened she was, and how she frantically crawled away when we approached her. Hope had never known a kind touch. Humans had only kicked, dragged, and abandoned her. Gene and I spoke gently to her, and wrapped a blanket around her shivering body. She let out one small grunt as we picked her up, and then she nestled into my arms like she had always known me.

For seven years, Hope was a part of our lives. We cared for all her special needs, and she filled our hearts with love. Hope touched many other people too. Over the years, she taught thousands of Farm Sanctuary visitors that farm animals are just as capable of suffering from isolation, fear, and neglect as a dog or cat, or you and I. It is comforting to know that Hope reached so many people, especially now that she is no longer with us. Hope passed away at our shelter, surrounded by those who loved her. After two years, I still find myself glancing in the direction of her favorite corner. I will never forget how she rolled over for belly rubs at the touch of my hand, or her distinct "thank you" grunt when I placed her food bowl in front of her. Most of all though, I will always remember how her life inspired us to continue the fight for farm animal rights.

It's easy to lose hope when you've just been to a slaughterhouse or factory farm and witnessed so much cruelty. I will never forget the first time I went to an egg factory and saw the horror of modern-day egg production. To produce eggs, four to five hens are crammed into a cage about the size of a folded newspaper. The cages are stacked by the thousands in row after row. Between 80-100,000 are housed in a single, windowless warehouse. Feed, water, and manure disposal are completely automated, so just a handful of workers oversee the entire production. There is no individual care or attention. The birds endure this misery for two to three years; unable to stretch their wings, walk, or even lie down comfortably. After months of intensive confinement, the birds lose most of their feathers, because their bodies are constantly rubbing against the bare wire cages. With little feather protection, eventually their skin becomes covered with painful bruises and sores. When the hens become too sick or injured to produce eggs at peak production levels, they are literally thrown out of the cage and left on the floor to die slowly from starvation. We found Lily on the floor of an egg factory, waiting for death to end her nightmare. She was standing in a corner, trying desperately to keep from falling on a mound of feces and decaying feathers and bones. Lily had given up all hope. Her entire body was hunched over, and her head drooped close to the ground. She was covered with sores, and her left eye was swollen shut. I reached out, and gently lifted her into my hands. She trembled as I lifted her. I kept whispering to her, softly telling her I was a vegan and her misery was over. My "vegan reassurance speeches" always seem ridiculous to me after a rescue, but no matter how foolish I feel the next day, they've become one of my rescue rituals.

For two weeks, Lily received intensive rehabilitative care. She was too weak to walk, and throughout the day, I would hold her up to help her regain strength in her legs. She also had bruising over 75 percent of her body, and four times a day we wrapped heating pads around her to reduce the swelling. Since Lily was severely emaciated, she could only eat small amounts of liquid food through a dropper every few hours. On more than one occasion, I wondered if we were doing the right thing, or if we were just prolonging her suffering. It is "the" shelter question whenever an animal is near death…but then one morning I had "the" answer. I opened the door to Lily's rehab pen, and she walked over to me and looked up. I immediately sat down to get as close as I could to "chicken height," and Lily climbed onto my lap. I reached down, and this time, I was the one trembling as I stroked her chin. Lily gave me her love in a way that I could understand, just like a dog "talking" with his or her tail, or a cat's soothing purr.

Rescuing an animal like Lily always fills my life with precious moments, and carries me through those times when we cannot save a suffering animal. Like the time Gene and I visited a California slaughterhouse in the Chino Valley south of Los Angeles. This area has the highest concentration of dairy cows in the world, which means it has one of the highest concentrations of beef production too. Dairy cows are not being retired to Farm Sanctuary; they are slaughtered and ground up for hamburger. The majority of hamburger sold in the United States comes from dairy cows, not rainforests.

We stood near the unloading area, watching the cows come in one by one. Gene was videotaping the scene, and my job was taking photos. They put the cows into one killing pen and then a worker came around and shot a cow in the head. It was a slow process, several minutes would pass between each killing, and the ones that were alive had to just lie there and watch. There was one cow who looked a lot like Maya, a cow at our New York shelter. She was shaking from fear, and I wanted so badly to put my arms around her and comfort her. Later, when I was in the car, it was unbearable. I kept thinking of Maya and how much she loves life.

Well, actually, how much she loves my husband, Gene. Maya adores Gene and is actually very jealous of me. She pushes me out of the way whenever Gene and I are in the barn, and since she's an 1800 pound woman, she's even knocked me down a few times. Of course, Gene has to be careful too. When Maya goes into heat, she tries to mount him. In the bovine family, the females take charge of the mating situation. (Perhaps we humans could learn something from our bovine sisters)! She'll stand there and gaze adoringly at Gene, softly mooing to him, and then turn around and give me the evil eye.

I thought of Maya and her likes and dislikes, her unique personality, and I thought of that poor trembling cow who wanted to live as much as Maya, or you and I. Farm animals are living, feeling animals. They are not breakfast, lunch, and dinner. Americans have drawn an imaginary line and classified some animals as "pets" and some animals as "dinner." Our society is horrified (and rightly so) when we hear of other cultures eating dogs and cats, and most people would never be intentionally cruel to a dog or cat. I have to hope that they would never be intentionally cruel to a cow or chicken either. People who love animals called pets would not eat animals called dinner, if they looked into the eyes of a suffering farm animal.

The production of "food animals" is the single largest and most institutionalized form of animal abuse. Billions of animals suffer tormented lives, and millions of people participate in the cruelty. But Hope's life, and now her memory, reminds me that we can stop food animal production...one life at a time, one law at a time, and one more person at a time who becomes a vegan, because they met an animal like Hope.

If you saw a laying hen like Lily, or a frightened dairy cow, wouldn't you do everything you could in your power to stop their suffering? Well, every person can stop dairy cow suffering, and every person can shut down egg and chicken factories, because every person can be a vegan.

The dairy, egg, and meat industries abuse and kill animals because people buy those products. If you don't buy meat, eggs, and dairy products, they won't produce them. It's that simple, and that direct. Food animal production is entrenched, but that is why we also have the greatest opportunity to stop it. Anyone can take immediate action, and maybe that is why being a vegan is such an empowering experience. When you stop consuming animals and animal by-products, you stop the slaughter of hundreds of animals. Your action saves lives, and it is as direct as going to a factory farm or stockyard and rescuing an animal like Hope yourself. When you become a vegan, you begin to share a special bond with farm animals. Vegan kinship is very powerful, and it will touch you and change your life forever. You may notice strange and wonderful things happening to you when you become a vegan. Like the time we rescued Jessie. Well actually, the time Jessie rescued herself.

Gene and I were making a cross-country trip with several turkeys during one of our annual Thanksgiving Adopt-A-Turkey Projects. Every year, we encourage people to save a turkey, rather than serve a turkey, for the holiday season. We adopt turkeys into safe, loving vegetarian homes and the media are invited to report on our unique way of celebrating Thanksgiving. We were going through Colorado (which is a major beef producing state) when I spotted her along the interstate. A young angus calf was just a few feet from whizzing cars. We pulled over, threw on our boots and started toward her. She was extremely frightened and started running away from us. An injured leg prevented her from moving too fast and we had her within a few minutes. Our new "baby" weighed about 150 pounds, and as we struggled to get her into the van, we heard angry shouting and saw a man running towards us. We soon learned that Jessie had jumped out of the trailer while it was traveling 60 miles per hour. When I realized what she had done to escape her fate, I felt like an angry mother cow, ready to tear her horns into anyone who tried to take her calf away. Finding it difficult to keep calm, I explained to the owner that we were anti-cruelty agents and would be willing to take this calf off his hands, because of course, he couldn't take her to the auction now. To my surprise, the owner agreed. I was gearing up for a major battle, since injured and sick animals are legally sold at auctions all the time. To this day, I don't know if he agreed because he was in shock, or because he saw a raging cow in my eyes. Or maybe, just maybe, he got a dose of vegan kinship.

The next feat was getting Jessie through the California border because she needed to be treated at a specialty veterinary clinic in northern California. We drove all night with her and four turkeys, through a torturous snowstorm, and just as it was getting daylight, we came to the California border...and the California agriculture checkpoint. Now every turkey mother knows that daylight is the time when turkeys wake up and start chirping, and we knew we didn't have much time. We turned up the radio, and inched cautiously toward the checker. He asked us if we had any apples or oranges. I smiled sweetly and replied "no," and drove on with the biggest grin I've ever worn. Jessie survived and is now a big healthy cow. I've never considered myself a very religious person, or one who thinks that everything happens for a reason. Still, I can't help wondering if she knew we were behind her when she jumped out of the trailer...at least I'd like to think so.

As a vegan, I have experienced so many incredible things, so many special bonds with farm animals. We all know that people bond with companion animals. Most people have loved and cared for a dog or cat, and experienced many moments of profound understanding and love. I know that whenever I'm feeling blue, my dog friend Suzy can always tell, and will come and sit by my side in sympathy. She will look up at me with such a forlorn expression, such concern, that I have to smile.

At Farm Sanctuary, we share special bonds with our farm animal friends, too. Most of the time, it's the little communications that we experience every day, but sometimes we are reminded with a powerful vegan kinship message. Our California shelter coordinator told me of one of these precious moments when she injured her arm while she was in the cattle barn. She didn't feel like moving, so she just sat on the barn floor and held her arm. Though they were not in the barn at the time, within minutes two of the cattle, Joni and Henry, suddenly appeared. Cattle have a distinct "distress moo," and both cried loudly when they saw Diane on the ground. They approached her cautiously, reaching out their noses. Their urgent mooing turned to soft, comforting moos. For over twenty minutes, they stood carefully around her, gently licking her face until Diane could move again.

    If you let yourself be touched, animals will touch you, and farm animals are animals. A cow or turkey, pig or chicken, is just as capable of feeling joy and sorrow, or pain and comfort, as a dog or cat. Like many people, I am fortunate to have the love and companionship of dogs and cats, animals who are truly a part of my family. But unlike many people, I have also known the love and friendship of cows and pigs, and turkeys and chickens...farm animals that suffered horribly at factory farms, slaughterhouses, and stockyards, and I was the one to blame. Every time I ate a pizza with cheese, or had a muffin with eggs in it. Every time I didn't care enough to feel their pain. We need to always remember the animals' pain, because that is how we find the love we need to stop it.

    The next time you want to eat meat, or cheese, or eggs, imagine living your life in a small, filthy crate, constantly in pain, unable to stand or lie down comfortably. After months of agony, your torture finally ends, but not at the slaughterhouse. Instead, two gentle hands reach down to lift you out of the darkness and bring you to a safe, loving place. For the first time, you can walk through green, sunny pastures, and rest in a comfortable bed of soft straw. As a vegan, you are providing the sunny green pastures and the soft straw bed. You are providing hope for a needy animal.

    I feel very fortunate to share my life with animals like Hilda and Hope. I am so thankful that my old friends never knew the terror and pain of a slaughterhouse, and that I was able to watch them grow old at Farm Sanctuary.

    Hilda died peacefully of old age at our New York shelter. While she lived with us, I would often find myself glancing out the window to watch her quietly grazing in the pasture. Sometimes I wondered what she remembered of that horrible trip to the stockyard. Hilda remained shy of humans, even after spending several years with us. It was a rare treat when she approached you, and an even greater privilege when she allowed you to scratch her chin. It took us a while to resign ourselves to this, and one embarrassing moment with Hilda (embarrassing for us that is, not Hilda). It happened about a year after Hilda's rescue. I was working in the barn, when Gene came running up to me, smiling ear to ear.

She likes me. Hilda likes me! he proclaimed grinning like a proud father. *She's following me everywhere I go. She won't leave my side.*

I couldn't believe it and, feeling a twinge of jealousy, I'm not sure I wanted to believe it. But as Gene walked into the sheep pasture, there was the evidence. Hilda trotted up to him, and even leaned up against him. Gene walked towards me and Hilda stayed by his side. Hours went by, and still Hilda stayed with Gene. Following him while he was painting. Following him into the barn. Following him to the compost pile. True to his nature, Gene kindly remarked that perhaps she had chosen him over me because I was the one who trimmed her hooves. But after several hours of adoration, even Gene started to wonder about this sudden display of affection. Then it hit us, and that day we officially turned from "city slickers" into "farmers." Hilda wasn't in love, Hilda was in heat. After hearing about Maya's story as well, you're probably wondering just how charming one human can be? But then you probably haven't met Gene.

So how can I, or Maya, or Hilda, possibly explain? We all share a special vegan kinship with him; there is nothing more to say.

Farm Sanctuary East is located in Watkins Glen, New York, and Farm Sanctuary West is located in Orland, California. For more information on Lorri & Gene Bauston and Farm Sanctuary, visit their website at www.farmsanctuary.org .

Lori Bauston was the first person to contribute to Softly On This Earth. Her impassioned message, along with the memories of our visit to Farm Sanctuary in California and a three-legged cow we met there, filled me with faith that this project would find wings of its own.

The day I sent off all my letters inviting people to contribute, I felt fear. All these incredibly courageous people and here I was, with my full-blown delusions of insignificance. I stood at the post office counter in James Bay Square, reluctantly handing over all the sealed envelopes. My last chance to draw back all these words. My last chance to back out of committing myself to this project. The words I had just written carefully to each of my prospective contributors danced through my mind and I could feel a cold sweat on my brow as Earle reached out across the counter and took the box of envelopes from my hands, nearly dragging them from my grasp.

I walked home slowly in the cool evening air, watching waves roll in toward the vanishing point where Menzies Street approaches the ocean. My mind was drifting back and forth between glee and terror. What if nobody responded? What if everyone did?

At home I leaned up against the kitchen wall and then slumped down to the floor with a whole new emotion washing over me. I had undertaken a zillion projects before, but never had I reached out and asked for help like this. Never had I invited the feelings of so many people into my life. For God's sake, I had given them all our address and home phone number!

For days I read and reread the journals I had written on our pilgrimage. I thought about our three-legged bovine friend from California, I thought about the thousands of brilliant red jellyfish we kayaked through off Prince Edward Island and I thought about all of the breathtaking beauty we encountered in between.

And then the phone rang. And it rang again. And the emails began and the letters arrived. One of the emails touched me so deeply that I printed it off and stuck it up above my desk to remind myself in times of despair. It read:

Your sincerity and kind words touched both me and my business partner more than you'll ever know.

It is so encouraging to hear of others out there attempting to better our world through their own personal path. There is so much out there that needs changing, it can get overwhelming at times. Your book will most definitely be a source of strength for people to draw on and an example for people to follow. It would be a great honour to be a part of that.

My partner and I are very excited about it, and would each like to submit something individually, if that is ok.

I thank you for the privilege to contribute, and I congratulate you on your own compassion, vision, and creativity. May you and your wife be blessed during every step of this wonderful journey you are taking.

Take care and God bless

My heart stopped and then raced with glee as I read that email and then others like it that arrived. These people were no longer separate from me. I had ended a mythical separation. And all it took was for me to screw on a little courage and write a letter.

When Lorri Bauston's essay arrived, it brought tears to my eyes. Not only was it a beautifully written piece, it was also my first contribution for the book and it confirmed that I was on to a good thing. It also marked a point in my path from which there could be no turning back.

Now it's time for another essay. Actually, two of them. It was Jessica Campanelli's email that gave me such encouragement through the early stages of this project and it seems fitting, after sharing her message, to share her essay now.

JESSICA CAMPANELLI

Jessica Campanelli is Co-Founder, with Diana Saakian Bokhari, of Naturalanimal & Pawtisserie Holistic Pet Centre. Naturalanimal is a unique business, a first of its kind in Quebec, that provides a truly holistic approach to pet care. From fresh-baked pet snacks and therapeutic massage to homeopathy and Reiki treatments, the Centre aims not only to provide compassion and health to its animal visitors, but also to educate their human companions as well.

A TIME TO HEAL

To be sure, I appear at times merry and in good heart, talk, too, before others quite reasonably, and it looks as if I felt, too, God knows how well within my skin. Yet the soul maintains its deathly sleep and the heart bleeds from a thousand wounds...
- Hugo Wolf

I was going to be a chartered accountant. I worked with numbers. I sifted through invoices. I typed out reports. I carried a laptop. I wore dry clean only clothing. When people asked me what I did - I was an auditor. My mother was proud, I lived up to everybody's expectations. But that was a lie. I was a good liar. I deceived them all – my teachers, my bosses, my colleagues. They all believed it as I continued lying for five years. Good liars believe their own lies – I was an auditor, yes, that is what I was.

I tried to feel like I belonged at business cocktails, with my nametag and my freshly ironed suit. My bookshelf included the CICA Handbook, Tax Guides, and university textbooks. I subscribed to CA magazine and read the business section in the newspaper almost every morning. All my poetry anthologies, journals, and animal magazines had been stored away in my closet. It was a painful reminder of my self-betrayal.

When I found myself in the hospital's intensive care unit diagnosed with a chronic illness a few years later, I stopped lying. My body was ravaged by disease, my mind was struggling for peace, and my soul was fighting for freedom. I wasn't who I pretended to be or what people expected me to be. I was a stranger to myself. Lost. Numb. I felt like I had been holding my breath; I wanted to breathe. I had denied my feelings and silenced my emotions for so long that I lost touch with my inner voice. As my family prayed for my life, I mourned the death of my spirit. I had been living an unconscious life or rather, a conscious death. It was time for truth. But, what was the truth? Who was I?

I left my job at the CA firm, withdrew from my courses, and announced to everybody that I was not an auditor. I abandoned my misguided quest to change myself. I had to let go of what I was in order to discover who I was. I had been defining my identity by illusions of self-worth. Among the wreckage of my lies was a lost soul waiting to be saved. But, to get to my toxic soul I had to get to my heart first. Every emotion, every lie, every denial had to be stripped away. My journey towards healing had begun.

I was afraid at first, not knowing what the future held. I had planned my whole life out for myself, no room for surprises. From university, I would go on to get my C.A., from there I would work for an auditing firm... safe, clear, and perfectly predictable. With the structure gone, I was lost. What was I going to do now?

For two years, I did nothing. In that nothingness, I discovered my fears, my passions, my desires, and my dreams. I began writing again. I started playing the piano again. I took animal behaviour courses. I reconnected with my spirit. As my awareness increased, my voice began emerging, and this time, I listened. With the laws of synchronicity at work, I met my business partner and friend, and together we created Naturalanimal Holistic Pet Centre, a place of healing and learning. I've come to believe that uncertainty is a gift. It is a sign of freedom. I thank God every day that I am able to help animals while doing something that makes my heart soar. But it is the animals who are the true healers.

Compassion without judgment, love without condition – this is the essence of a dog. Dogs do not pretend; they are pure emotion, pure love. They don't know resentment or hate. Dogs are the embodiment of our innate goodness, of all our potential for truth, love, and forgiveness. Everything is here to teach us. Perhaps that is their mission – to show us, to teach us about who we really are. They remind us that there is a piece of ourselves that we've lost...somewhere. They are reflections of our true nature, bearers of the human soul.

Through my journey to wholeness I learned many things. We all have guides and teachers – spiritual healers who will reveal to us our truth, spiritual leaders who will lead us to ourselves. Tazi, my seven-year-old Fox Terrier is one of those teachers. I found my truth in the eyes of a dog. As Goethe once said, *We are fashioned by what we love...* Through my love for Tazi, I found myself. I turned my passion for animals into my purpose in life. This has led me to peace and a feeling of connectedness to the world around me. The only truth is the one we carry inside ourselves. This is humanity's greatest challenge – to live by that truth.

When we choose to ignore truth, we face destruction. Humanity mirrors the individual. I had been destroying myself because I lost connection to my soul. I didn't hear the cries of my bleeding heart because I feared the truth. It was too painful to face the loss of my identity. So, I numbed my senses and continued lying. I was not alone in my fear. We, too, are a fearful humanity. We seek to destroy life. We exploit those weaker out of need for power. We rape the environment out of arrogance. We use and abuse animals without mercy. These are the acts of an abandoned soul. Why don't people hear the warnings from a dying planet or the cries of abused animals? We prefer the silence. We seek the comfort of irresponsibility. We fear the echoes in our heads. We close our eyes and our ears. The sounds are too strong, too deathly. Piercing. Loud and heavy is the sound of conviction.

But, we can choose to heal. We are creative beings with great power. Everything is a choice, and every choice has a consequence. When we choose hate, we, ourselves, become hatred. When we choose healing, we become whole. Every existence, every creation is an expression of the Divine. All is holy. When we live with that belief, we become responsible for our choices. The world today is the result of unconscious choice, creation without awareness. We can choose to create with love or we can choose to create through fear.

The reason we, as individuals, are in pain and suffering is the same reason the world is in pain and suffering. We are each part of the collective soul – cells within a body. We are responsible for our own healing. We have a contract with the world to use our gifts for the common good. When we follow our dreams, we assist the evolution of humanity. By healing ourselves we contribute to healing the world.

Naturalanimal & Pawtisserie Holistic Pet Centre is located in Westmount, Quebec. For more information, visit their website at www.naturalanimal.ca .

DIANA SAAKIAN BOKHARI

Diana Saakian Bokhari is Co-Founder, with Jessica Campanelli, of Naturalanimal & Pawtisserie Holistic Pet Centre.

AN OPEN HEART

The mark of a moderate man is freedom from his own ideas.
Tolerant like the sky, all-pervading like sunlight, firm like a mountain, supple like a tree in the wind, he has no destination in view and makes use of anything life happens to bring his way.
Nothing is impossible for him.
Because he has let go, he can care for the people's welfare as a mother cares for her child.
-Tao Te Ching (A New English Version)
Stephen Mitchell

I greet all of you with an open heart, and thank you for taking the time to read my message. Since I opened our holistic pet centre with my business partner, Jessica Campanelli, I have been blessed with opportunities such as this one to spread a message of hope and well-being; nothing could I possibly consider a greater gift than this.

For many of us who are on a spiritual path, the world today may often seem like a mad dash through a gigantic shopping mall where we are constantly bombarded with advertisements and information that the media are trying to sell. The North American continent has become the super mega market, the extreme end, of the duality pole where happiness is based on the material, and not on the spiritual essence of being. Our very governments promise us prosperity based on what they can do for us economically, not what they can do to ensure us a healthy, serene and peaceful existence. We have thus become a society of consumers, constantly wanting, needing, and purchasing. We are expected to accumulate onto no end.

As dismal as this may sound, it is actually very good news. It is my profound belief that the souls who have gathered in this part of the world have the greatest challenge to perfect themselves. Being amongst temptations is the greatest difficulty in remaining centered within one's goal to sustain spiritual perfection. How much more true could it be, that one cannot serve both masters! By no means do I suggest that we all choose poverty. I suggest that we do what we love, what we know to be wholesome and beneficial to all living beings, and allow prosperity to be our reward instead of profit being reason for our work. This is why when people live through traumatic or near-death experiences, they often end up completely changing careers. They realize that when we are not driven by desire for wealth, we remain ethical, compassionate, healing, and true to society and ourselves in every possible way. If we are not driven by desire for power, we become tolerant and accepting of every person and every thing around us, and thus we create a softer, happier world for ourselves.

    I will never forget the humble beginnings of our own business. With little money, we were the pioneers in an unexplored new market the likes of which did not even exist in our midst for comparison purposes during the creation of our business plan. I'll never forget the bank's loan officer's face when he asked, *You are opening a what?* On the wings of faith, and an iron will to make a positive difference, we opened our little Naturalanimal & Pawtisserie Holistic Pet Centre. We could have never imagined the impact that our work would have on our very own lives. Never did I, personally, dream that I could come home from work so exhausted and exhilarated at the same time. Never again will I question the reason for my existence and never have I ever felt so close to Divinity Itself. I see it in every corner of our store and in the eyes of every little creature that walks through its doors. The impossible became possible because the intention was good.

As long as man continues to be the ruthless destroyer of lower beings, he will never know health or peace. For as long as men massacre animals, they will kill each other. Indeed, he who sows the seed of murder and pain cannot reap joy and love.
    -Pythagoras

    To have the opportunity to work with animals is the greatest occasion to learn how much we need to improve as humans. Unfortunately, the entire human race, for the most part, has forgotten that the rest of the animal kingdom was not created to serve us. They are our equals in feeling a whole range of emotions, as well as the ability to feel physical pleasure and pain. All religions of the world call upon us to respect and treasure animals as living, breathing beings like we are. In our cravings for comfort, style, meat, and scientific "advancement," we have lost sight of the suffering that we cause. We have become heartless in our treatment of food and laboratory animals. We have chosen to do little or nothing to pass legislature that would help control any kind of animal abuse, and why? So that multi-billion dollar conglomerates can continue to sustain their profits. Barbaric treatment of these animals, as well as household pets, is for the most part unregulated in North America. If laws were implemented to protect Fido down the street from being beaten by his owner, it would really complicate the perception of the beagle being used in a cruel experiment by your local pharmaceutical company as a living being possessing the right to humane treatment. Most experiments are unwarranted with today's advanced technology, they lack ethical purpose and merit, and they exist mainly to create jobs and justify government grants (for in-depth information please visit www.animalresearch.org, www.factoryfarming.org, and www.lcanimal.org).

If animals could speak to us in our own tongues, what would they tell us about ourselves? Would we be proud to hear their assessment of our social evolution? If we were to listen to the words of great spiritual leaders like Gandhi, *The greatness of a nation and its moral progress can be judged by the way it treats its animals*, it would be frightening to gauge most nations by this measure. In Asia, for instance, dogs are gruesomely tortured for days, then skinned alive before they are slaughtered to be served in restaurants as a delicacy, which is believed to enhance one's libido. Throughout North America, puppy and kitten mills turn out millions of kittens and puppies in the most horrifying conditions where females are bred on every heat, without respite. These poor animals are kept in cages (too many animals per one small cage) their entire lives, never seeing daylight. They are barely fed (hungry, mothers will often eat their own dead offspring), and never groomed (their nails are so long that they cannot even stand properly on their feet, and their coats are so matted that they develop severe skin disorders) never mind them ever seeing a vet. Puppy and kitten mill operators make hundreds of thousands of dollars in profit from these sick and traumatized animals every year as 95 percent of all animals sold in pet shops come from them (please visit www.nopuppymillscanada.ca and www.nopuppymills.org for the United States).

These are just a few gruesome examples of how animals are treated around the world. We pillage and rape all nature in the name of our profit, success, power, or whatever else one may want to name it. Is it any wonder that our planet is revolting against us? In my view, if we are to find salvation, we need to shed our humanity and follow the examples that animals teach us. In their innocence, they trust and they love without conditions. In our guilt, we fear and judge. And we hurt...everyone. It is imperative that we realize that we all have an awesome individual power to change the world around us. We are each a microcosm within a macrocosm, and as a single drop of water within a great wide ocean, we can each make thousands of rings. And maybe even bring on a downpour! Goodness is contagious, and when we want to spread it, it makes itself ready. I bid you all love, peace, joy and prosperity always.

...Like giving birth, in agony, compassion's born of human heart.

Naturalanimal & Pawtisserie Holistic Pet Centre is located in Westmount, Quebec. For more information, visit their website at www.naturalanimal.ca.

Diana Saakian Bokhari's piece isn't easy for me to read. Reading about, or seeing, our demonstrated capacity for doling out cruelty to other animals and to each other makes me cringe inside. It makes me feel ill. And, as much as I would rather live in denial and join the throngs of people who choose to remain blissfully unaware, it grows increasingly intolerable for me to do so. I have seen cruelty. I have lived cruelty. And very few of us, if any, are exempt from causing pain to others. Likewise, very few of us, if any, manage to dance gleefully along their life path without being broadsided by pain once in a while.

Is it necessary? Must we suffer cruelty at the hands of others and must we hurl it back in their faces in order for our species to evolve? Are wars and oppression, slavery and imprisonment a natural course of events for humans? Or perhaps, are we so conditioned by our ancestors' behaviour that we have just managed to convince ourselves that this is natural?

There is, in my mind, nothing natural about cruelty. No matter who the victim of our cruelty is we do ourselves a great dishonour. We contribute to something ugly that's happened along the way, something we've all come to accept as natural. Because we haven't all taken the time to question the way things have always been done.

For a variety of reasons, I've seen a lot of cruelty in my life and I've spent a lot of time wondering how I could put a stop to it. Where does it come from? What possible evolutionary benefit can result from one being torturing another? We are all gifted with this incredibly beautiful world to live in, blessed with a vast abundance of life and endless possibilities. We are also blessed with the capacity to love. It is our greatest treasure. From love, all creativity is born. From love, all acts of kindness are born. From love, courage and compassion and honesty are born. Cruelty is the opportunity to love taken in the opposite direction.

Through my window, a full moon is casting its eerily beautiful radiance across the room. Its light bathes the surface of the Pacific with a golden sheen far below me. As the just-light of the morning begins to erode the darkness, the moon stands its ground firmly, as does the one remaining star in the sky. On closer inspection, I can tell that this is no star. This is Mars…our giant red neighbour. Closer to our Earth now, I'm told, than it's ever been. That's a very cool thing. As I write this, these two gigantic

36 Softly On This Earth

celestial bodies are hurtling through the universe in closer proximity than they ever have before. I wonder what sort of effect this is having on us. I wonder what sort of influences our enormous neighbour is playing upon our planet as I sit here gazing out across the water.

Time to introduce another incredibly courageous person. One who stands up for his convictions to overcome cruelty and has figured out a unique way of doing it. The result of his work is now widespread and the volunteers who carry on his vision are remarkable, courageous and inspiring.

KEITH McHENRY

Keith McHenry is Co-Founder of Food Not Bombs.
Food Not Bombs is a volunteer organization dedicated to nonviolence. They have no formal leaders and strive to include everyone in their decision making process. Each group recovers food that would otherwise be thrown out and makes fresh, hot vegetarian meals that are served in city parks to anyone, without restriction. They also serve free vegetarian meals at protests and other events.

WHY I DO FOOD NOT BOMBS

My parents were Republicans but they were concerned with social justice and the environment. My father, who was a park naturalist, gave me a copy of Walden by Henry David Thoreau when I was in the fifth grade and, being a young reader, I started the book by reading On Civil Disobedience in the back. My parents supported our town's Jewish family when our public school in Virginia had mandatory Christian education once a week. My father took us hiking and camping. I joined him at the founding convention of Earth Day and saw the power of community organizing.

I also think I was influenced by my family history. My grandfather's great, great, great grandfather was James McHenry. He was George Washington's assistant during the American Revolution, signed the U.S. Constitution and was the third Secretary of War. This gave me the belief that I could make a difference.

In high school I organized a student strike for an end to the dictatorial rule of a new principal. It was a success but I was suspended from school after the crisis was resolved. As a college student at Boston University I was active in actions against the tuition increases and school censorship of student publications.

It was while studying painting at Boston University that several things happened that influenced me to choose a life as an activist. I went to an art gallery on Newberry Street in Boston's Back Bay and, as I was looking at the paintings, I overheard a young wealthy couple discussing the resale value of one of the pieces of art. I could see that they were going to buy the painting and that they might store it in a safe rather than enjoy it so I took a hard look at my future as an artist. I wanted my art to have a powerful connection with society instead of becoming a good investment.

After class I worked as the assistant curator of the Old South Meeting House, which is where the Boston Tea Party was launched. One sunny day I took my lunch to the Boston Commons. There was a woman standing on a milk crate talking to a small group of people sitting on the grass. She told of the terrible things that we faced with the threat of nuclear war. She stated that there were thousands of nuclear missiles aimed at civilians, and that nuclear countries had a policy of Mutually Assured Destruction. She talked about how much money was taken from human needs and spent on weapons of mass destruction. She warned that Israel, India, Pakistan and South Africa were joining the nuclear community. Her name was Helen Caldicott and she made a powerful argument that nuclear war was the single most important issue facing society.

It occurred to me that using my art to address this urgent issue would be the most valuable use of my time. I joined Mobilization for Survival but it seemed like they mostly communicated with other peace groups but had little interaction with the general public. I would design and print posters that tended to stay in the office instead of getting out on the street. To me, if we were to end militarism, we really needed the support of the average person.

I began by designing a stencil with the image of a mushroom cloud with the word "Today?" next to it. My friends and I sprayed this all over the Boston area and included the outline of dead bodies painted in white to give the public a shock. I designed posters for protests and I designed posters with messages and startling images. My most effective was "War is Murder for Profit" with the famous photo of napalmed children running from the fire. Food prices were high at that time and we would spray-paint the words "Food Not Bombs" at the exits from supermarkets.

I was also helping organize nonviolent direct actions to stop Seabrook Nuclear power plant north of Boston. After the May 24th, 1980 protest, several of us decided to organize protests against the First National Bank of Boston because its board directors were investing in their own companies, which in turn were building the power plant. We knew members of The Living Theater in New York and saw street theater as an effective way to organize. We decided to set up a soup kitchen outside of the stockholders' meeting to send the message that their policies could lead to another great depression.

Lacking enough people to dress as hobos we visited the Pine Street Inn and talked to the homeless guys, inviting them to join us in our protest. That was a magical day. We had exciting conversations with stockholders, homeless vets and people walking by. It was inspiring and eight of us quit our jobs, rented a house in Cambridge, and started Food Not Bombs.

As we started to share free food on the streets and deliver food to shelters, we met people who were hungry, poor and suffering in the richest country on Earth. A political idea started to have a human face and it had a powerful effect on my soul. The joy of sharing food with the hungry, and the feeling that we are able to resolve social problems without the assistance of the government and corporations, changed my life.

Today there are hundreds of autonomous chapters sharing vegetarian food with hungry people and protesting war and poverty throughout the Americas, Europe and Australia.

Volunteers often tell me how the act of doing Food Not Bombs has changed their lives. Like me, they find a deeper understanding of the importance of working for social justice and peace.

Thousands of Food Not Bombs volunteers see the direct result of working as equals on a project that makes a difference. Volunteers find their experience a firm foundation for organizing in other groups. This is an education that contributes to a peace movement that will be more effective and lasting than the anti-war movement of the Vietnam era. Not only are we speaking out against the system, we are preparing the ground for a new system to replace the war culture. By example we promote the ideals of sharing, health and that the world is really a place of abundance, not the place of scarcity promoted in the corporate media.

Some have suggested that Food Not Bombs is the American version of Gandhi's Salt Marches. Police have arrested members of the San Francisco Chapter over 1,000 times in an effort to silence their protest against the Mayor's anti-homeless policies. Amnesty International states that it might adopt those

Food Not Bombs volunteers who are imprisoned as "prisoners of conscience," and will work for their unconditional release.

One reason I was so excited about co-founding Food Not Bombs was that I could focus on volunteering with one group while protesting all the issues that concerned me. Before Food Not Bombs I attended a different meeting each day. Food Not Bombs draws the connection between many issues and we work in coalition with groups like Earth First!, the Leonard Peltier Defense Committee, Anarchist Black Cross, the IWW, Homes Not Jails, Anti Racist Action, In Defense of Animals, the Free Radio Movement and other organizations on the cutting edge of positive social change and resistance to the new global austerity program.

We have a lot of projects besides sharing free food. One Food Not Bombs collective publishes a movement-wide newsletter called A Food Not Bombs Menu.

There is also a German language Menu. Food Not Bombs Publishing in Takoma Park, Maryland, publishes books like *On Conflict and Consensus*, which has been an important guide for group democracy.

Ronald Reagan came to power when we started in 1980 and we were very worried that his policies would cause tremendous poverty and an increase in military violence and we were sure right. Although the peace movement has grown and become more sophisticated, our job has become more urgent. Deregulation of the corporate media has made U.S. propaganda more pervasive.

Millions of uneducated Americans drive gas hogs sporting the Stars and Stripes made in China in a desperate effort to return to a time when they truly thought the United States stood for freedom and justice. Day by day, protesting against the regime becomes more dangerous.

The United States is waging a global war, threatening preemptive nuclear war against weak, defenseless nations. The definitions of human rights and justice are being rewritten by U.S. administrations. The Homeland Security laws make it legal to invade our privacy. Libraries must give the FBI information on who reads what. Four military intelligence agencies already claim that they collect all electronic communications and data including phone conversations, emails, bank accounts, criminal files, medical records and employment information. All electronic communications can be collected and reviewed by the government.

Another means of control is prison. The United States already has one quarter of the world's prisoners. The Red Cross states that they believe the U.S. may have more than twenty prisons outside the country holding an unknown number of people who have not been charged.

Our President has the authority to kill anyone anytime. In 2003, President Bush signed an executive order allowing the government the right to kill U.S. citizens when they are outside the country. Predator drones are used to strike human targets oversees while the soldier at the controls is sitting in Tampa, Florida.

It has been reported that one in 24 Americans are spies or snitches for the government. According to the Citizen Corp in Tucson, Arizona, the TIPS program is alive and well. The volunteers are given a special phone number to military intelligence in case they see any suspicious activity. The TIPS program trains meter readers, repair people, store clerks and all kinds of employees who have been enlisted in the fight against terrorism. The Highway Watch program has over 400, 000 truck drivers trained to be *the eyes and ears for the FBI counter terrorism taskforce*.

George Bush is terrorizing the world and our future is threatened so it's more important than ever to organize for positive change. Fortunately the peace movement is more dedicated and better organized than at any time in my life. Thousands of people have experienced the power of nonviolent direct action. We have created our own media so the corporate media are not as able to hide the truth from everyone. When Bush announced the doctrine of preemptive strike against Iraq, millions of people joined in protest.

I learn of a new Food Not Bombs chapter every day. In the past few weeks I discovered a Southern California website and a Chicago Food Not Bombs website with links to more than eight new chapters in each of their areas. I learned of a large German language Food Not Bombs gathering in Europe. There was an internet call for all European Food Not Bombs groups to help share food with the anti-NATO protesters in Praha. I get photos from Filipino and Malaysian chapters.

In my area we have Sonoran desert activist gatherings, which include Food Not Bombs groups from Phoenix, Prescott and Tucson, Arizona and Nogales and Hermosillo, Sonora (Mexico chapters). The book *Food Not Bombs, How to Feed the Homeless and Build Community* just came out in Italian and new chapters are already starting.

I think there are millions of people ready to take direct action towards creating a world free from domination, coercion and violence.

There are Food Not Bombs chapters in communities all over the world. Their head office is located in Tuscon, Arizona. For more information, view their website at www.foodnotbombs.net.

Long before I ever heard of Keith McHenry or met any of the Food Not Bombs volunteers who have shown up at several public events I've been at – resplendent with delicious food and great energy for those who might need it – I met a young woman who might have made a great poster child for their community.

I was on a Greyhound bus, taking an all-day journey from Banff to Vancouver. At Lake Louise, a young woman got on and made her way down the crowded aisle of elbows to sit next to me. She beamed at me through a mass of wild hair and offered me half of an aging cucumber. *It needs to be eaten soon*, she explained, breaking it in half and giving me the larger piece. Feeling somewhat guilty about all the half eaten cucumbers I had almost certainly let go to waste throughout my life, I obliged and accepted her offering. I nearly choked, though, when she told me where she found it. It turned out she had been dumpster diving behind the grocery store. A thousand varieties of food poisoning flashed through my mind but she assuaged me with the fact that she'd been living out of dumpsters for years and had never gotten sick.

By definition, my new friend and traveling companion was homeless, but she was the happiest, most free-spirited, seemingly healthiest hobo I had ever met. She didn't believe in wasting food. In fact, she didn't believe in wasting anything. To her, garbage of any kind was completely unnecessary. She claimed that she had been able to eat consistently healthy food and find plenty of warm, comfortable clothing simply by being aware of her surroundings and peacefully following the litter trail left behind by the bulk of our population. She lived simplicity and preached simplicity while grinning all the time. Her primary means of transportation was in the empty boxcars of freight trains that stream regularly through the mountains of British Columbia and into the prairies. She was on the Greyhound this trip simply because she met someone who had a ticket they couldn't use and she was missing the West Coast. I could relate to that. So was I.

On the ten-hour journey with her, I learned a great deal about trains, like the fact that you should never attempt to climb onto one unless you can still count the number of lug nuts on their wheels. Four is the right number. If they're spinning faster than that, you can be thrown off, or under, the train. She had never been thrown off a train, by momentum or by force, and lived for the thrill of watching the snow-covered Rocky Mountains rushing past as she hurtled through tunnels and over vast canyons, the cool air blasting her face with life.

    I asked how far she had traveled and she had been all over Europe, getting around much the same way as she did in North America. Hadn't anything ever gone wrong for her, I asked? There was a time in Belgium, she told me, when she had feared for her life. People seemed hostile and fearful around her and she couldn't find food or shelter. A man who offered to help her turned on her cruelly and she had to run for her life. Then she encountered more hostility when she sought help and wound up huddled behind a barn, terribly hungry in a driving rain. For many hours she curled up there, shivering uncontrollably and choking back great sobs. She had nothing and was wondering if she would ever see Canada again. She wondered if she would die right there, in this land that felt so far from anything resembling a home.

    Then strong arms and the smell of alcohol washed over her and she was lifted up by two men. She squeezed her eyes shut and decided to accept whatever was going to happen to her, too weak to fight and unable to understand the harsh sounding words they were exchanging. They carried her, limp and shivering, for what seemed an eternity, sloshing along through deep puddles and pouring rain. Then, with the creak of a door and the smell of food, her eyes popped open and she was inside an incredibly warm bungalow with oil lamps and a crackling fire. A family descended excitedly upon her, bundling her in warmth, feeding her body and nourishing her soul. They chatted non-stop with her, quite aware that she was understanding none of what they were saying. And, at the same time, she understood everything they said. There's something, she told me, very universally understood about helping someone who's down on their luck.

    After that night in Belgium, she never felt fear again on any of her pilgrimages. Everywhere, she said, a traveler can find a warm family to embrace them, if only they're patient enough.

    When our Greyhound bus pulled into Kamloops for lunch, I offered to buy her a meal. She laughed and invited me, somewhat predictably, to join her for a picnic instead. And that's what we did. We made our way to a grassy spot behind the bus station and she pulled enough food from her backpack to provide us with quite a wonderful feast. All of it, she said, came from behind the grocery store in Lake Louise and this time I didn't care. It was one of the best picnics ever.

In Vancouver, we hugged each other and parted ways. I made my way to the PCL coach bound for Victoria and I don't know where she went. I never saw her again and likely wouldn't recognize her if I crossed her path today. Though I might. There was something very unforgettable about her soul.

Time, now, to introduce you to another wonderful soul. One who has crusaded tirelessly to raise awareness about the world we live in, preserving its simplicity and beauty.

ELIZABETH MAY

Elizabeth May is Executive Director of the Sierra Club of Canada.

The Sierra Club was founded by John Muir in 1892 to protect the wilderness of the Sierra Nevada. Over the years, the activities of the Sierra Club have expanded to include issues ranging from climate change and energy to toxic chemical contamination and loss of biological diversity. The Sierra Club has been active in Canada since 1969, working on matters of public policy and environmental awareness. They have local chapters and working groups in every region of the country.

ACTIVISM AS AN ACT OF LOVE

Now that I have what is considered some sort of "status" within the environmental movement, I am frequently asked how I got started, and what sort of training is most appropriate to do the work I do as Executive Director of the Sierra Club of Canada. The tone of such questions is often one of seeking career advice – a green version of *How to succeed in business...*

I worry that young people, with freshly minted degrees in environmental science or policy, may believe that environmental work is a career, much as dentistry or real estate. It can be for some. There are jobs using environmental concepts working for industry or government, and even for some environmental groups, where the "job" is nine to five. But the only kind of work worth doing is work that makes a difference. It is definitely not nine to five. It may not pay a salary. It certainly will not generate an income that is the envy of anyone interested in such things. The work that is worth doing is the work of challenging authority, grassroots organizing, and, sad to say, conducting campaigns that are not "fundable."

My awakening as an environmental activist is probably related to an incident when I was twelve years old. Two of our sheep died in dreadful convulsions following an insecticide poisoning along the rural country lane in Connecticut, where I grew up. But I had been connected to nature in many ways before the word "environment" came into common parlance. Why certain children love being out of doors and in the woods and fields, I don't know. I do know that some love nature more than others. I always felt a kinship with other non-human life. I liked watching tiny insects on tiny flowers. I loved a grove of white birches behind my childhood home. I thought that if I could stay absolutely still long enough, they would speak to me. For my high school yearbook, I chose a quote from Henry David Thoreau, *The humblest fungus betrays a life akin to our own.*

Love of the natural world is a common thread in the lives of many activists. It is that affinity that calls some of us to drop our normal lives for something more compelling.

In truth, I have never thought I had a "career" in environmental work. I describe my commitment as more of a calling. I could not choose to leave this work. It would be like announcing that I had decided to stop breathing. I am an activist and an environmentalist because I have no choice. The same must be true for Paul Watson, an old friend of mine, who has risked his life over and over again on the high seas placing himself and his boats between harpoons and whales, between hunters and the hunted. Not all of us in the environmental movement take such risks, but many of us make sacrifices.

Colleen McCrory, vital firebrand for the Valhalla wilderness and forests in British Columbia, endured personal threats and, during the fight for South Moresby, a bullet through her living room window. Donna Smyth, working to prevent uranium mining in Nova Scotia in the early eighties, endured a debilitating two-year legal battle when a pro-nuclear spokesman sued her – unsuccessfully – for libel. Such SLAPP (Strategic Litigation Against Public Participation) suits have become more common since Donna's ordeal.

Grassroots environmental activism is very hard work. It can also be the most fun anyone can imagine. Concerts, fund-raising events, protest marches are all fundamentally social events and build a movement through fellowship and solidarity. Humour, friendship and good spirits are often the only things that can keep tired crusaders from packing it in.

Environmental work can be enormously fulfilling as precious areas of forest are spared eradication by mechanized harvesters, as poisons are not dropped from the sky to kill insects (and incidentally, other life forms in the way), as governments heed the call and do the right thing. The recent victory in Canada ratifying the Kyoto Protocol was the result of more than a decade's work in public education on climate change and applying pressure to government. We were elated knowing that our work helped bring Canada into line with more of the nations on Earth. We accomplished this even with pressure from the United States not to protect our climate from catastrophic de-stabilization, which made the victory more difficult and even more rewarding.

To live softly on this Earth, one should not be passive. The Earth needs us to reduce our ecological footprint, not our political one. We need to be actively engaged in the business of citizenship. While we put out our Blue Box, reducing to a bare minimum what cannot be re-used or composted, we must also look to the structural impediments to reducing pollution and waste. Many of those barriers come from out-moded policies derived from an anachronistic mind-set. Political awareness is the force for change — the unstoppable momentum of the new idea, the impulse to a better, more just society, without the entrenched waste and destruction of our current consumerist articles of faith.

If humanity is to survive we need a dramatic shift in consciousness. The nature of this shift will be as dramatic as that between when the enslavement of fellow human beings was considered normal business and when it became morally repugnant. We will not protect life on this Earth from our own greed and folly with half-measures. We need revolutionary change in how we think about the natural world. We need to re-orient the human assumptions about our place in the universe, taking us out of centre stage and with humility recognizing that we are a threat to our own survival.

Central to this shift will be a change in values. We must embrace the idea of having less, but being more. We need to reinforce that which is the best within us — sharing, love, compassion and cooperation — and explicitly reject those who claim that humanity's driving urges come from greed, competition, hatred and selfishness.

The first steps are to watch our language carefully. We are not first and foremost to be described as "consumers"; we should be described as "citizens." With global citizenship comes a responsibility to the rest of the human and non-human family. We are a blessed species with more senses than our relative, the fungus, to appreciate the beauty around us. We have the gift of appreciating what a miraculous universe we inhabit. Why then do we persist in despoiling it, preferring what we build ourselves? Or, as the old saying goes, *When a man wantonly destroys one of the works of man we call him a vandal. When he destroys one of the works of God we call him a sportsman.* (Joseph Wood Krutch)

So for those who wish to be of use to the planet, do not wait for a "job." The task is all around us now. Find a way, this minute, to make a difference.

The Sierra Club of Canada's National Office is located in Ottawa, Ontario. For more information about their organization, including links to all the regional chapters, visit their website at www.sierraclub.ca.

The Sierra Club's American headquarters are located in San Francisco, California, and their website is www.sierraclub.org .

> *All truth passes through three stages.*
> *First, it is ridiculed.*
> *Second, it is violently opposed.*
> *Third, it is accepted as being self-evident.*
> - Arthur Schopenhauer

Wrapping our heads around new ways of thinking takes great courage. As a society, we seem destined to evolve but, as individuals, we seem determined to resist change at all costs. Our little souls cling desperately to whatever shreds of comfort they can hang onto, demanding that we strike out at the evil infiltrators who threaten to raise our consciousness.

In choosing to reduce cruelty to all beings by avoiding the consumption of animal products, we have encountered ridicule and fairly staunch opposition. In choosing to reduce, reuse and recycle as much as possible to have a light impact on our Earth, we have again faced ridicule. And that one really amazes me. I understand why many people don't understand our vegan lifestyle, despite the fact that people are constantly dropping from heart disease and cancer directly attributable to meat consumption. But I do get that. And it is changing. Vegetarianism is growing rapidly and people are choosing greater awareness in their food choices.

What I don't understand is why Reduce, Reuse and Recycle seem to be failing so miserably on such a large scale. True, there are a lot of recycling initiatives in place in our society but they appear to be largely ignored by an alarmingly huge segment of our population. This one I've known for a long time so I get impatient when others don't get it. I see people with all their take-out coffee cups destined for a landfill when a coffee mug is so simple to carry around and it just floors me. I see people stuffing bottles and cans into their bulging bags of garbage behind their homes even though there are recycling depots in nearly every community and I start to feel a little sick. I see people buying pop and chocolate bars, prompted by cravings and boredom, resulting in needless waste and reduced health and I want to run up and shake them. *There are nine teaspoons of sugar in every can of pop*, I want to tell them. Just imagine how much there is in the big jugs. I want them to see what they're contributing to by supporting the consumption juggernaut that continues to grow more and more obese all around us. There is so much packing material, so much waste and so much cancer and heart disease lurking in every convenience store, it makes my heart reel. I want everyone to open their eyes and their souls and look at the choices they're making. Please, I implore, stop consuming so much of everything. Drink a tall glass of water, pick some blackberries, go for a walk through the park. Be a world citizen, not a world consumer.

These simple truths about our stewardship of the planet are becoming more and more self-evident to me all the time. I understand that I must be patient and hope from the bottom of my heart that people will grow beyond their ridicule and violent opposition and begin to accept and embrace a gentler, less consumptive, way of life. Many people tell me that they do in fact care about walking softly on this Earth. They tell me they love the environment and wish they could do something about it, as they sip their coffee from a take-out cup. They tell me they're worried about their health so they're avoiding all bread, even the ones laden with essential nutrients, and choosing to eat more protein instead. A doctor wrote about it in a book so it must be a good idea. Or they tell me they have chosen to avoid meat altogether and eat only fish and chicken. Because fish and chicken, as everyone knows, are vegetables.

I'm not giving people much credit and I apologize for that. I've just grown a little impatient. Sometimes I forget that there was a time when I was deeply embroiled in the throws of consumption myself. And sometimes, even now, the choices I make are more driven by my desire to avoid conflict than by my desire to support the causes I believe so very much in. Sometimes my own choices make me cringe.

So what can I do to raise awareness…to make people think a little about their choices? Well, that's why I'm writing this book. And that's only the start. I have a lot of work to do. So I'll step back down off my soapbox now and turn the dialogue over to one of my contributors. Another soul with a great deal of courage who has managed to live his highest choices instead of just talking about them.

BOB BANNER

Bob Banner is Publisher of HopeDance.
HopeDance reports on the inspiring activities of creative, pioneering individuals and organizations, regardless of their spiritual tradition or political agenda. They publish material that explores real alternatives to current planetary crises and network with others to strengthen progressive ideas and activities, whether it's social justice, peace, sustainability, personal/spiritual transformation or environmental activism.

To be blunt, what guided me to move to this beautiful bioregion of the central coast of California was an edict from a mad teacher. He simply required that all of us Americans move from Canada to a place between San Francisco and Los Angeles. He was the director/teacher/guru/master of a psycho-spiritual community/cult. So, when his word went out that all US citizens needed to return to the US, we complied. I agreed, not fully cognizant that in a short time the community would be gutted and exposed for its lurking shadows of deceit and abuse.

I fumbled around Shell Beach trying to figure out what to do next with my life, as I was still licking my wounds of apparent betrayal and disappointment with "spiritual communities" and teachers.

A shift started to occur when I became more responsible for my own path rather than remaining dependent on the crazy behavior of an egomaniac who relied on the alleged "crazy wisdom" tradition. All sorts of abuse and nonsense had been excused away, giving it a flare of a "lineage."

As I hung out in this beautiful resort beach town, washing windows to eke out a survival subsistence, it gradually dawned on me that I would once again start a magazine. I had published a national publication from 1980 to 1989 but gave it away to this "spiritual teacher" in order to transform it as well as transform myself. But nothing remained except window washing, a few close friends, and lots of grief to deal with.

Even though this area was new to me I needed to find out where the real people were, where the pioneers were, where the real spiritual teachers were, where the genuine social change agents were...I needed to continue on my journey. I needed to have hope in humanity that not all was lost. Also, the feeling and notion of not doing what I felt was my particular purpose for being here gnawed at me. Everyday I was confronted with the fact that if I did not do what I felt was my love and passion, I would die a miserable death. I knew I had to do something about it... even if it was an hour a day. I did not want to exist like so many others who lived in quiet desperation, who deeply buried their authentic self so no remnant was to be found. I needed to honor what I was listening to...day after day.

What better way to seek out those kinds of people than to create a journal and distribute it throughout the county. Almost three years later, on a shoestring budget, my beloved partner and I printed only 500 copies of a first-time 24-pager. I published articles about voluntary simplicity, meditation, mindfulness, health, and social change, and announced an intention to start building a community of like-minded, progressive individuals who wanted to see profound changes in our county. In a town where numerous publications were either very conservative, escapist new-agey, fundamentalist Christian, entertainment weeklies that paraded nihilism and controversy for the sake of the almighty dollar, or the very conservative daily that spoke to people who earned more than $100,000 a year while continually promoting consumerism, the new journal (which we named HopeDance) certainly appeared to be "underground." Or, if not underground, certainly it was off the radar of most people.

At that time I was fascinated with voluntary simplicity, a movement that slowly was making headway against a culture that had become frenzied with materialism, distraction, delusions, entertainment, consumerism and not comprehending how violent our lifestyles are at the expense of many others' suffering. It appeared that it would become a movement to embrace so many other movements: the environmental, social justice, peace and even the spiritual/transformational movements.

I thought it would become the new glue that was so important to fuse many of these separate and scattered ideological/activist camps. I was very wrong. Voluntary simplicity did not make a hit overnight, and neither did HopeDance. But it did allow me to meet people and start learning about the community: who the leaders were, the activists, the environmental organizations, the peace people, the different political parties, the Buddhist groups, the Catholic workers and on and on. The magazine became not just a useful tool to learn about change agents in the county but it gave me the opportunity to publish their ideas so more people could also learn of their existence, their projects, their courage and inspiration. I became a cheerleader of sorts – encouraging people to write their own stories with passion rather than simply having a reporter report about them. A small group of us started to put together workshops/forums about topics that we cared for dearly, that were not being embraced or even talked about in other media organizations. We embarked on creating all-day forums that dealt with permaculture, alternative media, voluntary simplicity and growing food. We had some of the magazine contributors speak at these events. We advertised workshops and presentations. With this publicity we got some of our contributors on the local radio talk shows. Even though there was a state university in town, community outreach from the local university was sorely needed. The communication between them and the locals was almost non-existent. When exciting events came to town it was as if we didn't even know each other. We needed to create our own media so that when a pioneer was coming through town or was someone we wished to come and speak, both academia and the locals would know about it.

It was a good beginning. I was always trying ways to keep the conversation and dialogue going. And don't ask me why. I had never done this before. I'm not sure what it was that was guiding me this time. Perhaps the community in Canada eventually taught me to listen to something else beside my egoistic desires. Perhaps I was finally getting out of the way and letting something else direct me. I no longer trusted human authorities so it had to come from somewhere else. Dead teachers were okay to trust since they never talked back to you. But real live teachers...? Well, I simply wanted to suspend that type of surrendering.

There was so much to do and I knew if a small core group could trust each other and work together we could do some wild things for social change.

We started an internet listserv that helped and still keeps helping the information flowing. If you have never heard of it, it's simply a broadcasting system whereby members join and have one email address to send their information to (instead of relying on 50-100 names and email addresses in your address book). For example, we have over 100 people who are members. We all get about 7-10 messages a day from members who post events, poetry, a meeting, a film, a party, or who wish to start a dialogue on some social issue or political campaign. Sometimes those postings get forwarded to other listservs or other email addresses. It can work as a well-oiled news and events distribution system. Sometimes there are angry voices and occasionally dialogues get messy and nasty. We have our guidelines and it is monitored gently yet forcefully.

The listservs (now we have two; one for national news and one for local news) helped many causes, e.g., contacting people to attend a city council meeting where certain decisions were in the process. When a local demonstration was happening at numerous stores or places, the listservs were quite helpful. They became conduits for social change agents even though many other topics might be discussed as well: what products to buy that were "ecologically correct," where could one buy fair-trade coffee, a poem by Rumi or Mary Oliver would oftentimes settle a dispute, an event for a dance would be posted to bring email buddies together so we could actually meet them in person, or where one could rent a room for a decent price or what type of hybrid car was the best deal.

The listservs also came in very handy after 9-11. There was so much vital information on the internet that did not make it to the mainstream networks. All the country was in a roar with a patriotic fervor to go to war immediately. Well, through the listserv I asked for donations so we could put together a special supplement on 9-11 called "Voices of Restraint, Compassion and Understanding." Within days we got enough money to go ahead and put together a 24-page special tabloid.

We ended up printing 20,000 copies and gave them away freely. We were the first publication to actually print some alternative viewpoints to the results of 9-11 (since we came out in mid-October). The same thing happened after the intensity of the Palestinian-Israeli horror show. We decided to put together another "Voices of Restraint, Compassion and Peaceful Resolve." Of course, we were accused of anti-Semitism by our own liberal leaders. But what else is new?

My idea was a simple one: to strengthen the sustainability movement by reporting on the actions and activity of pioneering creative and loving people and organizations, to network, to seek others who were doing similar projects so there was connection rather than isolation, to advertise green products or services so people could actually taste that a community was out there so they wouldn't feel so alone.

One of the characteristics of "cultural creatives" is that even though they have progressive ideas they frequently hide out. They are afraid to come out into the public sphere. Perhaps they are afraid of ridicule or of standing out like a sore thumb amidst the great omnipresent dominant paradigm. In any event, my purpose was to change that. I wanted to create a safe space where people could come forward and speak freely about ideas that oftentimes were dissenting in nature.

I became thrilled to know that I had something to do with having a standing room-only attendance for a Growing Food forum where different approaches of gardening were presented, where a workshop on vermiculture (worm composting) happened, or where we did our first seed exchange. It was sheer delight to see people coming out of their insular houses, shutting off the TV or computer, bringing their bags of seeds that they had collected perhaps over years and exchanging them with other seed savers! Or, more recently, when we showed a film of Michael Moore's speech to a standing room-only audience howling at some very funny commentaries. Or when we showed a number of Adbusters uncommercials to people who laughed silly seeing their first uncommercial on a larger screen in a motion picture theater while munching on their popcorn.

That gets me going... having fun while changing the world! As the people at the Billboard Liberation Front (featured on the documentary Culture Jam) commented, You gotta have fun doing this kind of stuff... If you don't, and you got a stick up your butt, then you're not better off than the corporations themselves.

Also, the various workshops and forums oftentimes coincided with a special theme of the magazine (now grown to 80 pages, 14,000 copies and printing six times a year). We did a special issue on Y2K and had an all day forum with speakers and booths and neighborhood associations all eagerly interested in how to survive the coming collapse (even though the collapse didn't turn out, the information was good anyway). We did one on Growing Food, Permaculture, Resolving Conflict, Sustainability and developed workshops that complemented the theme.

One time, we orchestrated a TV Turn Off Week and spoke at schools, wrote articles for the local papers, and were even invited to speak about it on radio. We encouraged students to sign an agreement that they would turn the TV off for an entire week and involve themselves in a plethora of other, more interesting, activities. At one school we got 80% of the student body to sign on. More fun stuff. I was even invited to some classrooms where I could show snippets of radical films and speak to the young people who were quite eager to hear something new. We orchestrated a Buy Nothing Day event inside a mall where we had a booth giving away BNDay logo T-shirts and where people could cut up their credit cards and discuss with us over consumption and how to simplify their lives. With Buy Nothing Day following American Thanksgiving, being the largest consumer day in the world, we got to see many outraged people as well as people who were eager to hear our message of simplicity.

We did a special issue on Diversity and published material from the Latino and Native American communities with ads about their workshops and events.

Also, on another note, we decided to form a network of green business types... actually anyone who was interested in making a livelihood while making a difference (or vice versa). At our second meeting we had over 50 courageous and committed people who introduced themselves for 45 seconds in a circle format before breaking for snacks and networking. It was truly awesome to see a gathering place of powerful people engaged in networking. Straw bale builders were speaking to alternative energy folks. University professors teaching about sustainability were seen chatting with young people who were eager to start a business with bio-fuel as an alternative to oil. And on and on....

We desperately need a green economy that social change agents can draw upon. Gone are the days when social change activists continually beg for money from the transnational corporation coffers. As Kevin Danaher once said, The corporate donors will shine your chains but they will not help you break them!

Despite all the great talk of the idealism of the 60's, much of it died away. But it all got reinvigorated in 1999 during the Seattle WTO protests. However, if the young anti-corporate globalists don't create an economy of green industries they will succumb to what the 60's flower children did.... sell out to the ubiquitous advancing technology industries and the corporate world.

The Green Business Networking gathering that we initiated helped start a conversation. The recent Green Festival in San Francisco had 10,000 people listening to social change agents while browsing the hundreds of green business booths!

We are getting to see a slice of the future and it's going to be beautiful... if we can keep the momentum and move it into the larger political sphere. Right now all this pursuit of a better world is considered "insignificant" by the mainstream press. But I'd rather be considered insignificant than sell out to some monstrous corporation eager to push me to work 80 hours a week so I can have my personalized SUV, a 2,000 square foot condo, and a 2-3 hour a day commute to get to and from work. No thanks...there are solutions!

There are happy people out there. And they are not all insane wacky people. There are sane models. You just have to know where to look, and the internet is great for that (or simply start talking to neighbors). I know many people who searched the web to locate interesting social justice/green business type folks only to find that some lived very near to them!

The key to insuring that all this activity keeps blossoming is maintaining a balance, not only a balance between the various camps of activism, i.e., peace, social justice, environmentalism and the spiritual/transformational camp (see my "Integrative Activism" article in issue #35 of HopeDance) but personally too: staying healthy, growing plants, meditating, doing occasional retreats (like the one I'm on right now so I have time to actually write this and type it into the computer), being with friends and having quality time with my beloved partner Selene.

It's a task for sure but very well worth it. Even though I don't make money doing this, I'm having fun (which can be more carefully defined as experiencing joy while aligning my livelihood with my passion and purpose). Fortunately for me, washing windows makes good money and I really don't need that much to live on. Who cares much about comfort and security when the planet is in crisis and we know we can truly do something about it? I certainly do not want to die knowing that I did not pursue my purpose... that would be absolutely miserable! I've demonstrated to myself that one person can do much (if they don't burn out). With a core group of friends, we can do much more.

It's also a balance between the internet (virtual community) and face-to-face meetings (real community). Often times, I spend way too much time on the computer: researching, networking, keeping the website's calendar alive and updated, sending out press releases for various events, orchestrating the next important documentary to show... at the expense of contact with people.

Of course, there have been numerous times when despair has taken its clammy grip. I need to listen to those times also, with as much equanimity as I can muster. There is a lot of resistance out there to living an authentic life...or even a life that is simply truer than what is expected from most of us.

When people ask me why I do what I do I simply say that this is a very selfish pursuit. I want to be happy (which is actually more difficult than the commercials portray) and I need to listen to my need for emotional sanity. I can no longer tolerate blaming and complaining and whining. And my threshold of reading depressing news is limited. And when we stop (or curb the diet drastically), it becomes very obvious while listening in on ordinary conversations how pervasive complaining and finger-pointing is. A form of lite nihilism seems to be right around the corner to seduce us to total impotence.

So I seek out people and organizations that focus on positive futures, focus on doing something about the problems they see and talk about, focus on creating the sustainability that they seek. Talk about inspiration! Talk about feeling a genuine sense of hope when I surround myself with courageous and committed people who have also slain the dragon of despair (or at least are working diligently to keep it at bay). So, hopefully my selfish endeavor becomes a path of service to aid others in discovering their happiness and joy so they too can kick butt with a smile on their face.

I'm involved in a small men's group. We have been meeting for close to four years every other week. That is genuinely nourishing. HopeDance oftentimes has potluck parties to celebrate another published issue. A group has formed in Santa Barbara where they meet every issue (every two months) to gather ideas, articles and announcements for their specific bioregion. And now we have been showing films/documentaries at a locally independent film cinema once a month and having discussions afterwards.

Make no mistake about it – people gatherings are exciting. For people to get up and announce an event or argue a point in the film or welcome people to continue the conversation at a local café is very cool – better than any chat group on the internet. And because the film showings have been so successful, some friends and I have purchased a video projector (that magical piece of technology that allows one to have a mobile cinema) so we can show films at more venues and more frequently reach out to more and more people. There are so many important social change documentaries that are not seeing the light of day. Especially in these critical and urgent times we have to become the media by doing it ourselves. The government or the transnational corporations certainly are not interested in critiquing themselves or coming up with genuine solutions outside of the box.

We are also interested in showing films and videos that have been produced by young local filmmakers who are becoming quite hip to what is happening. They might not read HopeDance but their form of expression is with sound and images. We are in the process of seeking out more people who are using diverse ways of expressing themselves as social change agents. They, like the pioneers before them, need cheerleaders and elder support just as much as the older activists did.

Our young people are no strangers to social injustices, and their voices, songs, words, videos and art need to be seen and heard. This is our next step as we continue on this everlasting journey of social and personal transformation. Having fun while changing the world!

HopeDance is located in San Luis Obispo, California. For more information, view their website at www.hopedance.org .

Tania and I bought a little piece of land this week. It's the first land either of us has ever owned so we're understandably quite excited about it. And the beauty of this little ¾ acre of forest on Pender Island is that it's wild and undeveloped. There was a time a long time ago when it, like most of this little island, was scalped of all its trees, leaving just a few majestic Douglas firs standing. And they're still here, gigantic and wonderful. I likely would've sobbed to have seen what our little forest looked like after it was first logged a century ago but today it is beautiful. The ecosystem here on the West Coast grows quickly and this piece of wildness has exploded with cedars and maples and more Douglas fir and an entire forest floor of lush ferns and deep, soft moss. It's also home to a myriad of life — spiders everywhere with great, intricate webs woven through the salal, along with woodpeckers, robins, bats, eagles, deer and great, slimy banana slugs. Walking through our new forest, we're able to breathe in the incredible smell of a lush seaside forest, all the time overseen by a few granddaddy Doug firs that have been standing in place for centuries.

So, now, how do we fit into this new little ecosystem we've purchased the right to be stewards for? To start with, we plan on moving onto the land next spring. We'll just find an old trailer and park it on the outside of the lot. Then we'll take plenty of time to just be there, feeling the energy of the land and its gigantic, mossy inhabitants. Hopefully, if we treat them nicely, they'll welcome us in.

This also creates an interesting timeline for me. Since I likely won't have the convenience of a home computer for quite a while once we move into our little island forest, I should probably finish Softly On This Earth in its entirety and get it off to be edited and published before we cut the lines of comfort and electricity we have now.

Which brings me to our next contributor. While sitting in the soft comfort of the forest floor, watching a veil of fog rise up through the conifers on the far side of the valley, I heard the words of Nancy Fresco. If she were to visit us in our new ecosystem, I think she would be able to provide some valuable insight into its preservation. And, Nancy, you are very much invited to do so.

NANCY FRESCO

Nancy Fresco is Boreal Forest Campaign & Local Issues Coordinator for the Northern Alaska Environmental Center. The Center promotes conservation of the environment in Interior and Arctic Alaska through advocacy, education, and sustainable resource stewardship.

Nancy Fresco has both a degree in Evolutionary Biology from Harvard University and a degree in Conservation Biology from Yale. She spent two years with the Peace Corps in Jamaica doing environmental education, and has done extensive work as an advocate for wilderness conservation in Alaska.

EVERYDAY EXTRAORDINARY

> *And what is so rare as a day in June? Then, if ever, come perfect days*
> --James Russell Lowell

I skied to the lake today. I pushed shut my cabin door behind me – no latch, no lock – snapped my boots into old-fashioned three-pin bindings, and shoved mittened hands through pole-loops. My skis slipped down onto the hummocky nameless trails. Left turn, right turn, quirky dip and drop, the crunching glide of crusted snow – and I stood in the lake's frozen center, ringed by an audience of black spruce, willow and alder.

I live here, I told myself. The lake is not mine, any more than the snow is mine. But this Alaska woodland is my home. How many people experience such a luxury? Even if I visit the lake every day, the experience is nonetheless rare. I turned my face up into the early afternoon sun, and let the scarcity of this ordinary experience soak through me.

Uncommonness is a form of currency. Our world is valued according to a human obsession with scarceness; we deride the unwanted and abundant, and covet what we have least. We rename our world as our values change. Rainforests were dark, forbidding jungles, until we realized they were vanishing. The US

Army Corps of Engineers worked hard to drain bogs, but the fast-disappearing bogs have lexically morphed into wetlands, which the Army Corps works hard to protect.

In early April, the lake is still solid enough to drive an eighteen-wheeler across, were it not a mile or more from the nearest road. The snow is tracked and pocked from the passage of skis and boots, paws and claws and hooves and dogsleds, but I stood alone today, inhaling a sense of space that is itself unusual amidst the burgeoning six billion of our species. The air hung still and cold enough to crackle dry in my lungs, but the sun-glare off the snow shouted, Spring!

I remember the lake in December, darkly different. Then, even during our three daylight hours, the sun hovers so low as to be muted dawn at noon, and the snow has a dim blue cast to it. Each sunlit minute is savored. At the year's zenith, in June, a whining density of mosquitoes amidst the cattails lurks in wait for any red-blooded beast lured by the waterside's succulent greens. The chemistry of mammals has changed little in a million years; I imagine that I taste just like a moose to a mosquito. I wonder how we might feel about mosquitoes if we saw them only singly, and fleetingly. If mosquitoes were rare, would we value them? The lake is different yet again in September; the edges first crust with ice, just as the cranberries underfoot burst ripe in the uncanny color of blood. The last drops squeeze from a succinct growing season, eagerly appreciated for its very briefness. Alaskans do not take summer for granted, for it too is in short supply.

I've read that when it was common, lobster used to be a poor man's food. Around the time New England was given that unimaginative name, armored bottom-feeders washed up on the shores in piles two feet deep, and sank into fishy-smelling decay. The grandfather lobsters, sixty or seventy years old, were each 40 pounds of irascible crustacean. Pilgrim children, undoubtedly less virtuous than we imagine them to be, whined at the dinner table as they worked to crack those menacing claws – *not lobster again!*

Twenty years ago, a different generation of children spurred parents to fight each other at shopping malls to bring home supply-limited cloth and plastic objects with names and birth certificates. I was the only little girl in my class who did not own a Cabbage Patch Doll. I relished that fact as a different form of uncommonness.

But craving rarity is not merely a game for children. Humans have enslaved whole generations and consigned thousands of lifetimes to scrabbling and blasting deep underground in a desperate quest for tiny crystals of pure carbon. If diamonds were as common as granite, they would be nothing more than sharp rocks to us – hazardous rough-edged pebbles amidst the warm and softly weathered beach sands.

I am no different. I have chosen to eschew diamonds and gold in favor of rock-jumbled mountainsides, paw prints in the snow, and the smell of damp moss, but my senses still clamor for the unfamiliar, the out-of-the-ordinary. I have heard scoffing directed at urbanites who want to protect wilderness, irritation at idealists in high-tech footwear, and anger at self-proclaimed environmentalists living climate-controlled lives. But I think I understand the paradox, and the apparent hypocrisy. We humans don't realize what we have until the last of it is trickling between our fingers. When all we see is tangled, thorny, predatory-fanged forest, we dream of conquering the wilderness. When all we see is concrete and girders, we beg to have our wilderness back, our bears and cougars and wolves back, at any price. How can I - how can anyone - learn to value what we already have?

Wanting what we do not – and cannot – have may be something unchangeable in the human makeup, as inbred a tendency as speech and fear. We may be eternal "questers," dreamers, coveters, hoarders of diamonds and dolls. But while we cannot change our nature, we can guide it. Billions of types of rarity enrich this world, and it is within our nature to reject fickle fads and self-imposed needs. In their place, we can choose to cherish those rarities that will nourish best: the sight of the first robin in spring; the one person in the world who loves us most; the taste of a thousand varieties of wheat near-lost to mono-crops; ephemeral streaks of aurora across an arctic sky; the one place, tucked between the mountains and the sea, where tens of thousands of caribou give birth.

I ski to the lake, as I have a hundred times and more. I stand on the ice and watch two squirrels chatter and chase in spring courtship. The average lifespan of a squirrel is only two or three years; for them, perhaps, this is the only spring, the only chilly sunlit day, the only chance. I turn my face up into the early afternoon sun, and let the scarcity of this ordinary experience soak through me.

The Northern Alaska Environmental Center's website is www.northern.org .

Nancy Fresco's beautifully written piece makes me want to strap on a pair of cross-country skis of my own, gliding off into the depths of the forest. Her words transport me back to a time many years ago, back in the valley of my childhood, when my sister and I would escape into the forest on our skis, smelling the freshness of a warm spring breeze and listening to the squirrels sing their blissful little songs of glee. Or maybe they were warning us to get out of their lair before they started hurling pinecones at us from above.

When Bucky left, I spent days on end searching for him. It was right after our first heavy snowfall of the year that he left us, the same day the rest of the deer moved down from the higher altitudes to find shelter and food under the forest canopy along our valley's hillsides. There were hundreds of tracks in the snow the morning he didn't return for his meal. Bucky's instincts had kicked in and he heard the wildness calling him from inside.

For days and probably weeks, I set off on my skis, hoping I'd see him and he'd follow me home. Occasionally, I was sure I saw him but, honestly, all his new friends looked a whole lot like him and, even when they'd cock their ears as I'd ski by them and look at me with big, inquisitive eyes, I couldn't be sure.

I missed my four-legged companion so much that I thought my heart would burst right out through my throat any moment. I skied through Christmas when it arrived, wishing more than anything for his return. Was he alive? If so, why wouldn't he approach me if he was with the dozens of deer roaming about through the fresh snowfall? Was he dead? Had a hunter picked him off? Surely not...he was just a scrawny little yearling. Had a cougar nabbed him? That thought was too horrible to entertain for long so I repressed it.

I remember my sister singing *Good King Wenceslas* and, although she sang it beautifully, I grew to associate that carol with Bucky's disappearance and started to get very upset when she'd sing it. *When the snow lay round about, deep and crisp and even*, conjured up all kinds of images of Bucky's hoof prints wandering off in a zigzag line into the darkness of a twilit forest, never to be seen again.

But Bucky did stay around the farm and he made it through at least that winter. After a while, he would show up, with a couple of other young bucks, on the hillside above our house. He wouldn't walk up to us but, if we skied nearby, he would regard us with a complete lack of fear, more of a revered sense of recognition. It only happened a few times but it was enough to satisfy me that he was alive and that his evolution into a wild creature of the valley was perfect. And, by the next Christmas, I was able to listen to *Good King Wenceslas* again without crying.

One night, after a warm day followed by a frigid night created a solid crust on the surface of the snow, a large buck was killed by a cougar right behind our house. The attack actually happened on the hillside above our house but the impact of the attack, and the snow's hard crust, resulted in the two animals sliding together to a resting place just above where we slept. We awoke to the sound of our dog, Aslan, frantically barking in the darkness. The cougar, after defiantly staring down Aslan for a few long minutes, during which I'm sure our old black lab aged many years, decided to retreat into the blackness of the trees. The next morning we lugged the deer's carcass (it wasn't Bucky) up the driveway to a place not far away where the cougar could finally claim his rightful kill.

And that was what life in the valley was like where I was fortunate enough to grow up. It was life and death and birth and it was very real. I don't know whether Bucky made it beyond that first winter in the valley. He may have lived to be an ancient Buck, fathering many wonderful fawns. His descendents might still be flourishing in the valley today.

Just a couple of weeks ago, a deer was eating the leaves off our apple tree here on Pender Island and I asked it to stop. When it completely ignored me, I picked up a small apple and tossed it at him gently, expecting him to run off into the trees. The apple thudded off his flank and he just stared at me with a completely incredulous expression. *I'm your totem animal, you idiot*, I imagined him saying. *You don't throw apples at your totem*. Then he flicked his ears in total indifference and went back to stripping the leaves from our tree. And I just laughed and walked away.

Ethan Smith 69

Our next contributor is an integral part of a wonderful organization. While camping along the California coast near Santa Cruz, we realized we were very close to EarthSave International's home office. Taking a break from the heat of the beach, we made our way to their office and met EarthSave's inspirational Executive Director. Here she is.

CARYN HARTGLASS

Caryn Hartglass is Executive Director of EarthSave International.

EarthSave promotes healthy and life-sustaining food choices, supplying information, support and programs to those who have learned that their food choices impact environmental and human health. They raise awareness of the ecological destruction linked to the production of "food animals," as well as advocating and promoting a delicious, planet-friendly diet.

Caryn Hartglass graduated from Bucknell University with Bachelor and Master of Science degrees in chemical engineering. She spent four years living in the south of France, during which time she won two international vocal competitions, one in France and one in South Africa, and recorded a CD with the French company, Ligia Digital. She returned to New York in 1996, and now divides her time between singing, engineering consulting and working for EarthSave International.

I grew up in a middle class family on Long Island. We were pretty typical in our American eating habits with lots of canned vegetables, TV dinners, and meat at almost every lunch and dinner. I remember Hostess Twinkies and Snowballs were the lunchbox delights. On the weekends we'd be treated to bakery rolls and doughnuts. There were the weekend restaurant outings where we would all come home overstuffed with stomachaches and rush for the antacid. And of course there were all the holidays with an overload of traditional animal-based Jewish foods: chopped liver, brisket, stuffed derma, gefilte fish, blintzes, chicken soup, etc.

We never had any particular connection to animals or pets. My sister and I used to beg to get a puppy but our mother wasn't interested in the extra responsibility and work. On two occasions we got a puppy from the pound and they lasted a week in the house. They were each too sickly to keep.

My parents raised us with good ethics and reinforced them by being good people themselves. My dad was always very responsible. When hard economic times came around he would take on an evening job to pay the bills until something better came along. He demonstrated through his actions the importance of responsibility and a good work ethic. My mother volunteered for Women's American ORT (Organization for Educational Resources and Technical Training) and the temple Sisterhood. We were comfortable and had what we needed and some special extras. We learned that if we really wanted something we would have to work for it.

I have to credit my sister for getting me interested in volunteering for good causes. She got us started raising money for the American Cancer Society by putting on shows in our backyard. We would sing and do silly skits. One year we raised money for muscular dystrophy and really wanted to get on the Jerry Lewis telethon. It didn't happen.

What did happen was I developed a sense of obligation to help those in need. Since we were fortunate, with a home, food and a loving family, it seemed essential to help others. It didn't seem like a burden, it just seemed right. As I grew up I didn't understand why everyone didn't feel the same way!

At 15, I announced to my family that I wanted to be a vegetarian. A friend of mine at school mentioned he was going to be a vegetarian and a light went on inside of me. I had suddenly become aware of the unnecessary cruelty involved in eating meat and no longer wanted to be a part of it. There was little information available about vegetarian nutrition at the time and my mother was concerned for my health. We negotiated deals – I would eat meat one or two times a week and she would try and get some cottage cheese down me on the other days. Had to get that protein! We visited the family physician, who insisted eating meat was healthy and was beneficial for animals, because more were given the chance to live. Fortunately, the physician's arrogant and patronizing demeanor was not convincing and I continued on the path towards eating a plant-based diet. Over time, I realized the benefits of improved health and the positive impact of the diet on the environment. As a child, I had frequent sore throats due to Streptococcus and had to take penicillin. My tonsils were enormous and I had them removed when I was eight. I know now that it was primarily due to the dairy products I was consuming.

Interestingly, persistent stomach ailments, anemia and premenstrual moodiness that I had experienced as a child and young teen all disappeared later with the plant-based diet.

Eating vegetarian became easier as time went on. I attended Bucknell University, majoring in Chemical Engineering. I will never forget Hank Ross, who ran the food service and did a spectacular job. A vegetarian meal plan was offered and I signed right up. Back then, vegetarian food was heavily smothered in cheese and contained a lot of eggs. But it was a beginning. My boyfriend, Richard, and I and our friends experimented with lots of vegetarian cooking. We made many new dishes all the time: mush #11, mush #34, mush #71, and so on. I'll never forget my first experience with tofu. It seemed so disgusting. I tried so hard to disguise it in this saucy bean recipe but the little white curds wouldn't disappear.

After college I worked at DuPont in Delaware for a year and a half. I had a strong calling to live in California. I quit and drove west.

I was still eating a little fish at the time. I remember visiting Epcot Center in Disney World with my sister Lori and my brother Barry when it just opened. There was an exhibit showing how food would be produced in the future. There were lettuce heads growing on spinning wheels. It was fascinating. Then I saw them – the white, rectangular tanks of farmed fish. As soon as I saw that I knew I couldn't eat fish anymore. If fish had to be grown in such a lifeless environment for me to eat them, then I didn't want to eat them anymore. *I have learned so much since then about the unhealthy conditions endured by farmed fish, living in their own waste, being fed antibiotics to withstand the filthy conditions, and being fed tons of smaller fish from the ocean that detrimentally affects the ocean ecological balance.*

The man I was seeing at that time in California, Jim, was very concerned about my eating habits. He bought me a subscription to Vegetarian Times Magazine. That opened a whole new world up for me. I also subscribed to the Vegetarian Resource Journal and started reading. I discovered how bad dairy was for my health and how awfully the animals were treated. I knew I had to give all animal foods up forever. I worked for an Israeli company for a short time and spent three months in Israel. This was the perfect time to make my transition to a vegan diet. I was eating alone a lot and didn't risk being pressured by my peers. Plus, due to the kosher laws, the servers in the restaurants were very familiar with what was in the food. And so many of the standard food items served everywhere there were vegan: hummus, tabouli, tahini, foul (a fava bean dish), salads, etc.

I was never a shy person. *People who know me would laugh at that.* I have always been outspoken and highly principled. I was not ready in the beginning to "proselytize" about a vegetarian diet. It was an evolution. At first, I was quiet about it. I didn't really know much and I was acting on feelings and instinct. Then, I thought I would talk about it only when asked. As time went on and I became more knowledgeable, I began to offer more information to people whenever possible. Today, there's little that can keep me quiet! Being so aware of the billions of animals that are tortured from birth until death annually, I cannot be silent. I look for opportunities to encourage people to eat more plants and fewer animals wherever I am – in airplanes, supermarkets, elevators, everywhere.

One of my close friends was diagnosed with breast cancer in 1984. She died ten years later, leaving a husband and a six-year old daughter. I was the maid of honor at her wedding and was present at the birth of her daughter. She's been gone almost ten years now and I still miss her very much. I know now that her diet and lifestyle significantly contributed to her death. She lived on coffee, vending machine food and lots of cheese. We joked about how she would never eat broccoli.

I wish I could have done more for her. I tried to encourage her to eat more healthfully. We worked in the same office and I made sure there were always healthy snacks around. Or, we'd go to lunch and eat salads. I signed up for spring water delivery at the office and the two of us shared the five gallons every week.

My desire to actively promote a plant-based diet and to be an EarthSave volunteer was triggered by my friend's untimely death.

I spent four years living in the south of France from 1992-1996. It was a very enriching time. My partner, Didier, and I had frequent guests and I was also cooking up vegan versions of French foods. I was new at it and was not always successful. My French friends and I had many lively discussions about food. I was struggling with the language, trying to make my message clear.

Many of the French are stuck on tradition. They are so proud of their cuisine – it is so heavily ingrained in their sense of selves. The idea of giving up cheese is almost sinful! Happily, when I go back to France to visit now I see that the health food stores are getting bigger and soy products are more widely available. Change is possible.

While in France I knew I had to start doing more to get the message out about the impact of our food choices. I wasn't sure what I was going to do but I knew I had to do something.

My brother had the answer when I moved back to New York in 1996. He said I needed to get involved with EarthSave Long Island and meet the chapter chair, Bob DiBenedetto. I had given my brother and sister copies of John Robbins's "Diet for a New America" back in 1991. They both became vegan after reading the book. It was only fair that my brother would return one good deed with another by referring me to John Robbins's non-profit organization, EarthSave, which had been formed in response to his best-selling book that I had shared with my siblings.

I was hooked. I loved EarthSave's mission of spreading the message of a plant-based diet in a loving, non-judgmental, compassionate way. There are so many worthy organizations that one could volunteer for, but EarthSave seemed to touch everything!

Helping people eat healthier food results in less disease, less pollution, less environmental destruction and certainly less cruelty to animals. When people realize they don't need to eat animals to live, they become more aware of our connection to everything on the planet. What I love most is that making individual changes in food choices doesn't require a change in legislation, convincing a politician to support your cause, or signing thousands of people onto a petition. It's something we all can do today, everyday and for the rest of our lives. We can all choose to make a decision to support pain and suffering – or not.

My involvement with EarthSave intensified quite rapidly. I was involved with the core group of EarthSave Long Island for three years. Bob DiBenedetto was very inspiring as a leader and he became a valued friend. I was asked to join the EarthSave International Board of Directors in 1999. I started the EarthSave

NYC chapter in October of 2001. We've got a great chapter and I have made many wonderful friends. I began my position of Executive Director of EarthSave International in November 2001. I spend most of my time now for EarthSave.

It's an ongoing challenge. There is no one slogan that will get the message to people to help them change their diet. Some people are solely interested in their own health. Others are horrified by the treatment of animals in factory farms. It's hard to understand how some people continue to eat animals once they know how they are treated. It's hard not to be angry. However, approaching people in an angry, judgmental fashion will never open them up to hearing what they need to hear. They need to be approached with love and compassion.

There are challenges within the movement as well. When someone starts a new EarthSave chapter they are concerned that they will be competing with other vegetarian societies or animal rights groups in their area. I always tell them to think outside of the box, to create different activities and events that the other groups are not doing. We need more groups doing more outreach to a wider variety of people. We are not competing – we are all in this together.

My best friend was diagnosed with multiple sclerosis about a year and a half ago. This was devastating news. I remembered my aunt who had endured it for over ten years and died after shriveling away in misery. The images of my aunt are very difficult for me and I could not see the same thing happen to another loved one in my life. I read up on the disease and learned about the diet connection. My consulting business was slow and I had a lot of free time available. With my friend's approval, I cleaned out her kitchen and taught her how to shop and prepare healthy food. We did this for several months. I am thrilled to say that she is doing quite well. She has never needed to take medication and has never had another incident since the first diagnosis.

I wish I could do this with more people. So many people say that if they had someone to cook for them it would be so much easier. I give free cooking demos and lectures whenever possible. I also try to sing a few songs when I give a talk. It ties everything together that I love to do and makes the message more effective. As a professional singer in opera and musical theater, I have a wide repertoire of material to draw from. One of my favorite pieces is the "Impossible Dream," from Man of La Mancha. I have performed the role of Aldonza in over 60 performances of the show. While listening to Don Quixote sing the song night after night, the meaning of the words became very clear to me. My mission, my quest, my dream is to help reduce pain and suffering, for people and for animals. I renewed my commitment during every performance whenever I heard the song. Now I end many of my talks with this song as well:

> *To dream the impossible dream*
> *To fight the unbeatable foe*
> *To bear with unbearable sorrow*
> *To run where the brave dare not go*
> *To right the unrightable wrong*
> *To love, pure and chaste from afar*
> *To fight when your arms are to weary*
> *To reach the unreachable star*
> *This is my quest, to follow that star*
> *No matter how hopeless*
> *No matter how far*
> *To fight for the right*
> *Without question or pause*
> *To be willing to march into Hell*
> *For a Heavenly cause*
> *And I know if I'll only be true*
> *To this glorious quest*
> *That my heart will lie peaceful and calm*
> *When I'm laid to my rest*
> *And the world will be better for this*
> *That one man, tossed and covered with scars*
> *Still strove with his last ounce of courage*
> *To reach, the unreachable star*

For more information on EarthSave International, view their website at www.earthsave.org .

It's hard to stay focused and even more difficult to remain vigilant in the world around us, treading as softly as possible. Life tends to gobble us up with its hurried pace and then we give up for a while. We don't believe in the work we do and don't believe we'll ever be able to support ourselves at what we do believe in. And then, having given up a little, it seems that we might as well just go with the flow. Undoubtedly, everything will just go ahead and unfold as it should without us.

Unless it doesn't. Unless the way things unfold does depend on the choices we make.

Tania and I had Thanksgiving supper with a large group of vegetarians at an event in Victoria. The meal was all vegan and it was incredible, without a turkey in sight. Joining us for supper and telling his wonderful story was Howard Lyman, ex-cattle rancher and author of the very successful Mad Cowboy. Howard said whenever he's asked why he's vegan, he simply answers that it makes him happy to know no animal has had to die for him to live. He said that every time he pulls his wallet from his pocket, he remembers that the money doesn't stop there. He thinks about who the money is benefiting and who it is hurting and that often stops him in his tracks.

I think that's perfect and succinct. Who does benefit from our money and who is it hurting? Is someone or something suffering so we can live? Can we avoid that?

We have interesting priorities, we North Americans. Many feel great grief when they see a cat that has been hit by a car but then think nothing of picking up some steaks on the way home for supper. Why is a cat's life more valuable than a cow's life? Or a chicken's? Is the fact that we don't allow them into our homes as pets the difference? Perhaps, but this isn't limited to pets. We see a newborn fawn in a field and we are in awe of it, never considering that it might make a good meal. And yet we'll scarf back a tender young lamb and pay a lot of money for that privilege. We give farm animals no rights to autonomy at all. Well, not all of us. I'm incredibly proud to say no animal has to die for me to eat.

And, after enjoying a wonderful Thanksgiving supper with 400 vegetarians, many of whom have been fully vegan for decades, I can confidently say that no animals have to die for us to eat. We don't need meat. Nor do we need leather.

Our choices don't really need to be so difficult. We can simply question who's suffering from our choices and who's benefiting. Fortunately, the answers do get easier as we go along.

Perhaps nobody spends more time caring for the animals we share life with than the veterinarians who nurture them throughout their lives. And this brings us to our next contributor. One who has dedicated much time to inspiring compassion for our furry friends.

TERI BARNATO

Teri Barnato, M.A., is National Director of the Association of Veterinarians for Animal Rights.

The Association actively works toward the acquisition of rights for all nonhuman animals by educating the public and the veterinary profession about a variety of issues concerning nonhuman animal use. AVAR is actively seeking reformation of the way society treats all nonhumans, and an increase in environmental awareness, as well.

It was 1983. I had just moved to Sacramento from Lake Tahoe. This was like a transition from night to day. Lake Tahoe seemed to have no woes, as it shines daily with beauty and life for the privileged. Sacramento, on the other hand, has many of the world's woes.

I took a job at an office building that was frequented by homeless people and their dogs. One of these was a man who had frequent seizures. His dog would protect him from people trying to help. So, it wasn't long before the animal control department took the dog and proclaimed him vicious. The dog was going to be killed, but the people in my office building decided that this was unjust. We went to the dog's hearing, each adding something to dispel the charges against the dog. I said to a co-worker, It is wrong that people can just take someone's dog and then kill it and that a dog's life is worth so little to our society. She told me to join with other people who were working in the area to protect animals. I did, and it was a rude awakening for me.

Shortly thereafter, I saw "The Animals Film" about how people treat all kinds of animals. I then decided to work for animals, giving up the profession of human counseling for which I had completed my education. It seemed to me that the way we treat nonhumans was so unconscionable that it could not even compare to the way we frequently treat other people, which is also pretty bad. So, I worked for a few different animal protection groups until I took the position with the Association of Veterinarians for Animal Rights (AVAR).

I've worked for AVAR for almost 12 years now and believe that its mission to make the veterinary profession more involved in animal advocacy is very important. All species are connected. I don't believe the world revolves around just one of these species. Therefore, it is my hope that, in my lifetime, I can help inspire people to end their prejudice toward other species, knowing that the many dozens of nonhuman beings who have shared my home over time lived in comfort and were loved.

The Association of Veterinarians for Animal Rights' office is in Davis, California. For more information, view their website at www.avar.org .

We've moved into our wet season, here on our little island. For several months, it was frighteningly dry. The lush greenery all around us had drawn to a halt, dry leaves rustling in the brittle warmth of mid-summer winds. But then the seasons changed, shifting wildly from hot to cool, from dry to wet, from silent to cacophonic. First a massive fog bank rolled in and filled the air we breathe with sweet coolness. A few days behind the fog, the rains began. Walls upon walls of water, drenching the forest as the giant Douglas firs and cedars threw their branches skyward and drank deeply of this oh-so-welcome gift. We're following a record-breaking hot summer all over British Columbia with record-breaking rainfall in the autumn.

I love these changes in season. They feel right to me. It's like an overhaul for the senses. We get too used to things feeling one way and our creativity goes all to pot. Life becomes routine and few wild imaginings fly from our hearts. But then the season changes and we do well to plunge right into it. To open our souls to the swing of the weather. I would love to see what might happen if everyone climbed up into the embrace of a huge pine tree, finding a perch on the highest branch they could reach, perhaps leaving their comfort level just a couple branches below, and then let an autumn rainstorm wash over them. From that one day of collective weather sharing, I believe great inspiration would burst forth, songs of incredible beauty being written by those who had no idea they had it in them.

Wind can grasp our depression and fling it away into the ethers, if only we allow it to. Rain can wash the deepest worries from our soul, if only we let it. Fog can comfort us and bathe us in life if we only remain open.

I've been fortunate enough to witness some pretty incredible weather conditions. I've watched the northern lights dance magically in the minus-forty degree darkness of a Northwest Territories winter. I've seen a water spout plunge from the sky over the turbulent waters off Florida's Gulf Coast. I've hiked through a coastal forest in the wild throws of a hurricane. It's seasonal change that brings this all on. These wondrous, sometimes frightening, blasts of weather shake us to our core and shake the cobwebs from our minds. Perhaps nothing reminds us more of what's important to us than watching a tornado in full flight. Perhaps nothing can soothe our soul quite so much as a cool summer breeze.

Perhaps then, nothing can nurture our state of mind quite so much as simply going outside. Simply raising our own branches to the sky and drinking it all in.

In the time it's taken me to write these past few paragraphs, the fog outside has lifted. Great, moist banks of fog are drifting away through the forest below our house and the sun has washed in through the window. Far below where I sit, off in the distance, the fog is rolling back across the eastern shore of Vancouver Island. The Pacific, from up here, appears smooth and shimmering. The vastness of the water looks so inviting, beauty reaching up to me from the Salish Sea.

Let's meet another contributor, now. Another who has followed her own dreams of helping others clear the cobwebs from their minds.

CATHERINE CARRIGAN

Catherine Carrigan is President and Founder of Total Fitness and author of *Healing Depression: A Holistic Guide*.

Total Fitness is an organization that offers training in mental, physical and spiritual health. Through personal training and seminars, the Total Fitness trainers help people achieve their goals of fitness, strength and flexibility, not only of their physical body but also of their mind and spirit.

DO LESS, BE MORE

The mission for my business, Total Fitness: To empower our students and clients to achieve total fitness of mind, body and spirit through personalized exercise and nutrition programs, ongoing education and positive partnership.

My personal mission: To be a light of God's love wherever I go, with everyone I meet.

For many years, my husband and I have been praying every night to be lights of God's love wherever we go, with everyone we meet. I don't know where that prayer came from – somehow we just began to pray for that. It's not like we are avid church-going folk – I have had several very bad experiences with organized religion, and I keep my spirituality to myself. Now, I frequently receive cards and letters thanking me for being a light. It's funny - I simply set my intention to serve God for the highest good of all, and then I watch what happens in my life.

On the surface, it is possible to look at so-called "achievements." I wrote a book about how to heal depression without drugs. Drugs almost killed me, but I thought they were the only effective method for healing depression. At the time I was writing, I battled two emotions, fear of talking about what had happened to me, and the desire to help others. The battle was neck and neck for a while, but the desire to help other people avoid what I had been through finally won out.

Now I teach people how to heal themselves. With the correct information, my clients become even healthier, even happier, than they thought possible - with natural, non-drug methods. I help people not only to heal their physical bodies but also their minds and their spirits. I used to wonder how my clients found me, because I do not have a big operation. Then, of course, there have been several instances where clients found out about me almost by accident. I can only say, God must have sent them!

As I become a healthier person day by day, my goals have changed. I used to want to have a play on Broadway, to change the U.S. medical establishment's status quo of drugging the mentally ill, to make a difference in a public way. Now I am a little less ego-driven. I see how so many people reach for what looks good on the surface, only to having nothing meaningful underneath. In my business, I see how integrity requires me to practice what I preach, and how being an example is far more powerful than anything I could ever say or do.

My number-one priority in life is to have a happy home, something that I did not have growing up. And it is! Our home is messy, disorganized, and full of love, light and peace.

My life is simple. I strive less, and I recognize that every interaction with every person is an opportunity to share peace and joy.

So many people are lonely. I say, Go to Waffle House and talk to the cook! Smile at the clerk at the grocery store.

There are many opportunities to help others, and in so doing, to heal your own spirit. Doing charity work is not necessary. Just be a good neighbor, a good friend, a good wife, a good mother. Practice loving more and judging less. Find the joy inside. It's there.

My favorite yoga teacher once brought tears to my eyes when he said the best reason to meditate is to connect to all the love there is, so that it will no longer matter that you did not get any when you were growing up.

I am now able to access peace, love and joy. It is no longer necessary for me to strive, prove or carry report.

I am learning to be OK with doing less and being more.

Total Fitness' head office is located in Atlanta, Georgia. For more information, view Catherine Carrigan's website at www.totalfitness.net .

The next person I invite you to meet is Mike Carriere. We visited his little store while traveling through Winnipeg and I was moved to ask Mike to write his story for Softly On This Earth. I'm pretty sure his story could have been a lot more detailed than this and readers would very much enjoy reading about it, but short and sweet is fine.

Stories like this are becoming more and more frequent and they're very important. They give people the courage to follow their hearts and do what feels right to them. Every time I enter a small business where the owners are clearly focused on raising the consciousness of the world around them, my heart sings.

MIKE CARRIERE

Mike Carriere is Co-Owner of Hempyrean in Winnipeg, Manitoba.
Hempyrean is a clothing store that promotes hemp products as an Earth-friendly alternative for consumers.

I became disillusioned with my role in the banking business and then as manager of a hotel and bar. I was dealing with too much alcohol, junky food, and smoking among my customers. One day, I realized I wanted to do something to leave the world a better place for my three children.

My wife first introduced me to hemp foods, primarily the seeds and oil. I thought, wow, this tastes great and it's good for you. Then I found out hemp grew all over Manitoba and you can make all types of things with hemp.

That's when I started doing some research. After six months of research and looking for a fresh start, we started the business of Hempyrean in June of 2002.

I guess my dream is to one-day see hemp being used for fuel and paper. It enriches soil and prevents erosion, it burns clean and sulphur-free hemp fuel maintains the earth's natural O_2/CO_2 balance.

It would be great to see hemp one day replace cotton in the clothing industry, since half the pesticides in the U.S. are sprayed on cotton plants.

I play but a small part in the solution for a sustainable planet and yet a larger part in its destruction. I must work to reverse this trend!

For more information about Mike and Hempyrean, visit their website at www.hempyrean.com .

Ethan Smith

From our briefest essay, we now lead into our most in-depth. This contributor is an amazingly driven individual who has dedicated his entire life to raising consciousness about the other animals we share this planet with. He needs no other introduction.

DR. MARC BEKOFF

Marc Bekoff, Ph.D., is Professor of Biology at the University of Colorado, Boulder. Dr. Bekoff's extensive work in animal behavior has been published in more than 175 papers and 15 books. He edited *The Encyclopedia of Animal Rights and Animal Welfare*. Dr. Bekoff is Co-Founder (with Jane Goodall) of the organization Ethologists for the Ethical Treatment of Animals.

MINDING ANIMALS AND MINDING EARTH:
MOVING TOWARDS A LOVE AFFAIR WITH ALL OF NATURE.

A clear distinction should be made between what is not found by science and what is found to be non-existent by science. What science finds to be non-existent, we must accept as non-existent; but what science merely does not find is a completely different matter . . . It is quite clear that there are many, many mysterious things. (His Holiness the Dalai Lama, The Path to Tranquility: Daily Wisdom)

Who am I, what do I do, why do I care?
When people ask me what I do, I first tell them who I am. I am a human being first and foremost. And, I also happen to be a professor of Biology at the University of Colorado in Boulder. I grew up in a very warm, compassionate, and loving household, and always felt very close to nonhuman animal beings (animals). My parents have told me that I've always "minded animals."

In a nutshell, the phrase "minding animals" means caring for them, respecting them, feeling for them, and attributing minds (mental states and content) to individuals. I've always wanted to know what animals were thinking and feeling and never doubted that they have very active minds. Although I wasn't raised with animals, I've always wondered what they might be thinking about or feeling as they went about their daily activities. The question that has continually motivated my research is "What is it like to be a ___ " (where _____ can be any animal), and in reality, this question has always been at the center of my interactions with the natural world, including trees, rocks, bodies of water, and air – *What is it like to be a rock?*

Deep ethology

I also continue to develop my notion of deep ethology. I use the term "deep ethology" to stress that people are an integral part of nature, and they have unique responsibilities to nature. Deep ethology means respecting all animals, appreciating all animals, showing compassion for all animals, and feeling for all animals from one's heart. Deep ethology also means resisting speciesism. Our respect for animals does not mean that we can then do whatever we want with them!

As an inhabitant of Earth, I'm a lover of the diverse and wondrous life on this splendid planet. As a scientist who has been lucky enough to have studied social behavior in coyotes in the Grand Teton National Park in Jackson, Wyoming, the behavioral development in Adélie penguins in Antarctica near the South Pole, the social behavior of domestic dogs, and the social behavior of various birds living near my home in the Rocky Mountains of Colorado, I've learned a lot about these amazing animals and many others. I am very concerned about what humans are doing to other animals, and to the planet in general. While some of my views may make it seem as if I want to stop all animal research, including my own, and the use of all animals everywhere, this simply is not so. I am just not very happy with what is happening to the wonderful animals with whom I am privileged to live and share the Earth.

My interests in the lives of animals, and how humans treat them, seem to be innate. I've always had deep feelings about them. Since I began working with animals, I have spent a lot of time pondering the complex and troubling relationships between animal and human beings. I am often terribly upset by the horrible things that humans do to other animals with whom we share Earth. I recognize fully that many people who harm nonhumans for purposes of research, education, food, or amusement also bring joy to some animals at other times. Of course, nonhumans do not always suffer at the hands of humans. I find myself focusing on horror stories not because I am a pessimist (whose glass is always half empty), but rather because it is important to call attention to the incredible pain and suffering of animals at the hands of humans. Of course, it's also important to remind people of the many good things that are done by humans for nonhumans' benefits.

Where I'm coming from

My early scientific training was grounded in what the philosopher, Bernard Rollin, has called the "common sense of science," in which science is viewed as a fact-gathering, value-free activity. Of course, science is not value-free. We all come to our lives with a point of view, but it took some time for me to realize this truth, because of our heavy indoctrination (and arrogance) concerning the need for scientific objectivity. In supposedly "objective" science, animals are not subjects, but objects that should not be named. Close bonding with them is frowned upon. However, for me, naming and bonding with the animals whom I study is but one of many ways to show respect for them.

With respect to the plight of the nonhumans who were used in classes or for research, I never saw or felt much if any concern for their well-being. Questions concerning morals and ethics rarely arose. When they did, these questions were invariably dismissed either by invoking self-serving utilitarianism (I call this "vulgar" or "facile" utilitarianism), in which suspected costs and benefits were offered only from the human's point of view (with no concern for the nonhuman's perspective); or by simply asserting that the animals really didn't know, care, or mind (or whatever word could be used to communicate the animal's supposed indifference to) what was going on. Only once do I remember someone vaguely implying that something beneficial for the animal might come out of a research project.

Killing rabbit

One afternoon, during a graduate course in physiology, one of my professors calmly strutted into class announcing, while sporting a wide grin, that he was going to kill a rabbit for us to use in a later experiment by using a method named after the rabbit himself, namely a "rabbit punch." He killed the rabbit, breaking his neck, by chopping him with the side of his hand. I was astonished and sickened by the entire spectacle. I refused to partake in the laboratory exercise, and also decided that what I was doing at the time was simply wrong for me. I began to think seriously about alternatives. I enjoyed science (and continue to enjoy doing scientific research), but I imagined that there must be other ways of doing science that would incorporate respect for animals and allow for individual differences among scientists concerning how science is conducted.

I went on to another graduate program, but dropped out because I didn't want to kill dogs in physiology laboratories and cats in a research project. My research centered on vision in cats. I truly enjoyed the challenge of determining how cats see their world. However, once the killing of experimental animals began, I also truly hated killing the animals to localize lesions in various parts of their brains. Recently I learned that the famous biologist, Charles Darwin, might also have left medical school after one year, because he was "repulsed" by experiments on dogs. In his book, *The Descent of Man*, Darwin wrote the following about those people who experimented on dogs: *This man, unless he had a heart of stone, must have felt remorse to the last hour of his life.*

The eyes of Speedo

One morning I woke up very disturbed about the whole thing, and decided that I could not continue to kill the cats. The eyes of the cats, especially one I'd secretly named Speedo, tormented me as they were being prepared to be killed. What an undignified end to a life! But what sort of life did they really have - live in a small prison (a.k.a. research facility), learn to negotiate a maze, sustain brain damage at the hands of researchers, run the maze again to see if there was any decline in performance, and be sacrificed – die. Naming animals was taboo because it was thought that one might become too attached to an individual and might actually care about his or her life. Objectivity was the name of the scientific game and subjectivity had no place in reliable scientific research.

Here's a brief story about my short life with Speedo, taken from Jane Goodall's and my book, *The Ten Trusts: What We Must Do To Care For The Animals We Love.*

When I first began conducting research in neurobiology and behavior, trying to figure out how cats processed visual information, I had no idea of what I was getting into. I'd teach cats to make discriminations among different visual patterns, for which they were rewarded with food for making the correct choice. Each cat had his or her own way of learning, some slowly, some rapidly, and some, not at all. I'd (secretly) name the individuals as they ran the maze, paying attention to their personalities and learning abilities. I remember Speedo looking at me when I lifted him from his small cage and anesthetized him, and then proceeded to remove part of the visual cortex of his brain. As he succumbed to the anesthesia, his eyes looked at me and asked, *What are you doing*? His gaze is forever burned into my heart.

For a very short time I was able to continue this research - train a cat on a particular task, remove part of the brain, and see how well they remembered the task after recovering from the surgery. But, it was when I had to euthanize them (sacrifice - kill with a minimum of pain, distress, and fear) to make sure that the damage I caused was localized in the correct area of the brain that it all came to a sudden halt. I did indeed regretfully euthanize four cats, Speedo being the last. When I went to get Speedo for the final exit from his cage, his fearlessness disappeared as if he knew that this was his last journey. His boldness and cockiness melted as I picked him up, and tears came to my eyes. He wouldn't break his piercing stare and it broke my heart to kill him. I wish I could have taken him home. To this day I remember his unwavering eyes – they told the whole story of the pain and indignity he had endured.

I simply didn't want to kill animals as part of my research. I couldn't justify this murder using any form of utilitarianism. I (and three medical students) also refused to partake in some physiology experiments that used dogs, and to our amazement, we were excused without prejudice from doing so, although the distinguished professor couldn't understand why we didn't want to kill the dogs. He asserted that they would have died in an animal shelter anyway. To his credit, though, he remained true to his word and I applaud his permissiveness and his open-mindedness. At the end of the term, despite these reprieves, I left this program because I could not do the research that I wanted to without killing animals or being responsible for their deaths. If I must forego learning something because I must kill animals to do so, then so be it.

The use and abuse of nonconsenting animals

The issues on which I spend a lot of time include the horrible lives of animal prisoners in zoos, wildlife theme parks, aquariums, and research laboratories. I am also very concerned with the use of animals in education. I am a strong opponent of dissection and vivisection in the classroom. These are the issues closest to my heart. I want people to learn about the awesome and magnificent lives of "wild" animals, not their captive relatives, whose impoverished lives in zoos are seriously compromised. They have no freedom of choice; they can't go where they want to go, they are nonconsenting victims.

My interest in the lives of research animals stems from some of my own research; I know how horrible their lives are. The arrogance of some of my colleagues also motivates me to question their goals and the ways they treat the animals on whom their lives and reputations depend.

Many biomedical models that stem from animal research simply do not work toward the goals for which they are intended. Unfortunately, the use of animal models often creates false hopes for humans in need. It's estimated that only 1 to 3.5 percent of the decline in the rate of human mortality since 1900 has stemmed from animal research. The prestigious publication, the New England Journal of Medicine, called the war on cancer a qualified failure. More than 100,000 people die annually from the side effects of animal-tested drugs. Early animal models of polio also impeded progress on finding a cure. As pointed out by the Medical Research Modernization Committee, Dr. Simon Flexner's monkey model of polio misled other researchers concerning the mechanism of infection. He concluded that polio only infected the nervous systems of monkeys; but research using human tissue culture showed that poliovirus could be cultivated on tissue that was not from the nervous system. Chimpanzees were used to study AIDS, but chimps do not contract AIDS! Many people die from biomedical models because the diseases produced in animal research are artificially induced, while the naturally occurring course of the disease is quite different.

Some guiding principles

I believe that our starting point should be that we will not intrude on other animals' lives unless we can justify an override of this maxim. Our actions must be in the best interests of the animals irrespective of our own desires. When we are unsure about how we influence the lives of other animals, we should err on the side of the animals.

Some guiding principles include:
- Putting respect, compassion, and admiration for other animals first and foremost, taking seriously the animals' points of view.
- Erring on the animals' side when uncertain about their feeling of pain or suffering.
- Recognizing that most of the methods that are currently used to study animals, even in the field, are intrusions on their lives, and thus, exploitative.
- Recognizing how misguided are speciesistic views, using very vague notions of intelligence and cognitive/mental complexity for determining assessments of well-being.
- Focusing on the importance of individuals.
- Appreciating individual variation and the diversity of the lives of different individuals in the worlds in which they live.
- Using common sense and empathy, which some say have no place in science.

Towards a compassionate new world: Moving toward a heartfelt science

I have a number of goals that I would like to accomplish in my short life on Earth. Some of my ideas have been presented in previous papers and books, whereas others are constantly being revisited and revised as I ponder more deeply just what it is that animals can teach us about Nature's wisdom. I am sure that some of the very ideas about which I write now will metamorphose when I revisit this essay and I discuss it with colleagues. It is precisely the dynamic, frustrating, and very challenging topics with which I am concerned that keep me working feverishly to gain a coherent perspective, at least for a short period of time.

There are many ways to travel the path of Nature's wisdom and to learn about her sagacious ways, and I hope that I can convince you that one path travels directly through the hearts and minds of our animal kin, and that we can learn much about Nature's wisdom if we open our own hearts and minds to her prudent ways. Given what some people do to animals, I often wish they were not as sentient and wise as they are. But the fact is that they are and we must change our ways and bond with, and love, animals because they are such wise and feeling organisms.

It is essential that heartless science be replaced with heartfelt and compassionate science and that all scientists take seriously their responsibility to be socially responsible and share their findings with nonscientists and the community at large. In my view, we need much more than traditional science — science that is not especially socially responsible, science that is autonomous and authoritarian, science that fragments the universe and disembodies and alienates humans and other animals — to make headway into understanding other animals and the world at large. We need to broaden science to incorporate and to be drenched in feeling, heart, spirit, soul, and love. Scientists need not be suspicious of things they cannot fully understand. Scientists need to exit their heads and go deeply into their hearts, and science needs to open its arms to people who love the world and who have a reverence for all life. Scientists should not be inhibited about being sentimental. We need a science of unity, a science of reconciliation, a compassionate science.

One must have a passionate vision. I would say that the most important starting point is to believe that it is always wrong to harm other animals intentionally, that humans are obliged to honor the lives of nonhuman animal beings even if it would benefit us not to do so.

My goal is to have people become more compassionate and respectful to all animals and the inanimate environment. We should view animals as our friends and partners in our effort to make the world the best it can be, for them and for us. We need to love animals and Earth. There really is ample room for "science with a heart."

Being concerned about animals does not mean we are insensitive to humans. The two are not unrelated in my view. For example, stopping animal research would mean that we would develop better models and cures for human diseases. Caring about animals means we will come to care more for humans.

I feel success will come when animals are no longer eaten, imprisoned in zoos, used in research, cut up in educational pursuits, and otherwise exploited by humans for their own anthropocentric interests.

I also advocate patience. Telling others what to do never works. Long-lasting changes are more productive than short-term changes. The changes must be changes of the heart—deep changes—and not superficial changes that are temporary or ephemeral.

The importance of activism: Activism is healing

There's an old saying, *After all is said and done, much more has been said than done.* While this is so for our interactions with animals, the human community, and Earth, and is among the many reasons that we wrote this book, we have indeed made much progress in making this a better world, a more compassionate world in which caring and sharing abound. By our "minding animals" and "minding Earth," numerous animals, people, and habitats are far better off than they would have been in the absence of an ethic blending together respect, caring, compassion, humility, grace, and love. Caring about some being or some thing, any being or any thing, can spill over into caring for every body and every thing. If we focus on the awe and mystery of other animals and Earth, perhaps we will be less likely to destroy them. Allowing ourselves to sense the presence of other animals, to feel their residence in our hearts, brings much joy and peace and can foster spiritual development, a sense of unity and oneness. And this happiness, this sense of bliss, allows for Earth, bodies of water, air, animals, and people to be blended into a seamless tapestry, a warm blanket of caring and compassion, in which every single individual counts and every single individual makes a difference. The interconnectedness of individuals into a community means that what one does affects all – what happens in New York influences what happens across the world in Beijing and other distant locales.

I ask the people with whom I interact to imagine that they carry a suitcase of courage, compassion, and hope and that because they receive what they give, the supply of courage, compassion, and hope will never be exhausted. It is easy to have one's spirit and soul weathered by the "bad" things that happen around us. It seems as if we are addicted to destroying the very animals and landscapes we love. But many, many good things are happening each and every day all over the world that can (re)kindle our spirit and impel us to act.

One makes a difference: The importance of hope, dreams, peace, and love

It's very important to realize that each and every individual counts. As Jane Goodall puts it, One makes a difference. In addition to teaching at the University of Colorado, I also leave the ivory tower and organize and take part in protests against animal abuse. Because of my efforts to call attention to the poorly organized program to reintroduce Canadian lynx to Colorado, one state employee attempted to get the University of Colorado to censure me.
(www.bouldernews.com/opinion/columnists/bekmarc.html).

Roots & Shoots

I also am regional coordinator of Jane Goodall's Roots & Shoots program (www.janegoodall.org). I work with students of all ages and also senior citizens and inmates at the Boulder County jail. All of these individuals make a difference; all are sources of wisdom and hope. Roots & Shoots is about building appreciation and respect for animals, people, and the environment. It originally focused on youngsters but now there are thousands of groups for all age groups in more than 70 countries worldwide. A major aspect of this program stresses that all individuals matter – that the voice of each and every individual needs to be heard. Those who lead Roots & Shoots programs, strive to empower participants.

My work with prisoners has been unbelievably educational and inspiring. Crossing the divide into a habitat in which I've never lived really has been an education for me. In my groups we talk about animal behavior and spend considerable time discussing ethics – how humans should interact with nonhuman animal beings and how we should interact with the environment. Discussions of sustainability rival those that I have in my university classes and debates about animal thinking, emotions, pain, and ethics are informed and moving.

It never fails to impress me that most of the men with whom I work are also incredibly hopeful individuals. And they're helping to nurture hope among youngsters by writing letters and poems telling kids about the mistakes they made, stressing that jail just isn't the place to be if they really want to make a difference, if they want to be able to work for a better world.

Many of the men with whom I work enjoy sharing messages of hope, for their voices are often silent on these issues. Many have families and want them to develop and sustain hope in what often is presented as a bleak and hopeless world. And they do indeed have much wisdom to share. Their messages often bring me to tears. Sincere outcries to try to make this a better world for all beings. These are messages that stress the importance of "being a kid" and the overriding importance of having a positive self-image and of boundless love. Some of the drawings that accompany their prose are outstanding works of art.

A few weeks ago, during one of my visits, one man couldn't wait to tell me about a wonderful bilingual project he'd begun called "The Book of Hope" - "El libro de la esperanza." It began with a well-known verse: *We are the world, we are the children, we are the ones to make a brighter day...so let's start giving...There Is Hope - Hay Esperanza.* A very accomplished artist did incredibly detailed pencil drawings to accompany the text. Some of the messages go as follows:

*Kids out there – you don't want to be like us – it's up to you to change the world and make it a better place.

*Tell your teachers that you want to help stop the destruction of your heritage.

*I hope that I can help those in need of help, as I would want others to help me when I need assistance.

*Obtaining an education will help unlock the doors to gaining opportunities.

*If I could do my life over these are the things I would do. Love yourself; go to school to learn how to live, be a good friend, love and respect your family...you can feel in your heart what is right. Have faith and hope for the future. Be happy. Time passes very fast so please don't waste it. You are all very special.

*Be a kid, have fun, play ball in the afternoon sun...climb trees and care about the birds and the bees...have simple days and simple ways, a kool-aid smile to light up your face.

*The future is like a bottled promise...the single greatest commodity known to man is HOPE. Hope is like dancing in stiletto heels – how it takes all your fears and breaks them down to make you feel good about yourself.

We can all learn from one another and we need to build bridges that carry messages of hope, peace, respect, compassion, and love. Perhaps more now than ever everyone should be encouraged to spread the word, for there are many reasons for hope. And silence is not always golden. As the late Martin Luther King, Jr. said: A time comes when silence is betrayal. He was right. Silence and indifference can be deadly for our animal friends, for Earth, and for youth who will be our voices and carry our messages into the future.

So, if you're looking for something to do, consider going out and building new bridges, dare to cross frustrating and challenging divides. It isn't always easy but never say never, ever. Sharing messages of peace and hope with everyone certainly is a good road to travel starting now – not tomorrow because "things" might get in the way, but right now.

I hope that others and I have inspired you to act, to do something – anything – to make this a better world. As Margaret Mead noted: *Never doubt that a small group of thoughtful committed citizens can change the world*. Indeed, it is the only thing that ever has. It is never too late to do something. Even if you have only one minute, or ten seconds a day, you can make a difference. Talk to friends and families while taking a break, while taking a walk, while just "hanging out." The small fraction that we each offer can contribute to larger solutions. Even a tiny ripple – a little agitation – can spread wide and rapidly. Even if you only have time to help one individual, you can make a difference. It is thought that North Atlantic right whales might survive if only one or a few females are spared each year –one whale matters.

Old big brains in new bottlenecks: Why we seek Nature's wisdom

As big-brained, omnipresent, powerful and supposedly omniscient mammals, we are the most powerful beings on Earth. We really are that powerful, and with that might are inextricably tied innumerable staggering responsibilities to be ethical human beings. We can be no less. I think that the influence of our big brains can lead us in a number of different directions.

Why do we feel good when we're out in Nature? While I was preparing my presentation for a meeting called "The Path to Nature's Wisdom" convened by His Holiness the Dalai Lama as part of his Kalachakra for World Peace 2002 (www.kalachakra-kultur.at), I discovered the following quotation by the renowned author, Henry Miller: *If we don't always start from Nature we certainly come to her in our hour of need.*

Perhaps there is not only one reason why Nature's wisdom is frequently sought when we feel out of balance, when times are tough. Perhaps we can look to evolution to understand why we do so.

I find I am never alone and neither do I feel lonely when I am out in Nature. Her wisdom easily captures me and I feel safe and calm wrapped in her welcoming arms. We converse with one another. Why do we go to Nature for guidance? Why do we feel so good, so much at peace, when we see, hear, and smell other animals, when we look at trees and smell the fragrance of flowers, when we watch water in a stream, a lake or an ocean? We often cannot articulate why, when we are immersed in Nature, there are such penetrating calming effects, why we often become breathless, why we sigh, why we place a hand on our heart as we sense and feel Nature's beauty, awe, mystery, and generosity. Perhaps the feelings that are evoked are so very deep, primal, that there are no words that are deep or rich enough to convey just what we feel. Joy when we know that Nature is doing well and deep sorrow and pain when we feel that Nature is being destroyed, exploited, and devastated. I ache when I feel Nature being wounded.

What about our ancestors? Surely, there must have been more significant consequences for them if they fooled with Nature. They did not have all of the mechanical and intellectual know-how to undo their intrusions into natural processes. Indeed, early humans were probably so busy just trying to survive that they could not have had the opportunities to wreak the havoc that we have brought to Nature. And the price of their injurious intrusions would likely have been much more serious for them, because of their intimate interrelations with, and dependency on, Nature, than they are for us.

Nonetheless, I imagine that our psyches, like theirs, suffer when Nature is harmed. Human beings worldwide commonly lament how badly they feel when they sense Nature and her complex webs being spoiled, and ecopsychologists argue just this point. It would be invaluable if we could tune into our old big brains and let them guide us, for our brains are very much like those of our ancestors. However, our socio cultural milieus, technology, and Nature have changed significantly and we face new and challenging bottlenecks. Cycles of Nature are still with us and also within us, although we might not be aware of their presence because we can so easily override just about anything natural. Much technology and "busy-ness" cause alienation from Nature. This breach in turn leads to our wanton abuse of Nature. It is all too easy to harm environs to which we are not attached or to abuse other beings to whom we are not bonded, to whom we don't feel close.

Our brains can distance us from Nature but they also can lead us back to her. Perhaps there is an instinctive drive to have close ties with Nature – biophilia, if you will – and when these reciprocal interconnections are threatened or ruptured, we seek Nature as a remedy because our old brains still remember the importance of being an integral and cardinal part of innumerable natural processes, and how good these deep interconnections felt. Perhaps our close ancestral ties with Nature offer a reason for hope, a reason for being optimistic about healing deeply wounded Nature. It just does not feel good to cause harm to Nature. Perhaps the intense joy we feel when Nature is healthy, the joy we feel when we are embedded in Nature's mysterious ways and webs, is but one measure of the deep love we have for her, a love that might offer us one more chance to change our ways, a love to awaken us from a dangerous and pitiful apathy that amounts to the betrayal of our collective responsibility to act proactively and with passion to save Nature for our and future generations. Activism, whether it involves calling attention to our destructive ways or conducting research that can be used to right wrongs, can be healing for us and Nature, and is but one way for us to return to Nature some of the wisdom and solace she provides, to allow her to continue to exist for all to relish.

Minding animals, minding ourselves: We are basically a cooperative species

By minding animals we mind ourselves. Personal transformations are needed and will serve us well. We owe it to future generations to transcend the present, to share dreams for a better world, to step lightly, to move cautiously with restraint. We owe it to our children and theirs to take care of animals and Earth. We all can be dreamers and doers at the same time.

I deeply believe that, fundamentally, humans are a cooperative species. I've argued elsewhere, and in more detail in a book I'm now writing on the evolution of cooperation and social morality in animals, that cooperation is not always a by-product of tempering aggressive and selfish tendencies and attempts at reconciliation.

It's a flagrant misappropriation and misunderstanding of Charles Darwin's agenda to argue that nature is solely red in tooth and claw. *Cooperation, fairness, and social protocols can evolve on their own because they are important in the formation and maintenance of social relationships.* This view, in which Nature is sanitized, contrasts with those who see aggression, cheating, selfishness, and perhaps amorality as driving the evolution of sociality. The combative Hobbesian world in which individuals are constantly at one another's throats isn't the natural state of affairs, and altruism isn't always simply selfishness disguised. Richard Dawkins, Mr. Selfish Genes himself, recently told an audience at a professional gathering: *A pretty good definition of the kind of society in which I don't want to live is a society founded on the principles of Darwinism.* But there are principles of Darwinism that allow for cooperation, empathy, and morality.

We are all part of the same deeply interconnected and interdependent community. We are one among many. We are all woven into a seamless tapestry of unity with interconnecting bonds that are reciprocal and that overflow with respect, compassion, and love. I feel blessed when I open myself to the heart, spirit, and soul of other animals. When I study coyotes I am coyote; when I study birds I am bird. Often when I stare at a tree, I am tree. There is a strong sense of oneness. Compassion and hope are two essential ingredients for making this a better planet for all life. My own spirituality is based on a deep drive for a seamless unity, a sense of oneness, motivated by compassion, respect, and love.

The social matrix in which I am defined is an integrated tapestry, a dynamic event of monumental proportions that might currently (or forever) resist being totally intelligible given the evolutionary state of my and other human's brains. My spiritual quest has taken me to the arena in which science, ethology, spirituality, and theology meet. Much of my journey owes itself to my interactions with other animals and their willingness to share their lives with me. Watching a red fox bury another red fox, observing the birth of coyote pups and the tender care provided by parents and helpers, watching dogs blissfully lost in play, and nearly stepping on a mountain lion have made me realize how much of "me" is defined by my relationships with others.

We owe it to ourselves to keep in mind the power of love. We owe it to ourselves and to other animals to whom we can, unfortunately, do whatever we choose. I want all beings to be wrapped up in a tightly interwoven community, to be wrapped in a seamless tapestry – a warm blanket – of love. I want humility, grace, respect, compassion, kindness, generosity, respect, and love to be as natural and reflexive as the knee-jerk response. Surely, we will come to feel better about ourselves if we know deep in our hearts that we did the best we could and took into account the well-being of the magnificent animals with whom we share Earth, the awesome beings who selflessly make our lives richer, more challenging, and more enjoyable than they would be in the animals' absence.

Love

On our journeys we will discover that we can indeed love animals more and not love people less. We need to be motivated by love, and not by fear of what it will mean if we come to love animals for who they are. Animals are not less than human. They are who they are and need to be understood in their own worlds.

It all boils down to love. The power of love must not be underestimated as we try to reconnect with nature and other animals. We need to love the universe and all of its inhabitants – animate and inanimate. We need to follow the heat of our hearts and live love. Our continued disrespect, and abuse of animals, and our relegation of them to hapless and innocent victims of human greed and arrogance, will make for much loneliness and a severely impoverished universe.

Giving and receiving within the community of Earth

No people ever knew the Earth as well as we do in terms of its mechanistic processes, but no people have ever had less intimacy with the planet. We are shriveled up in our souls.
(Thomas Berry, 2000)

In the grand scheme of things, individuals receive what they give. If love is poured out in abundance then it will be returned in abundance. There is no need to fear depleting the potent and self-reinforcing feeling of love that continuously can serve as a powerful stimulant for generating compassion, respect, and more love for all life. Each and every individual plays an essential role and that individual's spirit and love are intertwined with the spirit and love of others. These emergent interrelationships, which transcend individuals, embodied selves, foster a sense of oneness. These interrelationships can work in harmony to make this a better and more compassionate world for all beings. We must stroll with our kin and not leave them in our tumultuous wake of rampant, self-serving destruction.

It is essential that we do better than our ancestors and we surely have the resources to do so. Perhaps the biggest question of all is whether enough of us will choose to make the heartfelt commitment to making this a better world, a more compassionate world in which love is plentiful and shared, before it is too late. I believe we have already embarked on this pilgrimage. My optimism leads me in no other direction.

Let us all make a pact to do no intentional harm, to treat all individuals with compassion, and to step lightly into the lives of other beings, bodies of water, air, and landscapes. It will be difficult and challenging and also frustrating to achieve win-win solutions all of the time, but if we set any lower goal we can be sure that we will not be able to accomplish win-win agreements. Moral progress requires moral choices. Let us expand our relatively closed human clubhouse to incorporate all of Earth.

We are one: Replacing mindlessness with mindfulness

We are one. We really are one closely integrated community. We are a single community in which the loss of a single individual matters. We are part of the rest. "We" means animals, plants, trees, soil, rocks, water, and air. "We" means everyone – every being – and every thing. Harming other animals matters. Changing the course of rivers matters. Moving rocks matters. Cutting down trees matters. We must strive for selfless unity. We need to be mindful of all of our actions. We need more compassionate and respectful contact with all of Nature. Each individual is defined by the presence of others. We need wise

Nature and we need wise animals. We need them greatly, more than perhaps many people realize. Let us not lose our animal kin and only then discover what they truly mean to us because of who they are. Let us not lose them and only then discover that their absence robs us of our own identity, of our own place on and in Earth, and of our own wisdom.

Some directions for the future

When I finished editing *The Encyclopedia of Animal Rights and Animal Welfare* I realized how much work is left to do in the area of animal protection. I hoped to expose more youngsters to the critical issues in my children's book *Strolling with Our Kin: Speaking for and Respecting Voiceless Animals*. I develop many of my ideas in two recent books, *Minding Animals: Awareness, Emotions, and Heart* and *The Ten Trusts: What We Must Do to Care for the Animals We Love* (with Jane Goodall). In June 2000, Jane and I founded the organization Ethologists for the Ethical Treatment of Animals/Citizens for Responsible Animal Behavior Studies.

Some of the material in this essay has been excerpted from my piece in *People Promoting and People Opposing Animal Rights* (edited by J. M. Kistler, Greenwood Press, 2002).

For more information on Marc Bekoff and Jane Goodall's EETA (Ethologists for the Ethical Treatments of Animals) organization, view their website at www.ethologicalethics.org .

Another good website for information on the extensive work of Dr. Bekoff is www.literati.net/Bekoff .

I've been writing music as a hobby for about ten years. Before that, before I even learned to play guitar, I wrote poetry. I used to get a huge energy rush from frenzied writing, letting all my youthful angst rush out through my fingers. At the same time, I loved music but never made the connection between the two.

If I have one regret, it might be that I didn't pick up a guitar at a much earlier age. It was certainly in my blood. Both of my parents are very musical souls. My mom used to play us folk songs on her guitar and banjo when we were little. I would often hold her guitar and strum wide-open chords although it never occurred to me to ask her to teach me how to play. Or, if it did, I certainly never stuck with it.

My attraction to the guitar happened many years later, when I met a musician who had climbed to the very top of the charts doing what he loved. Les Emmerson, lead singer and songwriter for the late 60's band, The Five Man Electrical Band, wrote the song *Signs*, that put his band on the map and still rides the airwaves today, more than 30 years after its release. I interviewed Les while I was in college in Ottawa and wound up becoming friends with him. My friends and I would go hang out in the little pub where Les and his buddies still played, not because they had to but because they absolutely loved what they did. In between sets, Les would sit with us and tell us stories from the rock and roll highway while we all listened to him with rapt attention.

Not long after I graduated from college and left Ottawa, I walked into the Alberta Guitar Company in Calgary and bought myself a guitar, built by hand in their store. It had no brand name on it so I took a sticker of a fox someone had given me and stuck it to the outside of my guitar case and thus dubbed it the Fox.

I enrolled in a guitar class and quickly extended my knowledge from one chord to three, a point from which there was no looking back. Over a decade later, I can now play four chords with confidence. Actually, I can play a few more than that, although I have never taken the time to really apply myself to learning 40-minute instrumentals and breathtaking, beautiful ballads. I did though, early in the game, figure out that my old poetry writing hobby applied itself very nicely to my guitar. I began writing songs on the Fox, using the words from my old poems and finding rhythms for them. Then all my youthful angst began to flow again, this time through my newly written songs. For quite a while, I wrote prolifically, even sending various demo tapes of my music out to publishers. Through my twenties, when confusion, elation and bouts of depression ruled my days, my songwriting was frenzied and consistently strong. Even enough that several other musicians took the time to learn my songs and gave me heaps of encouragement.

My thirties brought with them a lot more happiness and a more laid back approach to life, translating into fewer songs of angst bursting from me. The songs have become fewer but I'd like to think they have also matured a little. I still send out demo tapes occasionally, not because I have any visions of strutting into a stadium of screaming fans but because I think hearing an established musician singing one of my songs on the radio would be an incredible experience. And I might be about due for another try.

The theme of Softly On This Earth is about sharing the stories of people who have found the courage to help the world around them, not about inspiring readers to achieve stardom. Unless, of course, someone can help the world by doing just that. What better platform is there, really, to get people's attention?

My next contributor is a kindred spirit who has followed her musical dream, applying herself to her art and raising awareness at the same time.

HEIDI HOWE

Heidi Howe is a Louisville, Kentucky, singer/songwriter. Her music is a reflection of her dedication to the environment and its inhabitants. With her Food Without A Face CD, she toured to raise awareness and promote the connection between the natural world and all who live in it, including humans.

What do you want to be when you grow up, is a question almost none of us escapes answering. When I was a child, my dreams for the future were based solely on what brought me Joy. This was, and continues to be, performing music. I began when I was young to pursue my dream every chance I got.

In my early teens, I had a good friend who I desperately wanted to emulate. She was a little older than I was, she played guitar and wrote songs, and she was a vegetarian. Because I looked up to her so much, I became a vegetarian too and also began to write songs and learn how to play guitar.

While studying vocal music at the Youth Performing Arts School in Louisville, Kentucky, in the early 1990's, I joined an after school group called "Youth for Causes." I began to learn how my daily choices affect the world around me. I became primarily concerned about animal rights issues and started to become involved in activism in some ways. Fighting for animal rights solidified my choice to be a vegetarian. I have since learned how my diet affects the environment and other inhabitants of this planet. I made the decision to become vegan (eating no animal products) in 1995 and have maintained that diet to this day.

As I mentioned, I always knew I wanted a career in music. Mostly motivated by desire for "fame and fortune," I never considered combining my ethical convictions and my music. I was afraid of alienating potential fans, and my career was without direction. I had good intentions but no objectives.

Before the release of my second album in 2001, I decided I wanted to donate a portion of the CD profits to EarthSave, an organization that promotes food choices that are healthy for people and for the planet. After selling some CD's, I was able to contribute some money. It felt really good to give to a cause I was passionate about through the sale of music I was passionate about.

I decided I wanted to write and release a song about the EarthSave message as a way to raise awareness nationally for both EarthSave and my music. I wrote and recorded the song "Food Without a Face." My team and I attempted to obtain sponsors for the project, but after the events on September 11, 2001, companies were reluctant to give donations. Eden Foods did contribute a multitude of coupons and recipe books, and Recycline toothbrushes gave us some coupons as well. We put the coupons in the CD packages and decided to give out the recipe books at shows.

I contacted vegetarian groups across the country and arranged to perform at all kinds of events (potlucks, festivals, vegan restaurants, coffeehouses, etc). I released the CD in April of 2002 at the EarthSave Taste of Health in Louisville, Kentucky. Then I traveled to many cities, from Seattle, Washington, to Los Angeles, California, to Miami, Florida promoting the project. I performed my last concert for the project in November 2002 at EarthSave Louisville's Turkey-Free Thanksgiving dinner.

The "Food Without a Face" CD project was a lot of fun and a lot of hard work. I learned so much about generosity and conviction from the kind, inspirational folks we met along the way. I also learned more about the music business the old fashioned way – by making mistakes. Perhaps most importantly, I learned that I want my career to be intertwined with my principles and ideals.

I believe that the way we treat the environment, the animals, our own bodies, and other humans is all connected. How can I tell my niece that I want a cleaner, better world for her if I do not recycle and reuse as much as I can? How can I say that I am devastated by the dilemma of world hunger while continuing to eat the beef it takes so much grain to feed, grain that could be used to feed people? We feed most of the grain we grow to livestock, and it takes sixteen pounds of grain to make one pound of beef. How can I say I care about the environment while supporting the meat and dairy industries – industries responsible for so much pollution and waste? How can I call one animal a "pet" and another "food" when it has been proven that animals feel and have emotions? (Chickens are smarter than cats and as smart as dogs. I have met many farm animals and watched them show both grief and joy.) How can I lament the lack of compassion for animals and continue to practice hatred toward my human brothers and sisters?

My answer is, I cannot. Although no one person can carry the world's burdens, there are things I can do to make a difference. I can have the integrity to stop paying people to do things I would not be willing to do myself – like hurt another living being. I can vote for the solution with my fork. A vegan diet helps to promote peace and prevent world hunger. It also helps save animals, the environment, and my own health. I can become educated. I can learn what to say when people ask me questions about my beliefs, and I can be kind to those who disagree with me. I can be an example of love, tolerance, peacefulness and health, because I never know who is watching me.

For example, one of my fondest memories from the "Food Without a Face" tour was at a Wendy's restaurant, of all places. We were traveling through Kansas with our cooler full of veg food and stopped in for some baked potatoes to round out the meal. We got our potatoes and brought in the rest of our dinner: salad, fruit and barbecue tofu. After we sat down to eat, a tall, young man in a Wendy's uniform came over to our table. I was afraid he was going to tell us that we weren't allowed to bring outside food into the restaurant. But he didn't. Instead, he asked us if we were vegetarians. We said yes. He asked us why. We cited some reasons, still unsure why he was asking. Then he told us that he had been considering becoming a vegetarian and wanted to know more about it. We talked to him for a while and gave him some ways to find more information. He was so excited to see vegetarians up close and in person (guess that part of Kansas needs some more of us)! Before we left, we asked him why Dave Thomas, the founder of Wendy's, died recently at age 69. We found that it wasn't because of an overdose of tofu, if you catch my drift.

This young man reminded me of the infinite possibilities that abound when we have the willingness to do things differently than the way we have always done them. This is where I believe that change begins. When we become even the least bit willing to place the needs of others before our own wants and desires, change begins. When we help others, we cannot keep from being helped ourselves. I think this is because it is an illusion that we are separate from each other. What I do to you, I do to myself. Likewise, what I do *for* you, I do *for* myself. There is no "us" and "them." We are one.

That is why I want my life to be about inspiring compassion for all living things.

I am indebted to the people who inspired me to walk through my fears and take this position, not only in my personal life, but also in my career. I am in the process now of finding ways to creatively make a positive impact with my music. I never really thought my journey would take me down this path, but I'm glad it has. I am constantly amazed at the blessings I receive.

My hope is that you find a cause that touches you and that your enthusiasm is contagious!

Lyrics to Food Without a Face, by Heidi Howe:
I believe the Earth can still be saved, if you want to participate.
I'll tell you how it can be achieved.
It's not a fib; it's not a fable, it all starts at our dinner table.
A lot depends on what we choose to eat.
There's a way we can feed everyone and keep our bellies full.
Your mom was right when she said to eat your vegetables
CHORUS
When you choose a food without a face,
You'll be doing your part to reduce our waste.
You can change the world by just changing what you taste.
You cannot lose when you choose a food without a face.
If we feed our amber waves of grain, to folks higher up on the food chain,
We'd be feeding people everywhere.
And these 99-cent heart attacks do little more than make us fat,
They're running up our bill for Medicare.
So be part of the solution when you hit the grocery store.
Some of your friends have two legs, but some of them have four.
CHORUS
What's it going to take to bring us to our knees?
We're already losing folks to hunger and heart disease.

112 Softly On This Earth

CHORUS

For more information on Heidi Howe, along with samples of her music and tour schedule, view her website at www.heidihowe.com .

So far, all of the essays in Softly On This Earth have been original and were written just for this book. This next contribution, however, is an exception. When I approached Robert Bateman for his story, he was getting ready to undertake a world wide promotional tour. He gave me great encouragement for my project and passed along a contribution he had already written, one that he believed would flow well with the essays I was collecting. He was right.

When I was a child, I remember my mom raving about Robert Bateman's artwork, his magnificent paintings of the wild world and his outspoken passion for life around him. It never occurred to me at the time that I would one day be living one island away from this very inspirational soul, requesting his words for a book of my own. The mountain he refers to in the following story…Mount Maxwell…is clearly visible from where I now sit. And from its summit, the vast splendor of the Salish Sea is truly awesome.

ROBERT BATEMAN

Robert Bateman is an internationally acclaimed artist and author.

An officer of the Order of Canada, his fascination with nature has been brought to life through his paintings, his numerous books, his involvement with many conservation organizations and his commitment to raising awareness about the natural world.

For his contribution to this project, Robert Bateman kindly gave me a copy of Thinking Like A Mountain (Penguin Books), and asked that I select some of his thoughts from it. I've chosen two passages from that remarkable little book: one, a look back at his early love of nature and, two, a current day look at the state of the natural world around us.

THE CALL OF THE WOLF

I've always been drawn to the North. As a boy, I read stories like The Call of the Wild by Jack London and The Feet of the Furtive by Sir Charles G.D. Roberts. Canada's great boreal landscapes loomed wild in my imagination and beckoned me to explore their rugged treasures. When my family bought a cottage in Haliburton, I reached the borderline between South and North, a place where pioneer farms rubbed shoulders with rockbound lakes and forests of pine and spruce. But I got my first taste of the North during the summer of my seventeenth year, the first I spent working at a wildlife research camp in Algonquin Park.

I'm sure my pay and job description would appall many: I filled in potholes, dug garbage pits and dried dishes that had been "washed" by the camp cook. (His method was to pour boiling water over the dirty plates and cutlery, which meant I had to clean the egg off the forks with the tea towel.) Because I was a serious young naturalist by then, I was given some "posh" jobs, too: I ran the bird count plots; operated the small mammal traplines, skinning and stuffing the mice to make a reference collection; and helped out with road kill autopsies.

Nature has its Romantic side, but I saw a lot of its uglier parts that summer. As we examined animals who had met their deaths on the highways, we discovered that the graceful, vegetarian deer were full of parasites, which had plagued their existence when they were alive. The bears, however, whose diet was less pure, were surprisingly free of parasitic pests. All the same, we'd find other things, like dishcloths and one Player's cigarette package, inside the garbage-eating bruins.

That first summer in Algonquin I cemented my sense of the kind of life I wanted to lead and the type of people I wanted to spend my time with. A middle-class kid from North Toronto, I had never before encountered the fascinating species known as the biological field worker, but my summers at Algonquin gave me ample opportunity to learn their ways. My newly discovered companions were as at home in the bush as in the laboratory, cultured and yet completely down to earth. They knew how to dubbin a boot and sharpen an axe. But after supper, the discussion often moved from the day's discoveries to talk of James Thurber or Immanuel Kant or Sir Arthur Conan Doyle's novel The White Company, set in mediaeval England, which became the basis for a group game we sometimes played. These men's musical tastes ranged from Beethoven to Gilbert and Sullivan to traditional folk songs.

For the most part, I enjoyed the work, but I lived for my spare time. Almost every evening after supper, I would take one of the camp canoes and paddle to a secluded spot so I could paint. By then, I was steeped in the legacy of Tom Thomson and the Group of Seven, and I took pride in paddling like Tom, kneeling just aft of centre and off to one side – Ojibway style. In this position, the angle where the floor of the canoe meets the wall forms a longer, sharper line in the water, and this helps you keep the canoe on course. And since you are close to the gunwale, you don't have to reach far to one side. So it's easier not to bump the paddle, and you can take little strokes by moving your upper hand out over the side on the down stroke and back across your lap on the upstroke, while pivoting on your lower hand. The paddle should sail like a bird's wing just above the surface, and the only sound should be that of droplets falling off the blade. If I wanted to be really quiet, I could keep my blade in the water for the whole stroke. This was the method I chose for observing wildlife.

One evening, after the chores were done, I took my canoe out to Lake Sasajewun and was lured north, past the narrows, to an island nestled among lily pads in a dead-end inlet. The island was a glacial erratic, a rock left behind many lifetimes before by retreating ice. During my last visit, I had been entertained by five snorting, indignant otters, but that evening, I was alone and far from shore. I was even relatively free of the mosquitoes and black flies that swarmed me and bungled into the gooey oils on the fresh paintings. (A half-century later, some of their mummified bodies are still part of those early works!)

Twilight descended before I finished. In those days, I worked only in the field and never retouched my paintings later, so as not to spoil the spirit of the moment. I'd found my scene that evening by looking north, toward the far end of the lake, beyond which lay a "wilderness area," out of bounds to the public. A hermit thrush was singing, its song spiraling upward, beyond hearing range, like the music from some reedy yet celestial pipe organ.

I always painted until dusk, stretching my time to the limit, but on this occasion, for some reason, I worked long past sunset, working in the darkness, waiting for…something. The moon began to rise, burnishing the edges of the black spruce spires with glowing silver, then emerging above the treetops in gleaming fullness.

And then I heard it. Starting as a low moan and moving up the scale to a full-throated contralto, a wolf's howl penetrated the darkness. Time stopped. I floated in a pool of blackness, alone with the moon and the soul-filling sound. My first wolf. The hair stands up on the back of my neck even now, as I relive the moment.

I returned to Algonquin for each of the three succeeding summers, the last as a university student at the park's fisheries research station. By that last season, however, I knew that the Algonquin Park I had come to know had been devastated by logging. Even here, commercial harvesting had irreversibly depleted the hemlock-clad ridges, destroying not only the natural beauty of the area, but also an important genetic pool. Scientists are just beginning to understand genetic particularity within a species, how trees have evolved to form their own intricate individuality, adjusted to their site. But once a stand of hemlock is cut down, its tiny gene pool is gone forever. Even though Algonquin hemlock has little commercial value, industrial logging takes it as raw material for cheap wood fibre that may or may not be marketable.

The story of the Algonquin wolves is also tragic. Even where they are protected, poaching is common because enforcement is inadequate. This is especially sad because recent genetic research tells us that Algonquin Park wolves may be closely related to the endangered red wolf, which some scientists believe is the original North American wolf. The Algonquin animals may even be a unique species.

The call of the wolf will last only as long as we protect this ancient creature and its habitat. Extinction is forever.

A VIEW FROM THE MOUNTAIN

I am standing on the top of Mount Maxwell. As mountains go, it is quite modest, only 1,975 feet high, but its almost vertical cliffs give it a certain topographic distinction, and the conglomerate stones beneath my feet witnessed the twilight of the dinosaurs. Mount Maxwell was once part of continental uplands that began eroding about 75 million years ago, leaving deposits on massive submarine gravel beds. These beds rested on even older formations – the roots of 360-million-year-old mountains, which, according to the latest theory, originated in Australia and now act as the foundation of our own little mountain.

The story of the creation of this mountain evokes permanence, patience, adaptability and nobility – characteristics worth emulating. If we looked at time and geography from a mountain's perspective, we would be able to see far and wide, and benefit from the experience of people all over the globe. If we thought in the way mountains were formed, we would treat the natural world with more respect.

As I walked to the top of Mount Maxwell, I passed through a grove of majestic Douglas firs, part of Salt Spring Island's original forest. In 1938, the Maxwells, an old pioneer family, set aside this wonderful piece of ancient nature for the enjoyment and benefit of the community. But nearby Maxwell Lake, an important source of drinking water for the island, met an unhappier fate. Part of the lake extends into a 5000-acre tract of land formerly owned by a German prince. When the prince died, his heirs sold the land to developers, who intend to log much of the mountain down to the lakeshore.

The developers have offered to sell the shoreline area to the community, but the price at last accounting was in the vicinity of half a million dollars. Will the island's residents be willing to pay that amount? The developers are not breaking any laws by making this offer or by logging the forest they now own. Are they to blame for not respecting the lake and its watershed and for ignoring the impact of logging on future generations? Or is society the culprit?

Thinking these thoughts of a lake and a mountain, I stand facing the view to the south. Salt Spring Island is spread out beneath me, a mosaic of farm fields (some dotted with sheep), a few barns and houses, and a little old white church. Rolling hills clad in dark forest frame the picture. Beyond the frame, at the end of the valley, stretches the long bay on which I live, its blue waters zigzagged with silver riffles that seem to reach all the way to the Pacific Ocean. Our house is a tiny brown wedge on the left, partway along the bay.

A bald eagle tilts its wings below me, then rides the air currents up the face of the mountain until it is a speck above me. With its fine-tuned vision, the eagle can see both me and my house in minute detail and considers both of us insignificant. It is watching for action in the water, a gleaming patch of herring driven suddenly to the surface by salmon below.

These days, the eagles have less occasion to plunge down to the bay to fish. There are fewer herring and many fewer salmon in the water. I wonder if the eagle's gaze strays out to the open sea, where the grey whales are migrating north to their summering grounds in Alaskan waters. My thoughts turn to a news item I heard on the radio this morning: This month, seven grey whales have been found dead in the waters of Vancouver Island. Seven dead in one month! Preliminary testing has revealed the presence of PCB's and other toxins – another link between pollution and declining whale and fish populations. Recently, another whale was found dying on a nearby beach, apparently of starvation. Perhaps the chemicals in its body meant it could no longer absorb nutrients properly; perhaps the mammal could not find enough to eat in the over-fished waters off the British Columbia coast.

Whales are not the only victims of damaged environments. I think back to my boyhood days, and my songbird-filled bower. The memory is all the more precious because migratory songbird numbers are plummeting as birds succumb to pesticides and deforestation in their tropical winter homes and their Canadian breeding grounds. Nature is resilient, but we are beginning to reach the limits of its endurance.

The eagle and I can see the snowy peaks of the Olympic Mountains of Washington State far to the south. Though it does not know it, as the symbol of the United States of America, the majestic bird represents a nation that has had great influence for more than half a century – sometimes for the worse, often for the better. All the same, we need to stop focusing on the notions of Progress and "bigger is better" that have powered North American society for so many years. By taking a longer view, we will discover healthier models of thought and behaviour in cultures around the world; models like the ecologically balanced communities of Holland, wildlife preservation in Israel, the sustainable practices of some tribal cultures – and thousands of others. Ideas like these are worth keeping; others must be thrown away. We must pick and choose.

At the beginning of a new millennium, we all stand at the top of a mountain that offers us spectacular views in all directions. We have more knowledge of nature than any other civilization in history. We can look beyond the sky and beneath the sea. We can see both the forest and the trees. We can count the rate of its destruction and tote up the cost of saving it. We can see all human activities – farming, fishing, manufacturing – their costs and their benefits. We can look back into distant history, to the origins of our behaviours and our beliefs, all the way to the birth of the human species itself.

We who live in the twenty-first century know more, own more and exert more power over our environment than any who have come before us. Our knowledge and our technology present us with a multitude of possibilities and choices. Why do we hesitate to decide? Does the sheer multitude of options overwhelm us? This may be so, but if we wait too long, our shift toward a more responsible ideology could happen too late.

The eagle is soaring above the mountain higher and higher; if it were to fly beyond the blue, beyond the place where eagles can go, it would see a wonderful world – a place of infinite variety and complexity and remarkable resilience. It would see the planet that every astronaut has said was infinitely precious. What is so wonderful about this sphere? It is surely our natural and human heritage in all its complexity.

If we begin to think like a mountain, we will keep all that is truly valuable in this world and pass these treasures on to succeeding generations. All we need to do is pay attention and pay the price. I'd say the cost is more than worth it.

For more information on Robert Bateman, view www.batemanideas.com. There are also many other websites dedicated to Robert Bateman's work.

For an excellent selection of his art, I recommend viewing www.artandnature.com/bateman .

These excerpts, from *Thinking Like a Mountain* **(Copyright Robert Bateman, 2000), are reprinted by permission of both the author and Penguin Group (Canada), a Division of Pearson Penguin Canada Inc.**

The internet still seems very futuristic to me. It is an incredible communication and research tool and, at the same time, it is saturated with mind-numbingly useless information. It's bringing billions of people together instantly and, at the same time, it's preventing people from walking outside into the natural world. It allows me to touch base with family and friends anytime at almost no cost at all. And it allows me to mire myself in an endless void of information that does nothing but overwhelm me and leave me deeply disillusioned.

The internet has increased the speed of the human race dramatically. Whatever destination our society is headed to, we're traveling there faster and faster by the minute. Our technology apparently knows no bounds. The energy I interpret as negative is speeding up rapidly and so is the positive. I have no idea what happens from here but I'm pretty sure the internet will be involved. It has to be. We now depend on it. A day for me without going online is quite an inconvenience. Funny enough, two days without going online begins to feel quite refreshing.

I grew up without electricity or an indoor toilet. We didn't even have a telephone until I was in my teens so today's level of communication would have seemed completely impossible to me. Once every couple of weeks, we'd make a trip into town and pick up mail and that was how we communicated with the rest of our family. There was generally a one-month turnaround in any family news we shared by regular mail. Now I can do it within seconds.

Granted, my childhood was not indicative of what other children were experiencing in the 70's. But even theirs was vastly different than children's experience today. Kids in town did have access to computerized games, but they were rather cumbersome. TV Tennis is the only one I remember. White balls bouncing back and forth across a black screen. Much has changed. Today's children can check their emails on their cell phones, to which, it seems, all teenagers are now entitled.

I remember seeing my first television, a fuzzy black and white image of the Dodgers playing the Giants on a generator-powered set at our neighbours' house. Every time the old Briggs & Stratton engine coughed, the picture would surge either clearer or snowier. Midway through the eighth inning, with the Giants clinging to a narrow lead, the generator conked out and, with a mighty groan from all of us kids, our first taste of technology ended suddenly. But we adjusted pretty quickly and found something else to do, creating our own ball game outside.

Don't worry kids, a futuristic voice could have told us. *One day you'll have cable and you'll be able to watch the game, and much more, in reliable living colour. Better yet, you'll be able to email each other from across the country, checking the score in between innings on a live video feed from Dodger Stadium right on your computer screen.*

Yes, that would have seemed impossible. But now it's not even strange. Now it's just a normal daily occurrence. So then, might all our hopes and aspirations for the future, which now seem impossible, one day be normal daily occurrences.

Where I was going with this technological rambling was to point out that there are a lot of wonderful places to visit on the internet. You don't have to mire yourself in mind-numbing overload to find what you're looking for. And there are visionaries out there, creating websites that exist to raise consciousness rather than dull it. With that said, let's meet one of those visionaries.

LYNN LANDES

Lynn Landes is Founder of EcoTalk.org and Zero Waste America, both internet-based environmental research organizations. She is also a member of the Society of Environmental Journalists and has written extensively about environmental issues.

WANT A BETTER WORLD? THEN DO SOMETHING

Progress isn't a one-way ticket to a better world. It's a living, breathing, ever-changing organism kept alive by the reaction of its positive and negative parts. Three steps forward and two steps back...that's what progress feels like.

Or so I've been told. In today's America it's hard to see any progress with the rich getting richer, the poor poorer, no universal health care, environmental protection that's a sick joke, and an Administration bent on taking the country back to the times of President Herbert Hoover.

But that's no excuse to throw in the towel. This is life. It's meant to be a struggle. And as Granny used to say, we should make the best of it no matter what the outcome.

I was a late bloomer. I didn't really try to make the world a better place until I became a housewife in 1978. I had graduated from college, worked for a few years, and then my husband and I decided to start our family in Bucks County, Pennsylvania. I finally had the time and energy to get involved.

At first I picked "safe," non controversial community activities. But in the 1980's my husband and I became active in the fight to save Eastern Air Lines from the notorious Frank Lorenzo. That experience was an eye opener. We learned firsthand how money and power can easily trump poorly organized unions. In the end, Eastern went out of business. But for many of us, Lorenzo's ruined reputation was some consolation.

In 1990 I joined a small local group to fight the building of a trash incinerator. That battle went on for years and in the end we lost. Not only was the incinerator built, but the adjoining landfills continue to expand to this day. In the meantime, I joined large environmental organizations and sat on state committees that gave advice on waste issues. There were even a couple of pieces of legislation that I wrote, but they never stood a chance in the garbage-friendly legislature. Pennsylvania has become the wastebasket of the United States, importing one ton of trash for every ton the state generates.

By 1996, my husband convinced me to publish a website, which I called ZeroWasteAmerica. It was a good place to file all that I had learned about the waste issue. I issued reports, did news interviews, and tried to educate the public as best I could. For the past several years, unique visitors to the website have ranged from 2000-4000 a week.

In 1999, I left the world of overt activism and began my career in broadcast journalism with a radio show on environmental topics at a tiny station (WDVR) in rural New Jersey. I started another website called EcoTalk.org. A year later, the British Broadcasting Corporation (BBC) hired me to do weekly environmental reports. And last year, Drexel University TV (DUTV) hosted daily environmental news spots that I produced.

Although I enjoyed the radio and TV jobs, I was not getting the feedback or sense of personal satisfaction I needed. Now I write an online column, which has received a pretty good reaction. And I'm writing a book about environmental choices and resources.

On the personal front, my husband and I abandoned the suburban life and moved into Philadelphia. We love it. We shed our conventional cars and bought a Toyota Prius Hybrid. We walk more, buy organic food and clothing, and purchase our energy from NewWindEnergy.com. We'll soon be installing some solar photovoltaic cells for our roof. We're trying to walk the walk, not just talk the talk.

There are a vast number of people, organizations, and businesses that are ready, willing, and able to make this world a better place. Will they overcome an equal number content to do nothing, or worse still, eager to make things worse?

I can't answer that. I can only be responsible for my own actions. And hope for a better world.

Lynn Landes' EcoTalk.org office is located in Philadelphia, Pennsylvania. Her web address is www.ecotalk.org .

Every day of my life, there has been a war raging somewhere on our planet. Most, but not all of them have involved my country of birth, the United States. I am fortunate enough to have dual citizenship, having moved to Canada at a very early age. With that, I can live and work on either side of the border. With half of my family living in the States, I have often considered living, at least for a while, somewhere south of the 49th parallel. My reason for deciding against that has always been because of the States' involvement in a war I didn't believe in, being waged somewhere, sometimes in several places, around the world. And that has never changed. I have never seen my homeland in a true time of peace...a time when no other country was being bombed or was having its dictator overthrown in favour of someone more in line with the current American president's ideals. The leader of the free world, it has always seemed to me, has held the consistent agenda of taking freedom away from people who don't serve their purpose. And it's been that way all my life and way before my birth.

Perhaps because my parents fled to Canada to get away from that very agenda, I have always felt war was hideously wrong. Over our crackling battery-powered radio, I would hear news stories about people dying and I would squeeze my eyes shut and imagine what those people looked like. In the fall, when we slaughtered our steers for our year's supply of beef, I would watch the life slip away from their eyes and I would visualize the same expression in the faces of the people being killed overseas. One moment, there is vital energy flowing through the glint of a living being's eyes, and then there is nothing...just a vacant stare.

I saw the same expression, many years later, when a small child was hurled off a ride at an amusement park into a crowd of people very close to me. Something happens to a soul when it is violently ripped from its earthly vehicle. It's like it lingers there reluctantly, resisting its heavenly ascent.

War is wrong. Innocent people dying to satisfy someone else's agenda is wrong. I wonder if the various "leaders of the free world" who have been around in my lifetime have ever stood before another living being and watched the life vanish from its eyes. It's pretty motivational.

I've marched in peace rallies, where thousands of people flood through the streets together in a goal of reaching out to the leaders of the free world in a gigantic plea for peace. I truly have no idea whether or not our goals have been reached. It would seem not, at times, although the means to the end is certainly worth it. Being around all that energy, all these people marching together and singing together, sends chills of excitement up and down my spine.

Peace can be found all over. I've found it in large groups of people and I've found it in complete solace. Some of the greatest feelings of peace I've encountered have been spent drifting in a boat in the middle of a lake. I think that the energy of floating aimlessly, contemplating the clouds overhead, sets the perfect stage for a peaceful world. Perhaps I'll organize a peace float, rather than a march. Perhaps we'll get through to the powers-that-be more effectively by all just joining in a group float. And we'll invite the Presidents and Prime Ministers and benevolent dictators to join us. I know of a lake or two that couldn't possibly nurture any thoughts other than those of peace. Of peace with no opposite.

Our next contributor is one who has gone far beyond just talking about peace. She's even gone far beyond marching. And I'm pretty sure she'll join us in our peace float if we invite her.

HONEY NOVICK

Honey Novick, is an accomplished performer and peace advocate. She begins her thoughts with a personal introduction so I'll leave that to her.

Thank you for this opportunity to share the story of the New Songs For Peace project. First, I'd like to introduce myself to the dear readers of this book. My name is Honey Novick. I am a singer/songwriter/voice teacher who lives in Toronto, Ontario, Canada. I direct the UNESCO-endorsed "New Songs for Peace" project as well as the Creative Vocalization Studio. This story is how this project began.

In 1999, the City of Toronto, McGill University and the Soka Gakkai International (SGI – Japanese for the Society for the Creation of Value) hosted an event honouring the life and work of John P. Humphrey. Like many other Canadians, Mr. Humphrey wasn't well known even though Eleanor Roosevelt asked him to draft what has now become the Universal Declaration of Human Rights. At the opening of that event, I was one of many who either sang or spoke. One speaker, Marilyn Ashby, of the United Nations (UN) Association in Canada, and I became friendly. Marilyn encouraged me to attend a UN Culture of Peace training sponsored by the Voice Of Women organization. The United Nations had proclaimed the decade 2000-2010 to be the Decade for the Culture of Peace and Non-violence for the Children of the World.

At the training, we were all asked to make a commitment to the UN proclamation. I was asked to collect new songs for peace. I thought about it and decided that just collecting my own songs was something I would do naturally, organically. Why not use this opportunity to connect with others? I proposed opening the concept to others so that we could create a book of new songs for peace. Thus, the collective Let's Sing Together for Peace and the New Songs For Peace projects were born. One of our founding members, Susan Berry, was able to get an official UNESCO contract. Eventually, Kofi Annan sent his best wishes and congratulations. It was a very heady and a very humbling experience for this daughter of a homemaker and Judaic scholar who delivered milk for a living.

Softly On This Earth

> *When you sing, you can't sing outside the song.*
> *You've got to be the song you sing.*
> James Baldwin, Just Above My Head

As James Baldwin says, *You've got to be the song you sing.* I really want world peace. I really want to learn to enlighten my sufferings and the sufferings of others. I really want to learn something about myself in relation to the world. Japanese educator Josei Toda taught that a change in the character of just one person can affect his or her friends, family, society and ultimately the world. I believe that working on this project will help me learn to develop myself and become more positively effective in the world.

Since the inception of this wonderful project, the history of the world has changed. September 11 happened and Iraq was invaded. Many people have contacted me because they want to feel hopeful and useful and part of something for peace. Something as simple as writing a song or expressing a feeling or taking a stand for peace or against war is invaluable when one is threatened with a sense of hopelessness and frustrated feelings.

I sent out emails and letters and faxes to every resource I could think of. Would Pete Seeger support this project with his name? He sent a handwritten note of encouragement with a list of names to contact. Would the Woody Guthrie Archives allow me to use the following quote from Woody? Yes, they would. Woody Guthrie has said, *I hate a song that makes you think that you are not any good. I hate a song that makes you think you are born to lose, bound to lose, no good to nobody, no good for nothing… songs that run you down or poke fun at you on account of your bad luck or hard traveling. I am out to fight those songs to my very last breath of air and my last drop of blood. I am out to sing songs that will prove to you that this is your world and that if it has hit you pretty hard and knocked you down for a dozen loops, no matter what color, what size you are, how you are built, I am out to sing the songs that make you take pride in yourself and in your work.*

These words of Woody's have been one of my life's guiding lights.

I asked composer Philip Glass, actor Ron Glass, Canadian Minister of Heritage Sheila Copps and Canadian Member of

Parliament Svend Robinson and many others for endorsements. They all have sent confirmation.

Asking for financial assistance was a big lesson for me. As an artist, I'm uncomfortable asking for money. Yet, how could I pay for the internet, postage stamps, fax ink and many other necessary expenses? Well, I just had to learn how. Pete Seeger once encouraged me to start my projects by looking at what I have at hand. So, I asked my friends and family first. I steeled myself for the possibility of people not giving money so when money did come, it was always a surprise and a blessing and an opportunity to be grateful.

The Voice Of Women, an inspiration to many women, offered seed money. The visionary new music organization, The Music Gallery, offered to act as trustee and issue tax receipts for any amount over $50.00. It was coming together.

Initially I collected my own songs: "I Am a Winner," "Where Does a Man Go to Be Free?" "Tell 'Em I'm Strong," "I'm a Fortune Baby," "War Ain't Nothin' but the Blues," "Oh, Mother Earth," "Gulp! War" and many others. Marcia Iwasaki, an honours student in fine arts at York University designed a cover for our fund-raising CD "New Songs for Peace" (a CD collection of my original songs). It may also be the cover of the completed book. Her artwork was used for her 4th year design project and part of her graduation exhibit.

SOCAN, the Society of Composers, Authors and Music Publishers of Canada, the SGI Quarterly and Sing! Out magazines have all posted notices. The Toronto Star published an article about this project.

The very first web pages were designed by thirteen-year-old Jeff Schmidt (with help from his father, Bernie) as a high school class project. Not long ago, Jerry Chong became our insightful and energetic webmaster.

All of these efforts and many more have been made in the name of peace. I have gone into schools and bookstores and art galleries, wherever I'm invited. I ask people to define what peace means for them. I ask people to talk about peace, to think about it and hopefully write a new song that we will collect. When I was invited to sing and speak at a mosque in front of a congregation of about 140 women, I knew this project had real meaning.

All things are connected. Eleanor Roosevelt knew John Humphrey. Mr. Humphrey was also a friend of poet Daisaku Ikeda, International President of the Soka Gakkai (of which I'm a member). The Soka Gakkai is an NGO (non governmental organization) of the UN. The Voice Of Women (VOW) is also an association of the United Nations.

It's all connected. I think that's the real message. We are all connected. All living beings have an interconnected relationship with one another. You and I could not exist without air and water, and water and air could not exist without an interconnected relationship with one another.

The Voice Of Women started about 40 years ago because many women had a vision that they could affect the history of the times by protesting against nuclear warfare. They wanted to offer kindness and assistance to those affected by war because we are all affected by the inhumanity war brings. When one living species is at war, all living species are affected. Isn't it clear? I am grateful that this organization is an active force that has survived the latter half of the 20th century and exists to this day.

If someone were to ask you what is the greatest gift you've been given in this lifetime, what would you say? In times of great sadness, I often think of this question.

Maybe the real question should be, *What is the greatest gift we could give in this lifetime?*

Whatever the answer is, I want it to be in the name of peace. I want to challenge, provoke, instigate thought in the name of peace, human rights, respect for the dignity for all living things, for idealism, for poetry and music and the sanctity of individual life choices. We all have a choice, every moment. The great boxer, Rubin "Hurricane" Carter says, *When people wake up in the morning, it's a miracle. They just don't know it's a miracle.*

This story has no ending. It is a constant challenge for me to define and re-define the meaning of peace, for myself and in relation to others. I want to reach out to others and have them reach out to others. Maybe through song, maybe through a simple smile. If anyone wishes to comment or send a song, please reach me at honey@newsongsforpeace.org .

I'd like to leave you with the words to my song, "Don't Get Sad, Get Mad."

Don't get sad, get mad
Get going, do something (about it)!
Are you blind to the circumstances of the world?
Do you live your life, like an ostrich with your tail to the sun?
If you do, this song isn't for you. So…
Don't get sad, get mad
Get going, do something (about it)
But don't hurt anybody, not even a tad when you're mad
'Cause that won't help anybody.
Do you let other people tell you what to do –
Fall in line, monkey see, monkey do?
Don't get sad, get mad
Get going, do something (about it)
But don't hurt anybody, not even a tad when you're mad
'Cause that won't help anybody. If you do, this song isn't for you, so…
Don't get sad, get mad
Get going, do something (about it)
But don't hurt anybody, not even a tad when you're mad
'Cause that won't help anybody.
Do you speak up loud when there's something to say?
Is your upper lip stiff while you bite your tongue?
If you do, this song isn't for you, so…
Don't get sad, get mad
Get going, do something (about it),
Like write a poem, or sing a song, call someone close and give them a dose of what's on your mind,
Ask for help, and pray for courage, do a dance, take a chance,
shake your fist; give someone just the gist of what's on your mind,
Make up your own things to do
That would be best for you!!!

Honey Novick makes her home in Toronto, Ontario. More information on her New Songs For Peace project can be found at www.newsongsforpeace.org .

The aim of Softly On This Earth was, and is, to be representative of people who are raising awareness about the environmental, social and ethical health of our world. It would seem, from looking over the stories of my contributors, that I'm including more thoughts on the welfare of animals than I am on people or the environment.

This is not intentional. Of all the submissions I have received, by far the greatest number have been from those dedicated to animal rights. Even those who I thought would write about something quite different have spoken about the importance of the way we treat all beings on Earth, regardless of how many legs they have, and just how unbalanced we have become with the animals we share this planet with.

Through the work I've done so far, I've been amazed at just how quickly awareness is increasing about the animals we live with and the animals we consume. This excites me to no end. But I am also very concerned at the same time that the incidences of heart disease, cancer and childhood obesity are increasing at approximately the same rate as the growth of the fast food industry. So many people are failing to make the connection. It's not just about how we're treating animals by consuming them. It's also about how we're treating ourselves by consuming animals.

Now I'd like to introduce you to another extraordinary soul doing her part and much more to raise awareness about our relationship with other animals.

SINIKKA CROSSLAND

Sinikka Crossland, RN, is a nurse and animal rights advocate with TRACS.

TRACS (The Responsible Animal Care Society) is a non-profit organization dedicated to the kind and compassionate treatment of all living things. They actively promote public awareness in areas where animals are abused, exploited for profit, or denied natural conditions.

Long ago, as a five-year-old living with my family in a two-room cabin along the banks of the Similkameen River, I happened to look outside one autumn morning to see a wounded deer fleeing for its life. Blood flowed from a wound on its side. Horrified, I remember asking my father what had happened. *A hunter*, he replied.

The memory haunted me...the frightened lance of the injured animal as its eyes briefly met mine through the window, and the image of a crimson gash against a soft chestnut coat. I often wondered if the deer had survived, and I thought about how much pain it must surely have suffered. Soon after this incident, I declared that I was going to be a vegetarian, that it was "wrong" to hurt and eat animals. But many years were to pass before I would actually take that step, and many more before my interest in helping animals was to grow into a driving force.

That is truly the best way to describe the motivation behind my work involving the rights of animals: a driving force, an energy and resolve that is not restricted to my person, but flows from a power far greater than myself. I am a tool, and a willing one. I am not in this world to take from it, to "harvest its resources" for my own gain or my pleasure. I am here to make a difference, and to the awesome power that has granted me life, I have given my commitment to do the very best I can while I walk upon the Earth. Herein lie my mission and my purpose.

Our world of incredible natural beauty is imprinted with the mistakes and violations of humankind. Evidence of this influence is to be found beyond the urban areas and farmlands (where animals are freely and often cruelly used for purposes of "benefit" to modern civilization). The abuses extend into the far reaches of our fields and forests, our lakes, streams and oceans. There, hunters, trappers, and fishers busily harvest living beings not only for food, but also for profit and personal trophies. Most animal "users" claim that they have an inherent right to continue their activities. Often they attempt to establish ethical credibility by referring to what they claim is "biblical" permission to use animals. They have a tendency to downplay or ignore warning signs – such as the health hazards associated with meat consumption, the environmental concerns when massive numbers of animals are "harvested," world hunger (which could be alleviated through a plant-based diet in the developed world), and the moral implications when humans become desensitized to the suffering of other living things. They "know not what they do," but the time will come when the problems created by humankind will be too critical to ignore. That time is not far away.

This will be the turning point, the dawning of an era that will herald another way to live, governed by a fair, inspiring, and permanent code of ethics for our world. Included will be all species of life.

Wars and terrorism will become a part of our nightmarish history, as will the slaughter of animals. One day, in meekness, we will deserve to inherit the Earth. As a mother loves her newborn, we will tenderly care for and nurture the intricate, wondrous world created not only for humans, but also for every living thing.

I am simply a committed part of that process, which many have dubbed a "movement." My purpose is to enlighten, to educate, and to help build and direct momentum, because a time of great fear and confusion is upon us. In desperation, many will reach out to grasp the cord that binds them to the power that created them; and those who advocate for a peaceful creation will guide their flailing hands. The movement is gathering strength in all corners of the world, and it will not subside until the work is done.

For all life,
Sinikka Crosland

For more information on the work Sinikka Crossland does with TRACS (The Responsible Animal Care Society), view their website at www.tracs-bc.ca . The TRACS office is located in Westbank, British Columbia.

In 1995, I was fortunate enough to be cast in a musical stage production for children called *Please Don't Sneeze*. This was undoubtedly the toughest theatrical production I've been involved in because I had to learn some fairly difficult choreography and had to be able to sing with others. While these two actions come relatively easily to some, they don't to me. But here I was, suddenly cast into a play I was very passionate about and I had to learn the role. What followed was a few exhausting months of physical and vocal training, until I could at last nail my routine without falling into the audience.

In the opening scene of the play, I had to race down through the audience, carrying a sledgehammer and shouting. Shortly after arriving on stage, I had to find my way through some much-rehearsed steps, sneeze and then break into song. If I made it through that opening sequence, I could generally coast for a while, up until a point where I had to carry the final note of a chorus of singers, my own voice rising a note and hanging on several agonizing seconds beyond everyone else's. Even long after the rehearsals had ended, and it was a real live show in front of hundreds of easily distracted children, this vocal piece was terrifying for me. I missed it by a hair the first few times until I finally found the motivation to hit the note and stay with it.

That motivation came from the audience members themselves. After each show, the whole cast would hang out near the theatre's exit and sign *Please Don't Sneeze* programs for any children who wanted them. These ridiculously adorable little people would come up to us with great, wide eyes, clearly in awe of meeting the characters who had just brought a fairy tale to life for them on stage. This one little person took my signed program and didn't want to leave, staring up at me with big blue eyes and a wide grin, until his laughing mother carried him away.

From there on out, it became easy. Show after show, I saw the children in the audience diving into the fairy tale we were creating and my heart would sing. And, night after night, I was able to nail that last vocal note with increasing ease. I was creating something that made someone else's world a little bit magical, if only for a moment, and that made all the rehearsals seem so very worth it.

Children are the ones who continue the work we're doing now. They are the ones we hand over the world to, again and again. What they do with it is largely up to what state it's in when we hand it over. Over and over. And you know what? I'd feel better about handing the world to most of the children I meet than I ever would handing it to many of the adults I cross paths with.

DAVE SMITH

Dave Smith is Executive Director of Special Love.
Special Love is a non-profit organization that sponsors camps and other services for children with cancer or HIV/AIDS and their families. Dave Smith volunteered for the organization during his summers in college and became Executive Director in 1987.

If you've ever been branded with the name "Underachiever," take heart. Sometimes luck, blessings, or a combination of the two is sufficient to put you in a place where you can do what you enjoy and still make a difference — and maybe even enough money to live on.

Take me, for instance. As a high school and college student, I was fortunate enough to make decent grades with only a modicum of effort (hence the infamous "underachiever" talk that my parents had with me during high school). Since both of my parents were college-educated, they had full expectations that I would be, too. Fortunately, obliging them wasn't too difficult and, since they taught at a small Baptist school in West Virginia, I also didn't have to worry about tuition money. I commuted from home so the usual distractions were minimized to allow just enough study time. I even had a writing job that gave me a little spending money. What I didn't have was a clue as to what I was going to do after college.

As it turned out, the old adage that "it's who you know" really was true, because I met another faculty member who would become the closest thing I would ever have to a mentor. When he left to become the director of a 4-H Center in Front Royal, Virginia, he asked if I'd like a summer job as a camp counselor and the building blocks for my future began to fall into place. Not that I knew that at the time, of course. In fact, after several summers of camp counseling, my father asked why I didn't get a summer job that had a greater bearing on my future career. Neither he nor I realized I already had it!

During the last week of my first year as a 4-H camp counselor, I met a local couple whose daughter had died of cancer and they wanted to start a weeklong camp for other children undergoing treatment. Within a year, that camp was a reality.

Within a year, Camp Fantastic was a reality, as was Special Love, Inc., the non-profit organization, that sponsored it. The first week of camp in 1983 hosted 30 children and was a smashing success. Any reservations I or the other camp staff had about working with critically ill children melted away when the first kids scampered off the bus. Four years and several new programs later, the camp's board of directors decided that there was more work to be done than volunteers could reasonably manage and that's when "destiny came knocking." Fresh out of college and already having served as a volunteer for the organization since its inception, I was truly "in the right place at the right time." I was hired as the new Executive Director in April of 1987.

I was fortunate to have the luxury of growing into this new position. My early days consisted of visiting with the camp founder and wondering if I should be creating more work for myself. At one point, I even spent an hour in my office practicing my softball swing! And I still have a very clear memory (one of few) of staring at the top of my desk and thinking that there was probably something I should be doing, but what? My days consisted of answering a few phone calls and making an occasional trip to a Rotary meeting to pick up a donation.

After 16 years at the helm of Special Love, I've seen the organization grow to a staff of six and an annual budget of over $800,000. Our audience has increased a hundredfold to over 3000 children and family members annually. Fundraising has evolved from a passive job of waiting for the phone to ring to a search for new resources in a troubled economy. Not exactly the United Way (is that such a bad thing?), but a far cry from the days when I kept attendance lists by hand and used board meetings to discuss shirt color preferences for camp.

It's not often in the current business climate that someone sticks with a job for nearly two decades, but I think I've discovered a secret. I still sleep soundly at night (at least when my two-year-old son, Andy, lets me), because I know that what I'm doing means something. For me, it is a hands-on projection of my faith in God and my belief in helping others instead of simply trying to accumulate wealth. Obviously, money is still necessary – anyone with kids can tell you that much. But the things that make me truly happy usually have very little to do with money. Watching my son sleep brings me far more satisfaction than the latest installment of reality TV, and on the rare occasions when my son lets us sleep in, the feeling of sharing a warm bed with my wife and my dog, Buddy, far outweighs any pressing work or personal issues. I like to think I can chalk up my appreciation for the present to the same laid-back demeanor that prompted the "underachiever" speech I got as a kid.

I make it a habit not to preach – let someone else get paid for it – but I do believe that the end of this life is the beginning of the next. And I'm convinced that what we do and learn in and about this life will have a bearing on what comes next. I don't think that winning a video game will end up on my permanent record (although that doesn't stop me from enjoying them immensely). I also don't believe that having the best toys, be they actual toys or the grownup equivalent of them, will make me more popular or a better person. I do think that who I spend time with will. And that's why I continue to devote my time to my charitable occupation and my family. Everything I need to know about this life, and prepare for the next one, is contained in the people I spend time with, if I know how to look for it. Fortunately for me, finding it is something else that often happens on its own whether I'm trying or not.

If I had to do it all over again – and who knows, maybe you do – I'd like to think my experience would help me keep my priorities straight. But I'd still be just as laid back. Even if that made me an underachiever.

Special Love's headquarters are located in Winchester, Virginia. For more information, view their website at www.speciallove.org .

Advocacy takes a lot of courage. It's all well and fine to talk about a cause but really standing up for it and acting upon it is something altogether different. Courage is the difference between living our highest choices and just talking about them. The contributors to this book embody courage and I admire that deeply.

Courage fascinates me. Why do some people have such an abundance of it and others seem to be so very lacking in it? Why do many of us so dearly wish we could find the courage yet wind up so very short of what we reach for?

I've worked on my own courage a great deal over the years. Not because I aspired to reach some distant plateau of greatness but because I seriously needed to do so. When I was little, everything terrified me. I was deathly afraid of heights, darkness, spiders, stink bugs and a myriad of other day-to-day obstacles. And living way out in the woods as I did, there were a whole lot of all those things to deal with.

I remember being up at the neighbours' house one evening and having to return home well after dark with no flashlight. I decided, that night, to stare down my fear of the dark and march bravely home on my own. It was a cloudy night so there was no moon or stars to help guide my way. Just the inky blackness of the forest and the eerie silhouette of the tree line against the night sky. Nearly home, with every little bump in the woods sending minor tremors along my spine, I walked smack dab into something large and hairy and nearly fainted from the shock. I yelped and jumped back in the darkness, my heart becoming lodged in my throat. The creature in the dark snorted back at me. His familiar snort eased my nerves and I realized I was standing right next to the neighbours' horse, who had also wound up out on the road after dark, just trying to make his way home. From there on, I always tried to remember that all bumps in the night might just be another soul trying to make its way home.

In my adult years, I've tried one thing after another to conquer my fears and develop more courage. I've gone hang gliding and scuba diving. I've skied in places where people, or where I, at least, have no business being. I've run two marathons and a bunch of other races. I've performed on stage, radio and film. I've sat on the summit of a couple of the highest of the Rocky Mountains. And yet I still get scared.

What scares me now? Well, I'm still not crazy about spiders. I do rather enjoy both darkness and high places now, something that still amazes me when I remember how those things used to curdle my spine. But fear is still very familiar to me. It's just transformed into something different. Now I fear things like rejection and failure. I don't mind failing at the stuff that I was just doing for fun anyway. But the stuff that's really important, the stuff I believe in and put all my love and passion into, that I don't want to fail at. And the fear isn't about getting eaten by monsters or falling to my death anymore. It's about not being able to make a difference.

So, time to strap on some courage and keep on. Let's meet another brave soul.

DON MORRILL

Don Morrill is Board President of the California Wilderness Coalition.
CWC's mission is to protect and restore California's wild places. Through public education and advocacy, they coordinate the efforts of conservation organizations, business people, policy makers and activists. The CWC has over 30,000 members and 80 member organizations.

My interest in the natural and "wild" world began as a child on our summer family home, which is on a ranch on the north coast of California. It began with an obsession with trout and fishing for them. My professional career began in 1972 at the Wilderness Society in Washington D.C., and, while I've been in business since 1980, I've continued my volunteer work throughout my life.

The California Wilderness Coalition (CWC) defends the pristine landscapes that make California unique, provide a home to our wildlife, and preserve a place for spiritual renewal. This mission is carried out by dedicated volunteers and staff.

My belief is that human beings from childhood have an inherent fascination with, and reverence for, the natural world. This is a natural part of being a human that gradually gets overridden by a desire for products and services that is inculcated by advertising. Our economic system is built on, and driven by, human desire to accumulate and consume products and services. This is not a "natural' phenomenon, but rather an artificial situation that must be corrected if we are to preserve the systems of the planet that provide our sustenance.

Wild creatures and wilderness provide humans an illustration of and a tie to the life systems that are vital to our, and all, life. We must educate human beings that the ideal behavior is love and reverence for all life – each other and all systems that sustain life, from the earth and the smallest microbes to large carnivores.

This is an enormous challenge, particularly given the ascendance of the U.S. and capitalism as the economic and social ideal. However, the U.S. has, more than any other country, the opportunity to lead the world to a better framework of living.

I'm optimistic in the long term that this will occur. However, it will not happen without serious and substantial ecological disruptions manifesting on the planet. This will occur in the form of global warming-induced changes in oceans and weather, and reductions in food supply.

I do have faith that humans will see the consequences of their actions before it is too late, and will change behavior and attitude to effect change. This will occur over many generations, and I'm sorry I won't be around to see it.

The California Wilderness Coalition's offices are located in Davis, California. For more information, view their website at www.calwild.org .

Softly On This Earth

I feel compelled to include something I wrote a while ago. I was reflecting on a brief encounter I had with a wildly smiling, tiny old soul earlier in the day. I started to tap out a drumbeat on the sides of my chair and this is what I came out with.

Early one morning without warning
on my way to a brave new day
a stumble walking mumble talking
little old lady swayed my way
cackle of laughter then right after
a smile of glee through ragged teeth
a gnarled finger paused to linger
a touch of grace upon my face
Got me running rhythm humming
rhythm gliding music sliding
my feet are flying my heart is sighing
on a crest within my chest
day or night it's always right
to run your feet along the street
when I tire chest on fire
I lie in the grass upon my ass
I walked a mile and stopped to smile
sat in the park 'til after dark
the rush of the river made me shiver
nighthawks cried as the daylight died
thought about life without strife
without reason to fight the night
made a vow to start right now
to raise the bar and reach the stars

KENNETH SHAPIRO

Kenneth Shapiro, Ph.D., is Executive Director of Psychologists for the Ethical Treatment of Animals (PSYETA).

For over twenty years, PSYETA has worked with social scientists, mental health providers and other animal rights organizations, using psychology and education to reduce the suffering and exploitation of both human and nonhuman animals.

EFFECTING RADICAL CHANGE BY CONVENTIONAL MEANS

Having grown up in the 60's, I belong to the generation that believed in and lived for radical change – not the gradual change of middle-class progressivism, but basic institutional change. However, it was not until my thirties that I found an area that captured my particular passion for change. In retrospect, I had some self-indulgent needs to work through before I constructively could apply that spirit of the 60's. In the late 70's, prompted by Peter Singer's *Animal Liberation*, I saw for the first time what has always been there – the suffering of animals other than ourselves. With that mini éclat, I gradually transformed my world until it was framed by a commitment to help change theirs.

Although someday it might be, the rest of the story of the Animal Rights Movement generally, and certainly my modest role in it, is not history. It is hard work for little pay with the only immediate "benefit" a large measure of social and political marginality. For to achieve a truly humane society requires a major shift from anthropocentrism to biocentrism. And, regrettably, despite its taxonomic incoherence, the polarity of human versus animal (humans *are* animals) is the categorical divide upon which we have built our religion, economy, science, and laws. However, arguably, it is our very marginality, our position on the periphery of conventional thought that allowed us to develop creative theories and approaches that question and would replace customary exploitative practices involving nonhuman animals.

In its first decade, until the 90's, the movement was optimistic about achieving major change quickly. It did not do that, but during that period it was above the fold, attracting much media attention and many followers. Since then, with less fanfare and, as yet, only modest institutional change, it has been developing an infrastructure of organizations, national, corporate and local grassroots, led by a new generation of activists who operate not on the street, but in the sophisticated spaces of legislative referenda, judicial innovation, socially conscious investment, economic boycott, and scholarly critique.

Despite the recent distraction of terrorism, the economic downturn, and the general ideological move to the right, the movement continues to develop infrastructure and is beginning to find its political legs.

My own niche in this effort has been influenced by my training as a clinical psychologist and my proclivity for the ivory tower of academia. I have been working to develop a field of Human-Animal Studies, comparable to Black Studies and Women's Studies, and currently edit two journals and a book series to that end. I also have written extensively on the science arguments against the use of nonhuman animals as models of human disorders. A final area of interest is the link between human violence and animal abuse.

In my view, effecting radical change requires long-term commitment on the part of individuals. They must be able to sustain themselves in the face of frustration; they must persist in projects that seemingly are getting nowhere. It also requires the use of a broad-spectrum of strategies on the part of organizations. To effect the institutional changes sought requires efforts on the level of economics, politics, and attitudes. Finally, it requires maintaining contact with the marginal position that is the original source and sustaining ground of the critique of established practices, while creatively exploiting all conventional means available to effect change.

Psychologists for the Ethical Treatment of Animals' (PSEYTA's) head office is in Washington Grove, Maryland. For more information, view their website at www.psyeta.org .

I ran across this following passage in a saved email. I don't know who the author is but I certainly thank them for writing it and I will gratefully reuse it here, with full credit to its anonymous creator.

If we could shrink the Earth's population to a village of precisely 100 people, with all the existing human ratios remaining the same, it would look something like the following.
There would be:
57 Asians
21 Europeans
14 from the Western Hemisphere, both north and south
8 Africans
52 would be female
48 would be male
70 would be non-white
30 would be white
70 would be non-Christian
30 would be Christian
89 would be heterosexual
11 would be homosexual
6 people would possess 59% of the entire world's wealth
and all 6 would be from the United States.
80 would live in substandard housing
70 would be unable to read
50 would suffer from malnutrition
1 would be near death; 1 would be near birth
1 (yes, only 1) would have a college education
1 would own a computer
When one considers our world from such a
compressed perspective, the need for acceptance,
understanding and education becomes glaringly apparent.
The following is also something to ponder...
If you woke up this morning with more health
than illness...you are more blessed than the
million who will not survive this week.
If you have never experienced the danger of
battle, the loneliness of imprisonment, the

agony of torture, or the pangs of starvation...you
are ahead of 500 million people in the world.
If you can attend a church meeting without
fear of harassment, arrest, torture, or death...you
are more blessed than three billion
people in the world.
If you have food in the refrigerator, clothes
on your back, a roof overhead and a place to sleep...
you are richer than 75% of this world.
If you have money in the bank, in your wallet,
and spare change in a dish someplace... you are among
the top 8% of the world's wealthy.
If your parents are still alive and still married ...
you are very rare, even in the United States and Canada.
Someone once said:
What goes around comes around.
Work like you don't need the money.
Love like you've never been hurt.
Dance like nobody's watching.
Sing like nobody's listening.
Live like it's Heaven on Earth.

DEBORAH WILLIAMS

Deborah L. Williams is Executive Director of the Alaska Conservation Foundation.
The Alaska Conservation Foundation promotes sustainable livelihoods while protecting the integrity of Alaska's ecosystems. They accomplish this by awarding grants and have helped over 200 organizations dedicated to the future of Alaska's wild places. They are also very active in offering various ecological programs, initiatives, training programs and internships.

THE ENEMY OF ALASKA

Every day I am guided by Eleanor Roosevelt's wisdom: *No matter what you do you will be criticized, so you might as well do what is right.*

Wild Alaska is my soul food, and protecting the Great Land's intact environment is my consuming passion. Like others who care deeply about social causes, I consider myself fortunate to wake up each morning with determination. As someone who has been publicly labeled an "Enemy of Alaska" for my conservation-based actions and beliefs, I also know that there is often a cost associated with conviction. It is a price worth paying.

Few places are more different than Alaska and the place where I grew up – Van Nuys, California. With heavily polluted air, cement-lined rivers, congested streets, and endless urban sprawl, the San Fernando Valley in the 1960's and 70's was Exhibit A for development gone amok.

Fortunately, my parents loved the out-of-doors, and we spent our vacations and long weekends backpacking in the Sierras, hiking in the San Gabriel Mountains, exploring the Colorado River, and camping in Northern Idaho. This is where I found joy – joy in breathing clean air, in drinking clean water, in listening to the songs of birds, and in observing the magnificent and beautiful complexity of every square foot of our natural world. Whenever I was outside, I felt at once elevated and humbled, and always at home.

I realized very early that every single atom in our body comes from our environment. By this and all other measures, we are truly inseparable from our organic and inorganic world. As someone who came from a small family, I also reveled in the feeling that we are all part of nature's vast, dynamic, and complex ancestry.

In my large public high school, however, I learned that not everyone supports efforts to protect the environment. As Commissioner of Campus and the Environment and founder of the school's first Ecology Club, I worked with a group of wonderful students to organize a massive Ecology Fair in 1970. By all measures it was a special event. Virtually every school club and class had a colorful, thoughtful booth examining how we can be better inhabitants and stewards of our natural environment.

Scheduled to last from Thursday through Saturday, the fair filled the entire "Old Gym," displacing for a modest period of time the practices of the B basketball team. On Thursday and Friday, the entire student body visited the exhibit-packed fair. On Saturday morning, when I opened the door to the Old Gym two hours before the public was scheduled to arrive, I stared in utter disbelief at a completely empty space. Everything was gone – everything. The Grinch had truly stolen the Eco-Fair.

Thanks to the indomitable spirit of the Ecology Club, we re-grouped, salvaged a few exhibits, and welcomed our speakers and the public to a diminished, but still educational, event.

Upon reflection, I began to understand that "this is what we are up against." There are people who will choose to destroy rather than do without – even when the self-defined deprivation is something as small as not having an Old Gym for one night's practice.

Similarly, I learned in high school something that is now well acknowledged by psychologists: there is no correlation between wealth and happiness. As a resident of the decidedly middle class city of Van Nuys, I attended high school with denizens of the upper-middle class town of Encino. Many of my friends lived in lavish homes with all of the trappings of the moneyed. After many sleepovers, it did not take long for me to realize that the driven and often materialistic parents of my friends were much less happy than my live-well-within-your-modest-means mother and father – much less happy.

Two years after high school, I discovered Alaska. During the summer between my sophomore and junior years in college, it was my turn to choose the family vacation and I selected Alaska. After spending two weeks touring the wild and awe-inspiring Great Land, I realized that I had found my future home. What a feeling of both exultation and responsibility.

In my short life in California, I had seen vast amounts of habitat destroyed, the air and water despoiled, and animals such as the condor go nearly extinct. As a daily reminder, the Golden State's flag itself featured the mighty grizzly bear, an animal that no longer existed in California because Homo sapiens destroyed its habitat and slaughtered it in fear, ignorance, and greed. Could we possibly take our relatively new knowledge of ecology, toxicology, and environmental economics and Do It Right in Alaska? I was hopeful.

When I graduated from Harvard Law School I had several choices. I could make really Big Bucks in a private law firm, especially if I worked in New York City, or I could go into government or public interest practice. Perhaps the most seductive choice, and one that was offered persistently by recruiters from the elite firms, was to work in private practice for "just a few years," learn "how to be a lawyer," and then leave to practice public interest law.

There was just one hitch, the Golden Handcuffs. As I talked to the recruiters in their impeccably tailored Brooks Brothers suits; visited their expensively furnished, mahogany paneled offices; and heard about their box seats to the Metropolitan Opera, I could see them locked to their solid walnut desks with Golden Handcuffs. Representing companies like Exxon allowed them to live in expensive homes, send their children to the best private schools and drink the most expensive single-malt scotch. But they were locked in; there was no ratcheting backwards to a much less expensive lifestyle, even if the demands of their job meant that they rarely saw their privately educated children and drank too much single malt scotch to relax or forget.

Fortunately, I chose government service, and became an attorney for the Department of Interior. With the promise that the Department would transfer me to Alaska after a year's service in Washington, DC, I joined a remarkable group of law school graduates in the Solicitor's Honors program, and had the privilege of serving under Secretary Andrus and President Carter while the greatest piece of land conservation legislation in our nation's history was being drafted – the Alaska National Interest Lands Conservation Act (ANILCA).

ANILCA – what an achievement. Following ten years of work by brilliant and dedicated citizens and Members of Congress, President Carter, as one of his last acts in office, protected over 100 million acres of land in Alaska when he signed ANILCA into law. Coincidentally, the entire landmass of California is approximately 100 million acres. Among other designations, ANILCA created over 43 million acres of national parks in Alaska and over 52 million acres of national wildlife refuges. In its application, ANILCA was designed to assure, among other achievements, that the grizzly bear would always thrive in Alaska – unless, of course, ANILCA is gutted.

A great law requires great defense, especially against those who, like members of my high school's B basketball team, are unwilling to share "their" habitat. Since 1980, I have had the privilege of working with many others to defend ANILCA lands, and the 50 million acres protected before ANILCA's passage, while wearing several different hats, most visibly when I served in the Clinton Administration as the Special Assistant to the Secretary of Interior for Alaska.

Not surprisingly, this has earned me the moniker of "Enemy of Alaska" by those who want-it-all. Right now these short-sighted power brokers especially covet: the dispersed and relatively insignificant amount of oil underneath the Arctic National Wildlife Refuge, the magnificent old growth trees in the Tongass National Forest's temperate rainforest, and the quiet biological heart of Denali National Park. They want to drill it, and clear cut it, and race their snow machines through it. And if they get this, they will demand more, much more, because we all know that greed is insatiable.

As the current Executive Director of the Alaska Conservation Foundation, I have the honor of working with women and men from across the country, who come from different backgrounds with diverse personal stories, but who all share a passion for protecting Alaska's great ecosystems, wildlife, and wild places.

There is something else that these compassionate citizens have in common; they all care about the future and our responsibility to posterity. Together the thoughtful patriots that I am privileged to work with appreciate that you cannot protect great places or other great things by inaction or default, but rather that you must be caring, vigilant, and engaged. And you must act, even when it will result in criticism or vilification.

I like to think in terms of 10,000-year units. It is always humbling and sobering to remember that Homo sapiens first crossed the Bering Land Bridge and entered North America a little more than 10,000 years ago. What will Alaska and the rest of the Americas be like 10,000 years from now? Dare we believe that the mighty grizzly bear will still be roaming through Alaska's intact ecosystems; that herds of caribou will be giving birth on the Coastal Plain of the Arctic National Wildlife Refuge; and that humans will still have the opportunity to take their children out to pick nutritious wild blueberries and to catch healthy, toxic-free silver salmon? Yes, I dare to believe this, and must act accordingly.

We have the capacity to live well and happily within our Earth's means, with due respect for other species and the intricate ecosystems in which we thrive. One testing ground for this theory is Alaska.

The Alaska Conservation Foundation was established by Denny Wilcher and Celia Hunter, two extraordinary human beings who wanted to demonstrate to current and future generations that we could be thoughtful, responsible and inspired stewards of our natural heritage. They also knew that to achieve this vision required hard work, strategically deployed contributions, and strong organizational infrastructure. Despite stinging criticisms, they "spoke truth to power" and prevailed again and again, while creating a public foundation that will support a wild Alaska forever.

I am fortunate, indeed, to carry on their legacy. Today, more than ever before, Alaska's gifts of unspoiled grandeur, vast forests, bountiful oceans, flourishing lakes and rivers, and unfettered wildlife are rare and precious resources. Alaska can serve as America's example, to itself and to the world, of economies and communities that share nature's bounty, without diminishing nature's capital. But the pressures to exploit Alaska have never been greater, and the need to protect the Great Land has never been more demanding. That is why, like many others, I wake up each morning, think about my child and future generations, look at the photograph of the magnificent polar bear in our home, gird myself against verbal assaults, and try very hard to do what is right.

The Alaska Conservation Foundation's head office is located in Anchorage, Alaska. For more information, view their website at www.akcf.org .

*What we want to see is the child in pursuit of knowledge,
and not knowledge in pursuit of the child.*
- George Bernard Shaw

George Bernard Shaw's words grace the front of HeartLight International's website. Momentarily, I'll introduce you to one of the people behind this remarkable organization.

Nothing, perhaps, is more important than how we treat our children, since, like it or not, they are the ones who will take all our hopes and dreams and carry them forward after we are gone. They will continue the work we are beginning today. Unless they choose not to. So it's up to us to show them the areas of life that we truly love and believe in nurturing.

Does our mainstream school system in North America teach nurturing? Imagine if it did. Imagine if there was a class every child attended simply called "Nurturing." Reading, Writing and Nurturing. And why not? What's more important in the big scheme of things...arithmetic or nurturing? I can see that being wide open to debate.

Actually, my mom taught me the difference between the two when I was only about seven. Because we lived way out in the middle of nowhere, we did all of our elementary schooling by correspondence. This was a challenging way to learn, since we were on our own time schedule and were in no way ruled by a clock. There was a lot of farm work to be done and a lot of woods to play in. With distractions running rampant, I would sometimes spend many days getting around to a single assignment. But then, give me a few days of heavy rain or snow and I would just get comfy up in my loft and catch up on a whole bunch of schoolwork. Or not.

Every couple of weeks, we would mail off our assignments in a yellow manila envelope to the central correspondence centre in Victoria and they would grade our work and send it back. It was a pretty good system. Finding time for the assignments was the hard part but having two well-educated parents around for guidance was certainly helpful. They would put their own spin on the process, adding assignments like encouraging us to read one article out of each magazine they subscribed to and then asking us to write an essay on it. Without the noise and clutter of television in my life, these additional assignments from our parents were the source of a great amount of education for me.

Back to how I learned the difference in importance between arithmetic and nurturing. One day I was working on a math assignment and just wasn't getting it at all. I asked Mom for assistance with the lesson but she was in the middle of a huge produce harvest, causing rather frazzled nerves. She took the time to explain the same lesson to me over and over but I just wasn't getting it. The little crosses and exes on the lesson page were just all looking the same to me and I was getting terribly frustrated. When Mom thought she finally had it through, I said something really stupid about math and she bonked me on the head. It was the only time in my life that my mother ever struck me and it was certainly not a violent act. I don't think it even hurt a little. But she immediately broke down in tears and apologized profusely, holding me warmly in her arms and filling my heart with love. Once she had released her embrace and returned to her work, the problem suddenly appeared clear to me and I was able to work forward, on my own.

Just like that, the difference in importance between arithmetic and nurturing was solved for me. If someone tried really hard, they could probably even come up with a mathematical equation for this. But that won't be me because I'm still not very good at math.

MAGGIE MACRO

Maggie Macro has worked as a curriculum designer and communication coordinator with HeartLight International.
HeartLight International creates educational models for schools, assisting in the development of enlightened and empowered learning. HeartLight's philosophy for education lies in the perception of the innate love and potential that lives within every human being.

I remember standing at my bedroom window, when I was fourteen years old, asking the heavens *Is this all there is?* I'd been voluntarily going to Sunday school twice every Sunday since I was four and I was still left empty. I knew there had to be something else, a grander vision and design to life. As an only child I felt trapped in a house where my parents fought and seemed miserable most of the time. I also resented that I was treated so harshly in school. I thought there had to be another way to interact with children. My heart cried out to be recognized!

The first avenue that I tried to change this was becoming a teacher myself. I thought "schools are the problem." I'll go and be a different kind of teacher. In my second year of study in 1964, while researching for a paper, I came across the book Summerhill by A.S.Neil about the progressive alternative school in England. I was so excited! It was an answer to my prayer. Here students were given freedom of choice. They could express themselves in many different ways. After completing my teacher training in the U.K. where I lived, I found the most progressive elementary school I could and began my teaching. I loved it and was able to give my students as much freedom as possible. However, my relationship with my first husband was a disaster. Its intricacies were beyond my ability. So I tried another husband and resolved to be a better person. I became a full-time mum and thought I would do a really good job now that I had my own children. But I soon discovered I still did not like how I was behaving with them or my husband. I couldn't understand why I did the things I did.

After I moved to the U.S. with my family and tried another marriage, my father in England committed suicide. This event was a springboard for me. No one should be so desperate that they should have no other option and I did not want my life to end like that. I found a women's support group run by a family therapist. During this time I decided that families were the problem and that if I could find out all about them I could change others and myself. I studied for and completed an M.A. in Family Therapy and combined this with my interest in education to become a counselor, providing a Student Assistance Program in elementary schools dealing with what were called "at risk" students. It was often exhausting, draining work. Too many huge problems with too little time and resources to deal with them. It was clear that what I was doing was making no significant difference. There had to be a better way. To continue to improve myself I tried personal therapy, 12 step programs, women's circles, Wicca, and many other explorations.

Then in 1996 my life was enriched by 2 major forces. I participated in the three-day course called the Landmark Forum presented by Landmark Education and began reading the Conversations with God series of books by Neale Donald Walsch. This was a powerful combination. A basis for both is that who we are being creates what we are doing and consequently what we then have, not the other way round. The understanding of this puts responsibility where it belongs. With me. It was the awakening I had been searching for. In my journal I wrote, *I have come to a place where I have always wanted to be.*

As I continued with Landmark courses and reading Conversations with God, life became so much simpler and clearer, exciting and vibrant. My journal in 1997 says, *So much is coming through right now I can scarcely keep up with it.* I saw many things at this time. I got God. Not as an idea but as a fact. Not as a religion but as me. I am God/Goddess expressed. My journal said *I see that my work in the world is not separate from what I do every day.* My life is my work. It is sourced not by a mission statement but by the declaration of a possibility stated as a way of being, in a specific way. For example, *The possibility I am inventing for myself and my life is the possibility of being an unstoppable stand for the greatness of humanity.* I invented this possibility ten minutes after I heard about the collapse of the World Trade Center.

In early 2000 I saw in the Conversations With God newsletter that a group of people were coming together to discuss and create schools based on the ideas in Book 2 of the series about how we could educate our children. On page 126 of this book it says, *Sit down together and collect your thoughts. Create the grandest version of the greatest vision you ever had about yourselves as a human race. Then, take the values and concepts which undergird such a vision and teach them in your schools.*

So we did, and HeartLight Education was created. It is an education based on the concept that *We are Love, Joy and Wisdom made manifest in human form* and that *Life is a continuous opportunity for declaring Who We Really Are.* The grounding premise is that *We are all one, There is enough, There's nothing you have to do.* Our four operating principles are awareness, honesty, responsibility and gratitude. What we are up to is transforming education on the planet, wherever people express an interest and a willingness to make it happen, with our support. To empower myself in this process I completed a seven month leadership training course with Landmark called The Introduction Leaders Program.

At the time of this writing, February 2003, we have opened our first ever HeartLight Learning Community in Port Elizabeth, South Africa with 35 students, with two more sites due to open in Chicago and Toledo in March, and there is a great interest in our educational ideas in Australia. My current role in this grand endeavor is to answer the web mail that is coming from all over the world and to be part of the team that is designing the vision and curriculum.

Based on the knowledge that We Are All One and therefore interconnected, HeartLight also espouses Honoring All Life, which means choosing to honor everything. I see this as including not only our environment, the way we treat each other and the interconnection of all, but also the way we are about our humanity and ourselves. Our evolution and possibly our very survival depends on us loving the way we are and the way we are not, embracing what we have previously thought of as "good and bad" within ourselves and recognizing that this is what it means to be human. Only then can we embrace and forgive those things in others, be they relatives, neighbors or other nations.

The idea we have had for so long that the world or anything in it needs to be fixed, changed or improved, or that we have problems to be solved, suggests that something is wrong, whereas there is, in every situation, only what is not working.

Looked at from this perspective there is no blame but an opportunity to take responsibility. Look for what is missing expressed as a way of being and be sourced by that. Both Landmark courses and Conversations With God books propose this and this is where my life journey has led me. This is what will make the difference, everywhere.

    HeartLight International's head office is located in Tyrone, Georgia. For information on HeartLight go to www.heartlightinternational.org.
    For information on Landmark Education go to www.landmarkeducation.com .

The American Southwest is an incredibly beautiful region. Even though I had heard about it for years, I wasn't prepared for the breathtaking vastness of its scenery. Tania and I visited there on our journey across the continent and wound up circling through the Southwest States, awestruck by their diverse topography and weird and wonderful little creatures.

We journeyed through Death Valley, across Southern Nevada and into Arizona, where we began our winding route around the Four Corners, visiting the Grand Canyon, Zion, Arches and Mesa Verde National Parks, as well as Moab in Utah and Taos, New Mexico. Utah, alone, has some of the most un-earthly landscape I've ever seen. Pillars of sandstone in a rainbow of colours from bright red to deep purple. Canyons that gouge so deeply into the earth that I felt I was resting atop a cloudbank, staring down at a miniature landscape, thousands of feet below. And vast open fields of nothing until you look more closely and see dozens of species of high desert life, surviving just fine under a big, hot sun.

In a very strange contrast to the natural beauty and utterly peaceful landscape is the eerie fact that Utah's largest industry is missile production.

The Grand Canyon, itself, may be the very centre of all of the Southwest's diversity and wonder. For those who haven't been there, I urge you to go there now. If you leave the tourist-busy rim and walk even a few metres down into the Canyon, the air becomes silent. Deep, deep within the silence, you will begin to hear the distant rush of the Colorado River far below you. Give yourself to this vastness with wide-open arms and I promise you that you'll leave with a gift from the Canyon itself.

This area of the world, an area that man has divided into States but really creates all its own boundaries with its canyons, plains and ridges, is home to our next contributor. He is an impassioned advocate for preservation of the Southwest. He speaks humbly but his efforts and his writing have influenced change and have raised awareness around him. Here is Lynn Jacobs.

LYNN JACOBS

Lynn Jacobs is an environmental advocate and author. His passion for the natural world has led him on many journeys, particularly throughout the American Southwest. His writing and wealth of knowledge about the environment around him have served as an inspiration and a reference source for many.

SAVE THE WILD

I was born and raised in middle-class America, in the suburbs east of Los Angeles in the 50's and 60's.

My childhood reality was contemporary American culture and early on I came to accept, like everyone else I knew, that our culture was the best. Not only was God on our side, but the United States of America was divinely preordained to spread our superior way of life across the planet, maybe even across the universe. This belief wasn't even conscious on my part; American society offered it to us kids as the *only* truth, and we assimilated it unquestioningly.

As my early years passed, however, my nationalism and my personal life clashed in a developing dilemma. A broken, dysfunctional family had produced a boy with very low self-esteem. So I learned to compensate for my feelings of worthlessness with feelings of patriotism – the concept that "we" are inherently better than everyone else.

Problem was, the "we" that was supposed to make me feel better about myself didn't really include me. I went through the motions of doing what I thought people expected, and I desperately wanted to be part of everything, but my self-respect was so low that I instead alienated myself from people and happenings around me. How could I feel that good ol' American patriotic pride when I couldn't even feel like part of American society? At high school football games, I cheered and shared feelings of "our" team's greatness, simultaneously feeling separated and alone sitting in the bleachers amongst a crowd of people I otherwise had little to do with.

I was lost, and lost on me was the fact that patriotism can provide only a false and fleeting sense of superiority at the expense of others. All I could think was that my life would be fine if I could be normal and fit in like everyone else.

Looking back now, in one respect I actually consider myself lucky to have spent my childhood estranged from the prevailing culture. Otherwise, I would undoubtedly have been absorbed into mainstream society and thus not been open to the alternatives that later led me to pursue what I now consider more worthwhile ways of living. Likewise, I probably wouldn't have become involved in environmental and social causes. And I sometimes wonder if I would have survived at all.

Whatever the case, the big change in my life's direction began in the summer of my 18th year, 1968. One sunny day (literally all summer days there were sunny), on a whim I picked up a hitchhiker alongside our local freeway and drove him to his house out in the nearby Mojave Desert. He shared some marijuana with me, and suddenly my reality experienced a profound shift. Soon I was using cannabis and other psychedelics as a tool to re-evaluate everything I believed and explore new possibilities.

An involuntary two-year stint in the US Army was thoroughly disagreeable, but at least it dragged me out of my Redlands, California, rut and shoved me reluctantly forward. As the other conscripts psychedelicized their brains for pleasure and escape, I often as not sat in quiet (not necessarily peaceful) self-contemplation.

Indeed, this process of deliberate mind alteration was as painful as it was pleasurable, as difficult as liberating, and as frightening as enlightening. It was gradual, ongoing, and maybe even necessary for my future sanity. Thirty-five years later, I'm still unlearning and redirecting childhood realities.

Early along the way, as my vision cleared I began to see something big: Culture Creates What We Perceive To Be Reality. The way we know ourselves and the world around us is determined far more by the inventions of the culture we inhabit than by "the way things really are," that is to say, by the more tangible, worthwhile, meaningful entities and situations around us. Indeed, as the years passed I increasingly realized that modern culture instead teaches its inhabitants to unthinkingly accept its version of reality — the established assemblage of traditions, customs, rituals, ceremonies, legends, myths, superstitions, histories, habits, behaviors, beliefs, faiths, tenets, dogmas, definitions, dictates, interpretations, imperatives, rules, routines, institutions, and so on that together constitute, define, and perpetuate a culture. And fueling modern culture's drive to further itself are its people of wealth and power — the elite — who have most to gain from preserving the status quo.

I began to see the correlations between the problems of my culture and those of my family, and to grasp the dynamics of my predicament. I peeled away like an onion layer after layer of my culture's predetermined reality, and each discarded layer left that paradigm a little smaller. What gradually emerged, as a more substantial reality during this process, was the natural world.

Culture wasn't always as we know it now, however. After evolving into more or less our present physical form a million or so years ago, we humans did live together in social establishments. But each tribe was unique, dynamic, and shaped mostly by its ongoing interaction with the natural world. Consequently, prehistoric cultures synchronized with their surroundings, providing us the most appropriate living circumstances possible and reflecting interrelationships between humans and nature most suitable to each habitat. And since there was an endless diversity of ever-changing natural habitats, a remarkable number and variety of corresponding local cultures developed.

When, relatively recently, the emergence of pastoralism and farming led to the rise of civilization, the numerous, diverse, small primitive cultures merged or were assimilated into much larger, increasingly homogenized regional cultures. These modern cultures were based not on an intimate interrelationship with the land, but on "anthropocentrism" — the belief that humans are inherently separate from and superior to nature. As a result, our cultural reality is now dictated overwhelmingly by the capricious desires, whims, and biases of people (again, predominantly people of wealth and power). Today little remains of our natural tribal cultures, of the ways we evolved to relate to our natural surroundings and to each other. Our modern cultures increasingly separate us from nature and each other with increasingly human-devised realities.

To make a long story short, although we humans now commonly believe we are above and beyond nature, that nature is little more than our servant, due to our million-year evolution in primitive cultures as part of nature, we still are and, regardless of how unnaturally we live, for millennia to come must remain physiologically, psychologically, emotionally, and socially attuned to living in primitive cultures as part of nature. Scientific studies conclude that evolution has genetically programmed us to be this way, and that it would take thousands more years of unnatural living to reprogram ourselves. Beyond that, more and more experts think that living separate from nature in an overwhelmingly anthropocentric environment is impossible in the long run. Time may tell.

    This discernment about culture was a revelation to me at the time. As my unsatisfying, prescribed cultural reality gave way to a more natural one, a literally and figuratively whole new world opened up. For the first time, I began to feel I belonged on the Earth, to perceive oneness with my surroundings, to sense real purpose in our lives.

    And though our natural ways were mostly gone, enough of the natural world remained that we still had a place in it. During my early 20's I spent more and more time outdoors, with like-minded people. I traveled around the US, especially the West, seeking out wild places. I learned to be comfortable there, to feel at home. I camped for free wherever I wanted on public lands. I slept under the stars and explored the universe. I hiked through all kinds of wilderness, swam in whatever wild water I could find, soaked in hot springs, scaled rocks and cliffs, boulder-hopped down canyons, climbed trees, crawled through brush, ate wild foods, drank from springs, stared at thunderstorms, napped under rustling cottonwoods, and generally immersed myself in whatever nature was around. I felt connected and alive.

    Just being in the wild was a learning and growing experience. Because our ancient interrelationship with nature basically created who we are, wildness helps us discover ourselves and gives us direction. Nature provides humans infinite lessons on many facets of existence, such as form, function, meaning, time, substance, structure, relations, sense, self, and awareness. These lessons reflect "nature's wisdom" – billions of years of creation and being.

    I was learning and changing, though my childhood problems didn't disappear. But they did decrease and become a lot more tolerable. And nature became a passion. My experiences in the wild enriched my life, and while they were to me the essence of physical reality, they simultaneously took on a transcendental, spiritual quality.

Things that I paid little heed to in the past began to affect me profoundly. I felt awe and wonder at the incredibly complex, functional, meaningful interrelationships amongst natural entities, between animals, plants, soil, water, and air. The ever-changing, never-predictable formation and dissipation of clouds amazed me. I was enchanted by the resonant, mellow songs of crickets on warm riverside nights. Dynamic, wind-blown ripple patterns and graceful curves of evolving sand dunes were fascinating. Gentle sensations of creek water swirling across my skin brought great pleasure. These kinds of things, I thought, are as natural and essential to people as good friendship, a helping hand, or a warm embrace. Yet, they are mostly missing from modern life.

Wildness was a natural high. Wherever I happened to be, even in the city, I sought out wild surroundings – the wilder the better. My goal was the most natural, intact, healthy, diverse, beautiful places. Was I a nature junkie? Maybe, because in the mid-70's, another developing dilemma – love of nature versus destruction of nature – began to bum out my wilderness experience. The more time I spent in the wild, the more intimate, enamored, aware, and concerned I became, the less I could disregard the environmental exploitation and degradation that I soon realized was pervasive around the planet.

The genie was out of the bottle, so to speak. When I tried to savor the splendor of a vast, unspoiled desert valley, I couldn't help notice the ugly blight of the sprawling new correctional facility. The peaceful whisperings of digger pine needles blowing in the breeze couldn't block out the violent roar of the US Air Force forcing me to suffer its intrusion. When I tried to enjoy a favorite swimming hole, it was hard to ignore that it was empty, that instead its water had been channeled to alfalfa fields.

Maybe it was partly selfish, but I felt driven to do something to counteract the ecological destruction that was emerging like an alter-earth all around me. Maybe I was naive to think I could actually make much difference. Looking at the world situation objectively, it's hard not to be hurt, angry, frustrated, and pessimistic. Many of us are. Someone advised back then, *All you can do is what you can, then put one foot in front of the other and live your life.*

At any rate, when I indulged in nature, I was now witness to its degradation, too. I read up on the various environmental issues and signed up with the groups working to protect and restore the wild. I wrote letters-to-the-editor, talked to people, joined demonstrations, committed civil disobedience, and practiced what was later known as "monkey wrenching."

Traveling around the rural American West I saw a lot of environmental abuse. What I gradually and reluctantly came to realize was this: Much more of it was caused by ranching than by logging, mining, off-road vehicles, litterbugs, or anything else. This was hard for me to accept because I was raised in America and *Americans love cowboys*, and ranchers, and ranching, and grazing cows, and anything else even remotely "Western." How ironic! I had discovered that livestock production has more than any other activity ruined the wild West. Cowboy mythology and rancher romance ended up in the trash bin of my mind, along with all the other cultural phenomena I'd come to disbelieve.

First-hand experience showed me many different things about ranching, but I did a lot of research as well: Stockmen use an incredible 70 percent of the West to raise livestock, and most of this land is publicly owned. The vast bulk is significantly degraded by grazing cattle and sheep, and related ranching activities such as fencing, road-building, stock-water development, vegetation manipulation, predator and competitor slaughter, pesticide and herbicide application, fire suppression, and so forth. Tens of millions of acres have been so overgrazed and mismanaged for so long that they are now essentially wasteland. Ranching has destroyed more wildlife and wildlife habitat, more native vegetation, and more riparian area than any other Western land use. It causes more soil erosion and soil damage, more ruinous flooding, more invasions of animal pests and non-native vegetation. It has destroyed, depleted, and polluted more natural water sources. It has eliminated more beneficial natural fire. On public land, it results in more developments, and environmental damage from developments thereon. Finally, it detracts more from other uses of public land than does any other land use.

What's truly remarkable is that, on America's public lands, all this environmental devastation results in the production of only a tiny 3 percent of US beef (a product that science tells us is probably the single main contributor to bad health in the United States). The other 97 percent comes from private property, 80 percent of this in the relatively well-watered, level, fertile East. Not only that, just 2 percent of US stockmen have permits to graze the 41 percent of the West that is public grazing allotments. These 30,000 ranchers who make up the public lands ranching elite comprise the most wealthy, influential special interest group in the rural West. It dominates much of the West, causing more political and social injustice than any other land-based business. No other commercial enterprise in the rural West wields such clout or commands as much special treatment.

Furthermore, public lands ranchers may be rich and powerful, but they are also extremely heavily subsidized; thus the term "welfare ranching." Foremost, they pay an average annual federal grazing fee only one-fifth fair market value for the public property they are permitted to ranch. Their myriad other subsidies (which would literally require a book to describe) cause a local, county, state, and federal tax loss of roughly one billion dollars each year. As well, their negative impacts cause a roughly equivalent yearly loss to the private sector. Public lands ranching actually detracts from most local economies, if all plusses and minuses are considered. Moreover, the industry produces just $550 million in livestock annually – far less than what taxpayers spend on it annually! Public lands ranching obviously makes no economic sense. And if we could put a price tag on the loss of biodiversity, suffering of animals, soil depletion, watershed damage, diminishment of recreation, aesthetic degradation, and so on, would it not be unimaginably huge?

In sum, public lands ranching is the most overall destructive, least justifiable land use in America (as well as Canada). That's how I came to conclude that ending public lands ranching is the simplest, best way to do the most good.

And so that became my special cause. Attention previously scattered thinly across environmental issues I now focused on ranching. In 1977, my family and I bought a few acres within the boundaries of a southwest New Mexico national forest, and plunged into the belly of the beast. As per legal requirement around most of the West, we erected a fence around our little "ranchette" to exclude stockmen's wandering livestock (raising the ire of the local rancher), and a year later what had been four-and-a-half acres of mostly trampled bare dirt and scraggly weeds magically transformed into a lush, diverse assemblage of leafy ground cover and wildflowers.

Surrounded by ranchers and their cattle, I was overwhelmed by their seemingly endless multiformity of malevolent influences: not only environmental, but also economic, political, and social. I began compiling a list, which I hoped to later copy and distribute, and planned to call it "1001 Harmful Effects of Public Lands Ranching," or something similar. It quickly evolved into a descriptive account, and eventually into a newspaper-style 48-page tabloid titled "Free Our Public Lands!" I had 100,000 copies printed and distributed them widely to anyone or any group that seemed interested or concerned. Surprisingly, the tabloid drew so much support that Free Our Public Lands! soon mutated into a small grassroots effort to end public lands ranching.

By now we lived in rural central Arizona, having been inspired to relocate partly by mounting threats and harassment by intimidating, well-armed stockmen. Over the next several years my little stop-ranching project seemed to expand exponentially. This led to an inevitable crossroads. I could try to lead a campaign whose potential was an organization with thousands of members, a big budget, offices, publications, and all the rest. Or, I could recognize my personal limits that in the end I knew I had to. I wasn't a leader; I wasn't even comfortable talking to more than one person at a time. As determined as I was, it didn't seem realistic trying to be something I'd probably never really feel like being, most likely just hurting the cause in the long run. It was painful, but through the late 80's I let the project die a slow death from neglect. Its supporters moved on to other stop-ranching efforts that later sprang up around the West (though that one, big national organization has yet to realize its potential).

Meanwhile, I still burned inside each time I walked out on the Western range and revisited the destruction. I still had to do more. My tabloid only scratched the surface in depicting ranching's impact on the West. Someone suggested a book. And so I spent the years 1989-91 mostly hunched over a computer keyboard. "The book" quickly dominated my life; I did little else for three years. In the end I self-published 7,000 copies of a 600-page, four-pound paperback behemoth named *Waste of the West:*

Public Lands Ranching – my only "claim to fame" and the likely reason I was asked to contribute to the book you are now reading.

Waste was generally well received, except of course in ranching circles. While not earth-shaking, it did help energize an already rapidly growing movement to end public lands ranching. Twenty years ago the idea of banning livestock from our public lands was unthinkable; today, it's a popular long-term solution that continues to gain support.

The book helped satiate my long-frustrated urge to reach out and communicate to humanity on some level, and to make some kind of difference in a world that needs all the help it can get. My decade-long compulsion to stop public lands ranching took a toll on me personally, but in the years following I've worked out a tolerable merging of activism and simply living my life.

I'm not sure I have The Answer to the world's problems. But I do know the natural Earth is going down fast; that's a scientific fact. And widespread social and political injustice obviously continues. In my opinion, if things continue this way, we humans will ultimately go down too. I can't imagine some all-powerful being descending from the sky to save us. We created this predicament; we'll have to figure a way out.

Each of us has some idea how best to do that. Trouble is, we have almost as many answers as people, so the solutions generally contradict each other. Seems to me this problem is inherent to anthropocentric thinking, and largely what got us into our plight in the first place.

Our attempt to mold the Earth to our human-centric, divergent wills is destroying the planet's health, integrity, diversity, beauty, and is, I think, futile in the long run. To my mind, only when we change our goals to harmonize with nature can we find a workable answer. Only a solution that sustains the natural environment, as well as our natural coexistence with it and between each other, can succeed over time. This means accepting our inherent unity with the Earth and moving toward re-establishing our ancient, time-tested interrelationships.

What it doesn't mean is what almost automatically comes to mind upon hearing the word "primitive" – huddled in caves, cold, filthy, and disease-ridden; barely surviving on greasy mastodon parts; clothed with ill-fitting animal skins; venturing out into the cruel world only to hunt game or club each other over the head. There is still widespread disagreement over just what life was like for primitive humans, but evidence increasingly indicates they lived far better than we imagined. Books have been written on the subject, but suffice it to say, our "suffering-caveman" concept is, I think, nearly the antithesis of most early human existence.

We moderns live a dichotomy; the farther we split from nature, the more we crave it. Consider a few examples:

We labor to make enough money to fly jet planes around the planet – so we may spend a little time in unspoiled natural settings living more like our ancestors did.

We seek social clubs, military service, and team sports – in a subconscious, mostly futile effort to recreate the communal satisfaction of our lost primitive tribalism.

To counteract the harmful effects of contemporary society – stress, physical inactivity, loss of control over our lives, emotional isolation, sensory overload, aesthetic blight, toxins, junk food, and so on – we pursue yoga, meditation, primal therapy, encounter groups, spiritual counseling, and a seemingly endless variety of "self-help" intended to restore our natural well-being. A report from one recent scientific study is enlightening; it concludes that going barefoot is better for your feet than wearing any shoe ever created.

Modern culture offers us extreme materialism, ever-expanding technology, increasing control over our surroundings, seemingly infinite lifestyle choices, instant gratification (for some desires), and more. Concurrently, it decreasingly satisfies our inherent need for long-term sustainability, simplicity, tranquility, aesthetic pleasure, wonder and magic, spirituality, interaction with our natural surroundings, a sense of place, a clean and healthy environment, quality family and group relationships, fulfillment of natural instincts, and other basics that nature provided for eons.

What most people want in life, I suspect, is basically and simply to feel good, as much and in as many ways as possible. Human existence has never been a bed of roses, but consider that the Earth's most "advanced" cultures have the highest rates of depression and suicide, while the most "primitive" peoples seem generally happy, content, and alive. We moderns can quickly travel to almost any spot on Earth, but do we feel the sense of wonder, adventure, camaraderie, and accomplishment that, say, a prehistoric group did when it spent a week walking down a wild river valley to collect shells, seaweed, and salt along the ocean shore? We currently work an average of two to three hours daily to make the money to buy packaged foods that we spend more time pulling off supermarket shelves, so we can spend another hour or so per day preparing the food, eating, and cleaning up. A primitive band might have spent a similar amount of time one day picking wild greens and blackberries by a creek, stuffing their bellies and drying the extra, having fun and feeling intimate with their surroundings and each other. Via modern telecommunications, we may now talk to family and friends instantly nearly anywhere around the world. But do we feel the emotions, the security, the sense of belonging, the community like our ancestors did for countless generations when we lived our entire lives with family, tribe, and nature, when we shared and experienced everything together? I don't believe in Prehistoric Paradise, but I am convinced that our overall quality of life is declining due to our alienation from our planet.

Yes, it is true, as the naysayers say, that we can't suddenly disown everything modern, go back in time, and live exactly like our forebears. Nature is nothing if not dynamic, so things would be very different now even without human influence. And humans surely have made huge changes (overpopulation, for instance). But, it isn't necessary to renounce every contemporary contrivance to achieve a basically natural existence; we can pick and choose. Things aren't black and white, and moreover, the point is to eventually re-establish a healthy, functional, natural interrelationship with the Earth, not pursue a carrot on a stick or some political agenda.

We *can* move forward, not into the past, per se, but ahead toward what we lost. We can rejoin the Earth. Committing ourselves to heading that direction is what's important. Although nature-based living may seem unthinkable to most of us now, we can reach that ultimate goal if we: First, admit that anthropocentrism doesn't work. Second, acknowledge that our ancestors' million-year existence was, on the whole, meaningful, satisfying, sustainable, healthy, safe, secure, open and free – not the opposite. Third, re-establish natural living in a determined but gradual manner, incorporating changes incrementally in logical, natural sequence, so the transition proceeds smoothly and at no point feels overwhelming or impossible. If at any time along that path the goal is hindered, then at least we made it that far. And we could take it from there further along the way. In progression, each succeeding generation could feel a little more comfortable being a little more natural.

The big danger now is that if we don't make enough change soon enough, it could be too late. Humankind is losing its remaining natural environment and ways of living so fast that we may in the near future reach a kind of "critical mass of no return." If this happens, there won't be enough healthy wild habitat or indigenous skills and viewpoints left to guide us back to nature and sustain us there. The whole concept of natural would then have no real meaning. We'd be lost in an inherently unsustainable, anthropocentric world of our own making, where everything we'd do (and think?) would be based on the dictates of those with power, in direct proportion to the amount of power they wielded. A greater scenario for injustice and conflict is hard to imagine, but this is indeed what has already started happening.

Further, as suggested, if our estrangement from nature continues long enough we will begin to lose our natural genetic programming, thus our natural attributes and abilities. It is no joke to surmise that at the rate we are going we will eventually reprogram ourselves so our bodies are physically designed more for sitting in chairs than walking upright. In the future, we may well lose our capacity to produce vitamin D from sunlight, tolerate temperature extremes, see in dim light, fight off disease, and even feel good without drugs. Many unhealthy, sometimes bizarre metamorphoses could and would occur. At risk are our natural instincts, physical characteristics and capabilities, family and social relationships, emotions and psychological make-up, and aesthetic sensibilities. The exact details of future scenarios are, of course, impossible to predict. However, these are more than fanciful speculations. It is scientific certainty that continued unnatural living inevitably will lead to genetic reprogramming and profound, mostly unwanted change in our physical and nonphysical composition. Humanized re-evolution would leave us desensitized, devitalized, diminished creatures. That such an existence could be sustained for millennia or even centuries, especially in the overall context of an inherently erratic anthropocentric culture and a dysfunctional, unnatural environment, is highly doubtful.

Modern humans, with their unique, analytical intelligence and contemporary cultural imperatives, seem no longer satisfied merely living out their earthly natural lives as their ancestors did for a million years. Now, we avariciously seek "higher" aspirations – newer, bigger, better, stronger, faster, more, more, and still more. But as much as we get, has it been, or can it ever be, enough to make us feel as happy, content, and alive as we were in the first place? If feeling good is our main goal in life, then what is the point of striving for pie-in-the-sky – or even eating every piece of the pie, if it doesn't truly satisfy – rather than simply accepting and being what we naturally are?

As for reaching for the sky, on Star Trek's futuristic starship "Enterprise," the crew explores the farthest reaches of the universe with currently undreamed of, nearly omnipotent technology. Their decks, halls, and quarters are flawless and antiseptically, spotlessly clean. Their climate-controlled atmosphere offers "optimum" temperature, humidity, ion content, and gas ratio. Their physical environment is perfectly planned and meticulously micro-managed. They want for nothing; all material needs are assiduously provided for. And a "replicator" magically materializes any physical entity a crewmember desires and verbally commands the machine to produce. With the starship's "transporter," a crewmember may decorporealize her or his body and instantly recorporealize at any location within (I'm guessing) a few thousand miles. Education, entertainment, and opportunities for communal interaction are all comprehensive and state-of-the-art. Social justice and cultural morality are strictly enforced with an uncompromising, all-encompassing set of rules, regulations, policies, parameters, and penalties.

For the pleasure, relaxation, and edification of the crew, the Enterprise is even equipped with a "holodeck" -- a large, fully computerized room where selections may be made from a programmed list of an almost infinite variety of human-influenced or natural surroundings known to exist throughout the universe. The specified computerized environment is a perfectly detailed simulation of the setting, complete with all physical sensations, and is fully dynamic and interactional, so that it functions similarly to the actual place and the participant seems to actually be in that place.

And so, with all their amazing technology and amenities, when earthling crew members of the Starship Enterprise have a little leisure time, what do they most enjoy doing? More than anywhere, it seems, you'll find them happiest on the holodeck running natural Earth simulations.

A final thought: Rarely do I truly enjoy writing. For me it's usually a tedious, laborious process. I don't consider myself a very good writer, either, though I've done a lot of it over the past 25 years. But I think maybe the best thing I ever wrote just popped into my head one day as I was trying to think of a short slogan for a bumper sticker. In just a few words I wanted to convey the importance of restoring our million-year interrelationship with the Earth and each other – that for both the planet's sake and ours, we must preserve what's still natural in our surroundings and within ourselves. The resultant bumper sticker reads, "SAVE THE WILD."

To get more information on Waste of the West and Lynn Jacobs, visit www.wasteofthewest.com .

This area of the world I'm fortunate enough to call home is surrounded by the Salish Sea and a myriad of islands of all shapes and sizes. Most maps you'll come across call this region the Strait of Georgia or the Gulf Islands. I prefer to call it by its traditional name though, in recognition and honour of the First Nations people who have lived here for at least 10,000 years. The territories of the Coast Salish people include both shores of the Strait of Georgia from Cortes Island south into Puget Sound, and extend far inland up the Fraser Valley in British Columbia and the river valleys of Washington State.

When British and Spanish explorers began flooding into the Salish Sea in the 18th century, they called the region the Gulf Islands, although we don't actually live in a "gulf" at all. They also applied their own names to each new island they discovered, not concerning themselves to any great extent with the people who were living on them and had been doing so for millennia.

I can only imagine how the First Nations people loved this archipelago, with its gently rolling waters, moderate climate and spectacularly lush ecosystems. The Pacific Ocean, powerful and temperamental on the west side of Vancouver Island, takes a rest on the east side. This is where the ocean comes for its naps. With high tide, the ocean rushes in through Juan de Fuca Strait, surrounds the hundreds of little islands that are nestled in the peaceful waters of the east side of the big island, makes a great, oceanic sigh and snoozes for a while. Then, ever so smoothly, it eases its way back out to the open water to begin its playful turbulence again.

The ocean here is full of life. Every shape and colour of sea star and anemone graces its tidepools for all the Earth's children to marvel at. Seals, otters, dolphins, sea lions, orcas, grey whales and fish of every kind call these waters home.

My favourite pastime here is finding myself a comfortable resting place along any shoreline and simply staring out over the gentle roll of the water. Under its surface, the sea is teeming with life. And every once in a while, I'm gifted enough to see that life up close, as ocean creatures pop up from the safety of the water and look at me with curious eyes.

These waters are precious and the lives they nurture are precious. That's what the life work of my next contributor has become – preserving life in our oceans. And what important work she does.

VIVIENNE VERDON-ROE

Vivienne Verdon-Roe is Co-Founder of SEAFLOW.
Seaflow is a San Francisco based grassroots environmental organization working with individuals and groups to build an international movement dedicated to protecting ocean life from man-made threats. One of their primary focuses is stopping Low Frequency Active (LFA) Sonar through educating citizens about its dangers, drawing on science, creative arts, and community for inspired political action.

Vivienne Verdon-Roe has earned an Honorary Ph.D. and over 20 film festival awards, including an Academy Award, for her work as an advocate for living in harmony with each other and our environment.

MESSAGES FROM THE WOMB OF THE WORLD

When I lived in England I thought social responsibility meant answering dinner party invitations. I came to the USA in 1978 and I had a rude awakening. Cowboy and Indian movies had not prepared me for the reality of the lives of Native Americans. After seeing the devastating consequences of uranium mining on Hopi land, I worked with the Hopis to publicize their plight and get help. Then in 1981, I saw a film called The Last Epidemic. It was about the danger of nuclear weapons. I became a full-time activist working in the peace movement. I wondered how children were affected by growing up in a culture that had the capacity to annihilate itself, and indeed, threatened to do so. I interviewed children and wrote an article about the effects of the nuclear threat on young people. It was published in EAST WEST journal.

The father and son team, Ian and Eric Thierman, who had made The Last Epidemic, invited me to collaborate with them on a documentary based on my article. That film was nominated for an Academy Award. We made three films together and Ian and I co-founded a non-profit company distributing social issue films.

I became a public speaker. I got really tired of being confronted with, My dear, aren't you being a bit emotional? Don't you think it's best to leave these military matters up to the experts?

This anti-democratic macho attitude infuriated me. The policies of the so-called experts weren't doing a very good job of creating real security for our country and our world. Being able to blow up the world more times than the Soviet Union could did not make me feel safe, and if it wasn't okay to be "emotional" about the threatened destruction of our planet, what was it okay to be "emotional" about?

I often heard women in the peace movement speaking with passion and common sense about the arms race. They pointed out how the bloated military budget drained resources from health care, from education for our children, and from taking care of the environment — basic security issues. Yet, despite the fact that 90 percent of the people active in the peace movement were women, our spokespeople were usually men. I don't think the men were especially chauvinistic; the women lacked confidence.

I wanted to make a film that honored the feminine perspective and encouraged women to speak up with the conviction and coherence I'd so often heard. Although I loved working with Ian and Eric, I was asking women to speak up for themselves and it seemed to me that as a woman I ought to take charge of this film.

Women For America, For The World won an Academy Award as best short documentary. I can still hear Ian's cheer in that great theater when it was announced. I got an agent to book more speaking engagements and my traveling increased. I was talking about living sustainably but I wasn't. I got sick. I burnt out.

After my health collapsed I started spending two months every winter in Hawaii, but I had a hard time not being an activist. After several years of being unable to work I felt very frustrated. I wanted to contribute to help create a safer, saner world.

One of the delights of coming to Hawaii each year was to see the whales. Every year the humpbacks travel thousands of miles to the warm waters off Maui where they give birth to their young and mate. Watching the whales helped to lift the depression that came with my being out of commission. Each time I witnessed a whale breaching — thirty tons of shining gray flesh rising up into the sky with flippers thrown out in abandonment like outstretched arms — my heart would skip a beat and I'd feel blessed. The whales remind me that this life is to be lived joyfully.

I became fascinated with whales. They have been on this planet for fifty million years. That's ten times longer than we have. These creatures are our elders. Whales have brains six times bigger than ours. They say three conditions have led to human intelligence: size of brain, expansion and complexity of neocortex, and social interactions. Carl Sagan wrote that these conditions in whales greatly surpass our own. We consider the possibility of other intelligent beings on distant planets. There may well be another class of intelligent beings on Earth beside ourselves.

I had just returned home from Hawaii when I heard that the United States Navy had tested a new type of sonar off the Hawaiian Islands. During the tests off Hawaii, whale calves died after becoming separated from their mothers and the humpbacks left the test area.

Unlike passive sonar, Low Frequency Active sonar (LFA) bombards the ocean with a burst of noise more intense than standing next to the launch of the Space Shuttle. I heard the Navy planned to deploy LFA sonar worldwide. The Navy claims the technology is needed to detect enemy submarines, but they have developed passive sonar that does the job without harming whales.

I knew that marine mammals communicate with each other using their own sonar. It seemed obvious that the calves and mothers had been confused by LFA sonar and lost each other. I knew that marine mammals also use sonar to find food and navigate. Could this new technology, deployed globally, threaten the very existence of marine mammals around the world? A world without whales.

March 2000. The effects of sonar on whales hit the national news. Using similar active sonar off the Bahamas, the Navy caused an unprecedented stranding of sixteen whales. Seven died on the beach. Tests on the dead whales revealed bleeding from their eyes and hemorrhaging in their ears and brains. In the past, there had been numerous whale strandings that coincided with the Navy's active sonar testing. The Navy had vehemently denied any connection. Now, the Navy's responsibility was clear, but they continued with their plans to deploy LFA sonar worldwide.

I was devastated. I knew I couldn't stand by and do nothing while these magnificent beings were tortured and killed. My health was improved, but I still was not strong and I tired very easily. What could I do?

For some years, I'd been studying Shamanic Journeying. Being weak, I spent a lot of time prone on my back. So I explored what I could do lying down and I was introduced to this ancient practice. Listening to a tape of a drum beating monotonously with your eyes covered, the idea is to leave this realm and visit the upper and lower worlds of "non-ordinary reality." Keeping a question firmly in mind, you call upon your animal guardians and spirit teachers to come and give you guidance. I learned that indigenous cultures all over the world used variations of this practice to get answers to questions about their survival and to bring healing to their communities.

I wasn't sure if I believed in spirits. Sometimes I thought it was all my imagination. However, I got good information from my journeys. Sometimes I got inspirations that I know I could never have come up with sitting at my desk. So I continued with the practice.

I decided to journey to the whales and ask what I could do to help. I listened to the drums and I felt myself sinking until I was in non-ordinary reality at the bottom of the ocean. I was in the center of a circle of whales. They thanked me for answering their call.

We need your compassion, just as we offer you ours.

Tears came to my eyes. Whales care about our species even after we have hunted and slaughtered them almost into extinction? I remembered being on whale-watching boats, and seeing mother whales come to the boat to show off their newborn calves. I thought that perhaps the big hearts of whales had given them a big ability to forgive.

I asked if there was anything I could do about the Navy's new sonar system. *Invite your community to an event and tell them what is happening.* I was given the format for the gathering, a mixture of politics and spirituality. A description of LFA sonar and its effects on whales and then a guided shamanic journey to the whales with drums.

I didn't want to be a party-pooper, but I suspected that an evening at my small town's community center with a few friends and neighbors wasn't going to have much of an effect on the U.S. Navy. Besides, I wasn't sure I had the energy to organize such an event. I expressed my reservations. The whales were patient but firm. If I wanted to help, this was the help they wanted. They told me not to be so focused on the outcome. They suggested I ask friends for help. *Give others an opportunity to contribute. Your caring and your intention to gather others who care will make a difference.* And the whales said they'd help me find the energy to organize the event.

Okay, okay. I replied. I still felt somewhat skeptical.

During the next few weeks as I organized "The Whales Are Calling," I had more energy than I'd had in a long time. Almost every person I talked to about the event wanted to help. A San Francisco television station had broadcast a ten-minute news story on the Navy's LFA sonar. I got permission to use it. I asked the members of my journeying circle to participate and drum for the journey. Thirty people attended. Despite the depressing subject, by the end of the evening the hall was filled with a sense of joy, community, and we-can-make-a-difference. A woman asked if I'd come and facilitate a similar event in her nearby hometown. Fifty people came to that event. A small group of us began meeting regularly.

One member of our group was an acoustician who'd been following the development of active sonar. He pointed out that it was not only marine mammals that would be affected. Fish use sound for survival too. Research has shown that just a moderate amount of noise harms fish eggs. The whole balance of ocean life is endangered.

It would have been easy to feel overwhelmed by the task ahead. Here was a technology that could cause a worldwide planetary catastrophe, and yet very few people knew about it. Other than the Bay Area newscast, there had been no mainstream media about LFA sonar. We discovered that the Navy had developed the system in secret, violating all sorts of federal environmental laws. We also discovered that many marine biologists were funded by the U.S. government and were apparently afraid to speak out opposing the Navy's plans.

Our group began organizing events all over the Bay Area. We met with local elected officials urging them to take a stand opposing the deployment of this harmful technology. We called ourselves the Council for Living Oceans. That was such a mouthful, we used the acronym C-flo. Then we decided to adopt the acronym as our name, spelling out the "C" as "Sea" and adding a "w." Thus, finally, SEAFLOW was born!

Our mission is to educate the public and stop the worldwide deployment of active sonar. Since we began SEAFLOW, we've discovered that there are other lethal forms of man-made noise (for example, seismic air guns) and no regulations that apply. Our long-term goal is to help build an international movement to create laws that restrict noise underwater.

From the beginning, we knew we wanted to be part of a sustainable activist organization. Being fueled by anger and taking on too much are ways that lead to burnout. Instead of blaming and demonizing the U.S. Navy and those who disagree with us, could we frame the issue in terms of our common interests? Can we do all the work that needs to be done – educating the public through events, media and direct action; lobbying elected officials; building coalitions with fishermen, the whale watch industry, kayakers, and other organizations concerned with the health of ocean life? Can we do all that and maintain our own health? We don't have all the answers, but we are asking the questions. We believe that setting very clear intentions will lead us to where we need to go.

We are attempting to follow Gandhi's advice: *Be the change you want to see in the world.* We realize that means paying as much attention to the process of the organization as to its goals. We want to be sure that our communications do not spread more violence in the world. Often, social change activists are combative when talking to "opponents" and they motivate people to get involved by guilt tripping. As I well know!

Several of us have trained in conflict resolution and mediation. We are acutely aware of the importance of clear, honest and compassionate communication, and of making our organization as inclusive as possible.

As our decision-making process, the Board of SEAFLOW has adopted Concordance, which goes one step further than Consensus. Any hesitation or a less than enthusiastic response to a call for agreement is discussed. The member who has a reservation about going along with a decision may well make an important contribution to the wisdom of the group. That niggle can lead us to an entirely new insight and a better final decision. When a decision is finally whole-heartedly endorsed, everyone is fully on board and enthusiastically responsible for that decision.

We want to create a sense of community in SEAFLOW. It is so common to feel isolated and alienated in a culture that has separated itself from the natural world, separated itself from the sources of life, and left so many people hungering for a sense of belonging.

We want people to feel appreciated, supported and empowered when they volunteer for SEAFLOW. We hope their lives will be enriched by working with us. We look forward to learning new skills and to growing at the same time as we are contributing to protecting life in the oceans.

Despite the enormity and gravity of the task we've taken on, our meetings and events are fun and full of joy and optimism. We often comment that the whales must be with us, guiding us and reminding us that life is to be played, not worked. This doesn't mean that we deny our anguish about the suffering. Far from it. We feel it is important to channel our pain for what is happening to our world into creative expression. We end our meetings with someone volunteering to entertain us with a poem or a song. We also host a monthly SEAFLOW Salon, offering people an opportunity to come and perform. In these challenging times, grief, anger and despair are appropriate feelings that come from our caring. We believe that sitting on those feelings can drain us of our energy, causing an overwhelmed feeling of hopelessness and paralysis, and that expressing our pain breaks through the despair, releases our creative juices and empowers us to act.

We recognize that our work is really about relationships. The way we relate to the world and to each other. We live in a time of profound change. The old way of viewing relationships is no longer functional. The old science and old social order have viewed nature in terms of discrete and separate entities, related in a hierarchical and competitive fashion. This has led many people to believe that we needed to dominate in order to survive.

This is the view behind the United States' military objectives. On the Defense Department's website the stated goal is "Full Spectrum Dominance" – control of the Earth's resources, landmasses, space and oceans. This policy of "Full Spectrum Dominance" will not lead to our security. This policy will inspire continual "terrorist" attacks by those who do not want to be dominated. Ultimately, systems based on force are destined to fail.

Based on the latest scientific understanding of the universe, there is a new story emerging of who we are and what our place is in the scheme of things. John Muir said, *When we try to pick out anything by itself, we find it hitched to everything else in the universe.* We are one strand in the web of life. Our genuine self-interest includes other beings and the health of the living body of the Earth. Our security will come from living in partnership with each other and in harmony with our environment.

This understanding is the next step in our continuing evolution, a lesson we must learn if we are to survive the destructive power of our own technology. We are a very young species. It's time for us to grow up and recognize that we have an amazing role to play. Because of our ability to reflect on what we do, we are the Earth, aware of herself.

Awareness is the key. I've seen the violence in the self-righteous attitudes of the old dominator worldview in myself. I've seen the violence in how I've pushed myself to do more than my health could withstand. I believe an essential part of our work is to leave behind these abusive tendencies that are so often alive and kicking within us, even as we espouse values of compassion and cooperation. I want to pay attention to the quality of the energy I am putting out into the world. I believe this is the transformation human beings need to go through to evolve and survive.

There are many myths that speak of how life sprang from the oceans. The whale is an ancient symbol of the creation of life. Connecting with a being that represents the source of life seems especially important at this point in the history of our planet, a time when we find ourselves faced with the destruction of so many life forms and the crumbling of our very life-support systems. Perhaps as more and more of us make a deep connection to nature we will experience life anew and we will be empowered to make the profound necessary changes, in ourselves and in the world. The fact is, we will make those changes or we will destroy ourselves. That is our choice.

As we appreciate the values of being cooperative and trustworthy, as we learn the benefits of respecting each other's well-being, our culture will change and reflect those values and that understanding. Times of great change are frightening times, exciting times. The transition from a system that relies so heavily upon force and domination to one that is based on good will and mutual cooperation seems to be a difficult labor. But that depends on us, all of us. We are the midwives, the mothers, and the newborn. It's up to us to keep in mind a vision of a world based on loving kindness, and to live our everyday lives knowing that the world is as we do.

Vivienne welcomes feedback on how to create a transformative activist organization. She can be reached at info@seaflow.org . SEAFLOW's website is www.seaflow.org .

A few years ago, while I was still living in Banff, I met Neale Donald Walsch for the first time at a lecture he was giving. Neale, the author of the *Conversations With God* series of books, has an incredible energy around him and spending an evening in his presence is beyond motivational. His words shake you up and bring you to life.

Although I had already read three of the CWG books, I was incredibly inspired by meeting this enlightened old soul in person and my life took a leap or two forward after that evening.

One of the things that evolved from Neale's visit to Banff was a weekly Wisdom Circle, a discussion group for people who had been touched by the CWG books and who wanted to continue developing the ideas therein. These weekly meetings were a great thing, with different people showing up each time to share their thoughts and explore new ideas.

On one of these evenings, I met a wonderful couple. They were passing through the Rockies on a pilgrimage they had named *Journey of the Heart*. They were relaxation expressed. They exuded a laid-back, positive energy that was wildly contagious. Listening to their stories from the road and how they had left their normal life behind to pursue their dreams was a great experience. The next day, after visiting a glacier on the Icefield Parkway, Tom contacted me and said, *Boy, God does good work, doesn't he*?

His words, for some reason more than anything else he or Kay said, stuck with me. Maybe it was his incredible sincerity. He was speaking from his heart.

Now, several years after they began their journey, they're still at it. And I'm proud to be able to include their contributions to Softly On This Earth. Here are Kay and Tom Seliskar.

KAY & TOM SELISKAR

Kay and Tom Seliskar are full-time travelers, having embarked on their Journey of the Heart in 1998. The mission of their journey is to "plant seeds of the heart" and make a positive difference in the world. Both Tom and Kay have taken their businesses on the road with them; Kay as a motivational/inspirational speaker and Tom as a nature photographer.

PLANTING SEEDS OF THE HEART - Kay Seliskar

Sometimes a dream takes hold of your heart and just grows and grows—especially if that dream comes from your soul. At some point you have to decide if that dream will only live in the "Land of Someday I'll…" or if it will become a reality. In 1989 my husband, Tom, and I made a commitment to respond to this calling and turn our dream into reality. Nine years later, after our children were grown (or at least we told them they were), we sold our house, gave away our possessions and began living on the road full-time in our recreational vehicle. We wanted to travel and see the beauty of this Earth, share it with others, and, most of all, make a positive difference in the world. Gandhi said, *Be the change you want to see.* We wanted to see a world where people weren't afraid of each other, a world where people took the time to help each other, even if they were strangers. And so we set out to create a kinder, gentler world. We figured strangers were just friends we hadn't met yet, and we wanted to meet them. We also knew in our hearts that there were a lot of good people doing good things (unlike what the media usually focus on), and we wanted to share those stories with others.

Before we launched this "Journey of the Heart," as we call it, Spirit told me to Be a Johnny Appleseed, so we set out to plant seeds of the heart. Throughout our journey, Spirit has guided us. We follow this guidance in deciding where to go and when – quite literally! We may make tentative plans to head one direction, and then find that Spirit has a different plan. For instance, we always talked about spending our first spring on the road at Lake Tahoe and Yosemite National Park – two beautiful places we had never been. We were in the Salt Lake City, UT, area getting ready to head to Lake Tahoe the next day. I woke up in the morning, turned to Tom and said, *Honey, I don't think we're supposed to go to Lake Tahoe and Yosemite now.*

Tom paused for a moment, then responded, *I think you're right. Tahoe and Yosemite don't seem right. Where do you think we're supposed to go?*

The Columbia River Gorge between Oregon and Washington. I'm not sure why, but that's where we're supposed to go, I responded with a knowing deep inside. So off we went. It became perfectly clear why we were called there after we arrived, and everything unfolded wonderfully so that we could connect with various people and plant seeds of the heart. That type of experience has been repeated often.

You might be wondering just how we've been making a difference. For one thing, we often stop by the side of the road to help people out, even in urban areas like Boston or Washington, DC. It's kind of funny when you stop to help folks, and they respond with comments like *Gee, you must not be from around here. Nobody stops to help here,* or *I'm so glad you stopped, but you know it could be dangerous to do that around here.*

A friend we stopped to visit in the DC area gave us a lecture about how we could get killed stopping to help someone along the road. I took a deep breath and told him this:

Well, I look at it this way. I can't control other people in this world and how they act. All I can do is choose how I want be. I want to live in a world where people will stop and help each other out. I want to live my life from a place of love and caring, not fear. And if that is how I meet my end, so be it. I'm not afraid of what comes after this life, and at least I will have done what I could to make this world a kinder place while I was here. I hoped I had planted a seed in his heart that would take root and grow.

Another time we stopped along an urban freeway to help a guy who had a beat up old car. We could tell by his colorful language that he wasn't too happy with it. Since we were in our RV, by the time we got stopped we were quite a ways down the road. Tom walked all the way back to the broken down vehicle to give the guy a hand. This crusty character was amazed that someone would care enough to stop. After Tom helped him get going again, he said, *You know I've breezed past hundreds of people broken down by the side of the road. Next time I think I'll stop to help.* Another seed planted.

Oftentimes we meet people who are going through one type of life crisis or another. We listen to their stories, let them know we care and give them hope. Sometimes we change our plans so we can stay and help them out doing practical things like taking care of their pets, watching over their place, cooking meals, making them laugh and just being there as extended family. We help them find the rainbows in the midst of their stormy days.

One of my gifts is helping people get more clarity about what they really want to do when they grow up through a workshop called "If the Shoe Fits." I conduct other workshops that teach people how to connect with their own Divine guidance. I also give seminars and speeches on turning dreams into reality that are designed to help people get in touch with what is in their own hearts. I love working with people who want to live more fulfilling lives – planting seeds and watering them with hope.

Tom does phenomenal scenic photography and loves to share the beauty of the Earth with others. His personal mission for his work is to bring the healing power of nature to others. His reverence for nature prompts him to help injured animals and birds, and he even catches flies and bees that have wandered indoors and releases them back outside. Whenever we go hiking, we take along a plastic bag to pick up trash. One day we were walking a beautiful beach in Florida, bending over to pick up trash and place it in our bags. As we got closer a couple who was picnicking on the beach called out, *Gee, you must be finding lots of great shells.*

We've been finding lots of stuff. Do you want to see what we got? we asked. When they looked in the bags they said, *Whoa, you got all that trash on the beach?*

Yes, we sure did. We just figure if we're out walking and enjoying the beach we can maybe leave it a little better than we found it...and it gives us great exercise, too.

The guy turned to the gal and said, *You know, we could do that when we walk, too. Let's take a bag along next time.* Another seed planted.

We've been on the road since January 1998 and have traveled 45 states and seven Canadian provinces so far. Spirit is expanding our mission now to include doing energetic and spiritual work to bring balance to Mother Earth. We've also been inspired by Spirit to spend several months in New Zealand doing planetary healing work. As we travel, we don't tell other people what to think or do or how to live their lives. We simply try to live our lives each day the best way we can and maybe inspire others to do the same.

To all those friends we haven't met yet, be sure to wave and say "Hi." We look forward to connecting with you. Just watch for us traveling along life's road, planting seeds of the heart.

Walk softly on this Earth…for this world is a gift from the Creator, given to you as a home for this sojourn into physical form. Love her, honor her, cherish her, for your destinies are entwined, your breath is one.

Walk softly on this Earth…being mindful of your thoughts and beliefs for they are the creational forces of the Universe. Speak only the words that will help create Heaven on Earth for all.

Walk softly on this Earth…knowing that you are remembering how to be Love in action. In every moment make your decisions by considering "What would Love do now?" for Love is who you truly are.

Walk softly on this Earth…taking time to help a neighbor or a stranger, for that stranger is simply a friend you haven't met yet. Dry a tear, help carry a burden, share from your abundance, and it will return to you many times over.

Walk softly on this Earth…with kindness, compassion, and tolerance toward those who choose a different path. Honor all others as fellow travelers on the roads of life. Look deeply in each other's eyes, and you will see yourself reflected. Take each other's hand and walk together into a future without fear.

Walk softly on this Earth…with joy in your heart, a smile on your face and gratitude from your lips, for your potential is unlimited and your blessings are infinite.

Walk softly on this Earth…and leave behind only footprints of Light.

MAKING LIFE MORE BEAUTIFUL - Tom Seliskar

Life is truly beautiful, and our short time here is a gift to be cherished and spent wisely. We need to recognize the beauty, not only of our own lives, but also of every single being on the planet. We can all make this life even more beautiful through many simple actions. Take time to notice people who need your help. When someone's vehicle is broken down on the side of the road, stop to offer a helping hand. If you see someone who needs help in any way, pitch in – open a door, carry a package, share a smile, hold a hand, wipe a tear. Being of service feels good!

And how about that bumblebee trapped behind a pane of glass? Do we squash it or do we set it free to go out and continue doing its service of pollinating beautiful flowers and trees? Or notice the banana slug, slowly making its way across a hiking trail. Offer it a leaf to crawl onto and then place it safely well off the trail. Yes, even these critters can use our help from time to time. After all, their lives add to the beauty of this world, too.

We can all make life even more beautiful. It doesn't have to be complicated. Just pick up that piece of trash instead of pretending not to see it and walking by. Bring a sack next time you stroll along a beautiful beach or walk a forest trail and pick up whatever doesn't belong there. That way the world will be even more beautiful for your having been there.

Life is truly beautiful. And there are so many simple little things each of us can do each day to make it even more so. How do you choose to add to the beauty of life?

For more information on Kay & Tom Seliskar and their Journey of the Heart, visit their website at www.appleseedenterprises.com .

Rain patters down on the skylight above my head. Its melody falls into my ears and soothes me deep inside. Through my window I see tiny droplets of water suspended from the tips of the leaves on our apple tree. This is a light rain, the kind that has evolved from a heavy fog into a heavier mist and now has actually developed a rhythm of its own, bringing a delicious morning shower through the forest. Far down below, the fog is receding slowly, rolling itself back across the saltwater vastness until it comes to a rest on the horizon as one great comfortable bank of softness.

This is our first wet season on Pender Island. How very green and alive it is. We're half way through November and most of the trees around the island are still covered in leaves, not yet moving into their autumn colours. The grass meanwhile is getting greener. From anywhere inland in Canada, where foliage withers and hibernates at this time of year, the role is reversed. Here, after a hot, dry summer, the forest is coming to life.

I can no longer imagine living anywhere else. I have fallen unabashedly in love with the Salish Sea and its vast embrace of life.

I am certainly not alone in my devotion however. The Pacific Northwest, between Seattle, Vancouver, and southern Vancouver Island, has over six million inhabitants. Here, on our little island, we rest within a 100-kilometre radius of six million people. And that number is growing rapidly. Even Pender, with its 2000 residents, is growing and many of the people here are nervous about that. Even I am nervous about the future population of the island and I'm one of the new people the rest of the residents are nervous about.

Why is the population of the Pacific Northwest growing so rapidly? I have no idea, unless it has something to do with its breathtaking beauty and moderate climate.

So perhaps I shouldn't be selling the virtues of this little paradise so strongly. Perhaps I should be deterring others from coming to our area, warning everybody about the biggest spiders in the country, the ever-present danger of earthquakes, and the ridiculously narrow, treacherous roads.

Meanwhile, we'll hold up against the advance of civilization from within the confines of our little forest – our refuge.

If I gaze out across the water now, I can see one of our neighbouring islands, one that happens to be home to our next contributor. A tireless campaigner for the preservation of the natural world around us, she is no stranger to residents of these islands. In fact, to the Salish Sea in its entirety, she is a true friend.

BRIONY PENN

Briony Penn is an environmentalist who divides her time between teaching, writing, hosting a TV show and public speaking. She is a tireless voice for environmental protection and has a wealth of knowledge about the world around us.

REFUGIA

Living on the edge of a continent on a small island has provided me with a rare clue for a small mission. When the glaciers covered every inch of Canada and flattened the place as if a 12-million-ton bulldozer had been let loose with an adolescent driver, one could say that things looked a bit hopeless for the future of life. However, nature is as bad at cleaning the slate as I am at washing the dishes; the scouring brush always misses a few places. A handful of islands and mountaintops missed the ice. Life in those microcosms clung on and when the ice retreated, the plants and animals (including humans) that had survived simply crept, swam, flew and lumbered back onto the continent to repopulate it. And the cycle started all over again.

Now that we are in the midst of the next minor ice age, caused by the rapidly-moving glacier of parking lots, suburbs, malls, clearcuts, monocultures, feed lots and strip mines, it is reasonable to assume that small refugia, like parks and backyard wilderness saved by the persistence of citizens (or the oversight of developers, forest companies and mining operators) will serve the same purpose. We can take comfort from the fact that these small patches of wildness can be of immeasurable value once the forces of mass destruction have melted, waned, been voted out, seen the light or otherwise desisted. I think of my small island as providing warm ecological raw material, and the conservation efforts of my fellow islanders like hot sunny days keeping the ice at bay. It gives new meaning to melting the ice at social gatherings and makes me laugh when faced with endless town hall meetings or hurling myself in front of bulldozers.

To have an ecological rationale for saving small patches of wildness, is what most of us need, since the problems with the environment are too big and too unfunny for any of us to grasp. We cannot personally hand out birth control pills to the entire world, we can hardly remember our own. Nor can we control the consuming appetites for stuff in a globalizing world, since we know ourselves that the discipline needed to catch the bus, not shop, recycle, stay put and cherish life, is shaky in all but the most holy. But saving small wild areas is within the grasp of anyone who likes to melt the ice with their neighbours and local politicians, especially if you approach it with the same spirit as one cultivates a love affair. And love affairs on small islands provide a good model for the ground rules of successful small missions; approach with passion but don't burn the ferries if you need to retreat.

For more information on Briony Penn's EnviroMental television program, see their website at www.thenewvi.com/programs/viPrg_EnviroMental.asp.

K. LAUREN DE BOER

K. Lauren de Boer is Editor of EarthLight Magazine.

EarthLight's mission and focus is to cultivate the awareness that Earth is a sacred community of life to be cherished, protected, and restored, not a commodity to be exploited.

SPIRITUAL ECOLOGY AND THE TULIP
Or, the Meta-Religious Autobiography of a Recovering Calvinist

I was thrown into early spiritual searching when my father, a Christian Reformed minister of 20 years, suddenly quit the church. I was a teenager at the time. I had grown up under the protective bubble of the Calvinist worldview, inculcated into a certain way of seeing. The sense of spiritual community with the church congregation I had experienced throughout my childhood quickly crumbled.

Growing up in that community might have given me some sense of certainty, but it had isolated me from certain truths. It had also isolated me, theologically at least, from the natural world. I had always loved being in nature as a child. So during the crisis that my father's departure from the ministry created in my life, I turned to the community found in the fields, forests, rivers, and prairies of the American Midwest. I didn't know it then, but I was seeking rites of initiation into a larger spiritual community.

No adult in my life at the time seemed to have the knowledge, interest, or sense of wonder I found in the natural world. Without a proper elder to guide me, it was a slow initiation, happening in fits and starts. But I was initiated nonetheless. Mother Earth was a haven and place of birthing for me. I crawled into the magnificent green robe of nature and emerged renewed, after many years, into a more refined spiritual awareness. My work and life has been dedicated, since then, to cultivating a sense of the Earth's sacred aspect, of attempting to reconnect others and myself to the reverence, wonder, and spiritual healing found in our relationship to the larger community of life.

Unpredictably, my father's break from the Calvinism of the Christian Reformed Church was a crisis that led me to a deeper sense of interconnectedness. It was ultimately a moment of grace that would define my life's work. To appreciate the significance of such a moment, it helps to have some understanding of the five basic assumptions of Calvinist theology. Summarized through the acronym TULIP, the theology goes something like this:

T—Total Depravity. We are shot through with sin. Our heart, emotions, mind, will, and body are all affected by it. This is the doctrine of original sin par excellence. It is also called Total Inability. Not only are we sinful, we are helpless. Not only is all of humankind fallen, but so is all of nature.

U—Unconditional Election. Some are elected into salvation, some are not. Some will experience glory, some are damned. It was determined from the beginning, and will be so for all time.

L—Limited Atonement. Christ died only for those who would rightly bear the name Christian.

I—Irresistible Grace. This actually has some allure through its appealing name. However, grace in this usage means that the Holy Spirit melts your resolve and makes you realize just how sinful you really are. Broken, you go willingly, desperately, to Christ in repentance.

P—Perseverance of the Saints. Once you are saved, you can't lose it, no matter what you do. You can drill in the Arctic for oil, wage war, abuse animals, and despoil the planet in a myriad of ways and you're still destined for glory.

To be entirely accurate, these five points of doctrine are a caricature, not a full exposition of John Calvin's theology. Put into their historical context, they were written later as a theological response to the challenges of 17th century Arminianism, a perspective articulated by Jacobus Arminius, who disagreed with the doctrine of unconditional election. However, the points are still used today as a quick handle for understanding Calvinism, and they are so severe, one has to wonder what historical circumstances would give rise to such an extreme, guilt-ridden theology. A partial explanation might be that Calvinism is theologically and temperamentally well suited to conditions of adversity and struggle. Thus, when it first emerged in the 16th century, Calvinism seems to have provided an alluring response to religious and political persecution of that time.

In my personal experience, the TULIP acronym permeates the Christian Reformed community with the potency of an unspoken, unquestioned family tradition.

REDEEMING THE TULIP, A BEAUTIFUL FLOWER

My complete spiritual rebirth might not have happened without a seminal experience at age 30. I was living in Toronto and reading up on my two passions at the time, ecology and literature. I was trying to piece together, through the writings of Barry Lopez, Annie Dillard, Loren Eiseley, and others, what felt like a powerful interplay of landscape and the human imagination. It was largely a secular endeavor. Spirituality was unarticulated and remote for me, although as I think back on it now, my reading was an attempt to find a certain meaning and depth to human existence.

I headed for Florida to study cultural anthropology, stopping for a week in North Carolina to do a workshop with Catholic priest and theologian, Matthew Fox. Here was a second moment of grace in my personal story. By the end of the week, I canceled my graduate studies with cultural materialist Marvin Harris at the University of Gainesville and was headed for California to study at Fr. Fox's Institute. I was coming full circle to a life of the spirit again. This time, my spiritual community was expanded to the whole of the Earth community. By the time I met Brian Swimme and experienced his course "Cosmos as Primary Revelation" at the Institute, it grew as big as the Universe. The sense that we live in a sacred story and come into the world as blessings, not depraved beings, resonated with my personal sense of spirit. I was able to bring my spiritual growth back into the human community, seeing the human as part of a sacred community on Earth to be treasured and cherished.

As a way of articulating what this orientation has meant to me, I offer the following reinvention of the Calvinist acronym TULIP as a kind of meta-religious testimonial. I do it in honor of Tulip as flower, a sacred, self-revelatory reality unto itself (not merely a symbol). I do it as well for my father, whose own unfolding life story gave me the gift of spiritual searching and a much wider sense of community.

Each point is based on aspects of the sacred Universe Story that move me. They show how the work of Thomas Berry and Brian Swimme plucked me from under the sway of an outmoded theology into the embrace of a functional cosmology. While only words, they reflect my journey into a joyful and profound feeling of purpose and meaning in my life.

T—Total Enamorment. (from en amour = to inflame with love). Also known as Complete Communion. Not only are we "in love" with the beauty of our Earth, but we are saturated, totally enfolded "within the love" of the Universe. Through the "amorization" of the Universe, we are blessings from our very birth. The process of "total amorization," that everything we see and experience has a "singular bias for transforming itself into love," progresses in complexity and depth into the essence of all spiritual activity. The affinity of being for being, present throughout time and space, is the psychic-spiritual dimension, beginning with the draw of two particles toward each other and culminating with Teilhard's supreme form of love when the Omega point coincides with the Christic. This is the ultimate point of transformation, where everything is flooded with divine love (quotes from Teilhard de Chardin).

U—Utter Delight. Also known as Continual Celebration. We are here as a species to be that aspect of planet Earth that is able to reflect on her own beauty and magnificence in complete delight and abandon. We are also the Earth reflecting on that phenomenon and thus able to consciously celebrate the wonder of this evolutionary emergence. We transmit this delight and celebrate through our transgenetic coding – through story, music, dance, and other artistic cultural memes.

L—Lasting Activation. Also known as Choice as Identity. What we choose, we become, and the Universe becomes. Far from helpless, we are agents in the Universe to such a degree that we are determining the very future and evolutionary trajectory of the planet itself. Our consciousness as a species is an emergent process in a Universe in process. Thus, we become an activating process through our very thought, emotion, will, heart, and bodies. This gives us a deep sense not only of the evolutionary legacy we enjoy, but of the gift we bring to the Earth Community—and to future generations.

I—Irresistible Grace. Also known as Amazing Differentiation. (Flip them and you get Amazing Grace and Irresistible Differentiation, which is ok too!) I find what Thomas

Berry calls cosmological moments of grace irresistible in the hope they carry. An example of such moments in evolutionary time is the crisis the early Earth experienced when the waste products of unicellular organisms were creating conditions toxic to life. That waste product was oxygen and one organism adapted, learning to use oxygen as food, a source of energy. Life not only survived, but learned to thrive and perpetuate the story.

Meister Eckhart wrote: *Grace is no stationary thing, it is ever becoming. It flies straight from the heart of the Divine, carrying the Holy Spirit on its back.* I see the Holy Spirit as the pervasive creativity of the cosmos. Grace transforms everything, using crisis as fuel. It gives us the miraculous emergence of life on Earth, photosynthesis, respiration, conscious self-awareness, and countless other transformative moments in the unfolding of the Universe. It works in the domain of liminality, the edge. Where the marginal moves to the Center, grace happens. Thus grace affirms our confidence in the future through centration of previously insignificant phenomena.

P—Perseverance of the Numinous. Also known as Undeniable Subjectivity. Everything has a numinous presence in the Universe, an inner sacred depth which is a unique and unrepeatable contribution to the unfolding Story. We are all bathed in glory and worth. There is no elite that has rights over other expressions of the Great Story. As humans, we do not have rights to exploit the other-than-human beyond our own basic needs for habitat, sustenance, and fulfillment. And we do not have rights to deny the same needs in other beings.

INTEGRAL MYTHOLOGY

My Calvinist background did give me something of value. Incongruous as it may seem with that theological backdrop, I carry within me the mythological image of Christ as a compassionate force in the Universe. For me, it is cosmogenesis personalized in the figure of Jesus. An example: I walked into a café one day for a latte. I purchased it, turned to leave, and was confronted by a homeless man who panhandled me. My immediate reaction was irritation because the forward motion of my day was disrupted. I brushed by with only a brusque acknowledgment of his presence.

Later, on the sidewalk, I was slowed to a stop by a feeling of regret. I wondered at my lack of compassion for a fellow human being and searched for an anchor to guide my behavior. Unbidden, the strongest mythological figure of my childhood emerged, followed by a question: *What would Jesus have done?* I don't know if Jesus would have given him a dollar. But I have a feeling he would have engaged his numinous presence as a unique expression of the Universe. He might have found some way of imparting compassion in a way that might have contributed to healing Hunger. Hunger is a great force of our time – hunger for connection, meaning, and belonging in a world addicted to consumerism. Addressing this force in each other is to help heal the brokenness caused by a dualistic worldview.

I have struggled for a way to name my evolving spiritual state. "Integral ecologist" is the closest I can come at this time. My practice is spiritual ecology, so perhaps "spiritual ecologist" describes it better. Spiritual ecology is a creative response to Earth's environmental crises. As a practice, it involves the human choice to cultivate an attitude of reverence and awe for the creative processes of nature. It is marked by attitudes of humility, simplicity, respect, and a sense of the sacredness of planet Earth and all life.

I resist a label for this orientation because Earth process is at the heart of my spiritual practice and idea of faith. My awareness is Gaian in the sense that I feel Earth is primary to everything we are and do. Human beings are a mode of the planet, the way in which the Earth is aware of itself, both in joyful celebration of its beauty and in pain for its destruction.

It will be a lifelong struggle to integrate the best mythology of my childhood with the emergent sacred Universe Story. Part of that struggle is about leaving behind the theological abstractions of TULIP, so that I might commune with tulips again.

For more information about EarthLight Magazine, view their website at www.earthlight.org .

What I seek now is a shortcut. I've been working on this project for quite a while and I'd like it to be done. Just like that – all the essays flowing together ridiculously smoothly, interjected with some happy banter from me, and there you have it...an irresistible creation that leaves its readers breathless with inspiration and anticipation. Then the next shortcut will be an editor, a publisher and an eager audience chomping at the bit to get their hands on what I/we have written.

Yes, please, bring on the shortcuts! I do love shortcuts. They bring such a great convenience along with them. *Hello*, they announce when I discover them, *I'll be your shortcut for today*. They kind of chuckle when they say that, tickling my senses chillingly. In fact, they usually look like a really bad idea at first impulse. But then they just keep grinning at me and I become seduced by their beauty. Just like a moth being drawn into a fatally bright light. *I can't help it. It's so beautiful.* Irresistible, these shortcuts are. None of this waiting for things to develop on their own. None of this waiting for the universe to unfold as it should. Better to take that good old shortcut.

Especially this time, because it's not just me. I've got all these other people involved in this project. They're waiting for me. They've done their part. And they expect me to follow through now and send their wonderful messages out into publication where they can inspire some potentially higher levels of consciousness in the world. I can't let them down – can't let them think Jeesh, this is taking him a long time.

I've always been kind of prone to shortcuts but I think I am improving all the time. I hope so, anyway. I used to be flat-out horrible about it.

When this happened, I was probably about 10 although I'm not sure. I sure remember the events surrounding the event though. I was on the plateau above our house. The Upper Flat, we called it. The Upper Flat was probably a hundred feet above our home, with a windy little forested path leading straight down to our house. We kids used to scramble up and down that path all the time. There was also a long, looping road that wound its way down to the farm but that was far too time-consuming for children with tiny attention spans. Anyway, on this particular day, I had a wheelbarrow full of tools from a project we had been working on. My role in this project was simply to roll the wheelbarrow all the way around the road and back down to the house. As chores on the farm went, this was actually a pretty simple one. Foolproof, one might say. Everyone else was down at the house while I was still on the Upper Flat and I overheard guests arrive. Guests arriving on the farm was a big deal to me. We didn't see people that often and my heart honestly did a somersault whenever anybody showed up. So here I was at the top of the shortcut with exciting visitors below. There would be laughter and stories and good times waiting for me down there and I was stuck pushing this stupid wheelbarrow all the way around the road. I'd be missing at least twenty minutes of this precious visiting time.

I made it about a third of the way down the shortcut, just long enough to get into plain vision of our very important guests, before the wheelbarrow and I took off. Having broken several laws of physics already, gravity took over and the wheelbarrow, its contents and I went tumbling head over wheels down the trail. With much clanging and banging and crashing, we tumbled, slid and came to a rest in the trees, with tools, wheels and a bruised ego strewn across the hillside.

There was laughing down there all right. And a story or two was certainly being told. Our visitors have likely forgotten that day. At least I hope they have. My family hasn't though. From time to time, if I seem to be riding a bit too high, they like to remind me about that shortcut. And a few others that happened along the way.

So here I am now. My wheelbarrow is full of essays. I'm making my way along a winding road and there are numerous little trails leading downhill, beckoning me seductively to a beautiful clearing just beyond my sight. A clearing in which a large bookcase rises up from the lush grass. The air in the clearing is full of birdsongs as kind people surround the bookshelf, gently drawing one book at a time from the shelves of the ornately designed tower of books. There on the centre shelf, right under the caption NEW BOOKS, is a book that keeps gathering more and more attention from the people in the clearing. If only I could make it there, I could read its title. Softly On This Earth.

Darn shortcuts.

CRAIG MILLER AND PAUL MOSS

Craig Miller and Paul Moss are co-founders of Cottonwood Foundation.

Cottonwood is an all-volunteer, charitable organization that awards grants to small grassroots organizations worldwide. They combine protecting the environment, promoting cultural diversity, empowering people to meet their basic needs, and relying on volunteers. The foundation dedicates over 90 percent of its expenditures for grants.

A JOURNEY

We wish we could share with you how it happened to us. But to be honest, we don't really know. Perhaps it is magic. We know that we saw a lot of urgent needs around us, and we wanted to find a way to make things better. It seemed critical to help our global community by addressing our declining environment and by encouraging people to empower themselves. Promoting cultural diversity and encouraging volunteerism were also important to us.

We weren't aware of any organizations that combined all of these areas, and so in 1992 we started Cottonwood Foundation to address these issues and as a way for us to give back. Cottonwood Foundation is an all-volunteer organization that provides small grants to grassroots organizations worldwide that are working for a sustainable future. In the past 10 years, through the combined energy of hundreds of people, Cottonwood Foundation has awarded 228 grants in support of projects in more than 45 countries. Cottonwood has evolved far beyond what we envisioned.

In 2002, we helped create a web site (www.creatingabetterworld.com) to encourage others to make the world a better place. We're hopeful that this web site can be a catalyst for self-exploration and change. Each individual change has a profound effect.

If we could help you to take action, it would be to encourage you to just take the first step. Your next steps will become clear to you if you listen to your heart and follow it. It's not necessarily the "big" things that make the most difference, but just that you make an effort. As you continue to walk forward, you will get to go on a

206 Softly On This Earth

meaningful journey that will change the world. Your special contributions are needed to create a better future for us all.

Look around you. Listen to your heart. Take the first step.

Cottonwood Foundation's home office is located in White Bear Lake, Minnesota. For more information, view their website at www.cottonwoodfdn.org .

More and more people are realizing that the way we consume and what we consume are ultimately shaping the future of our world. Nowhere, perhaps, is this more apparent than in our food choices, where vegetarianism and the demand for organic, non-genetically modified produce is increasing every year.

Yet this choice for a gentler diet — consumption without suffering — is far from being a new concept. Many well-known people from the past were devout vegetarians, likely standing up to far more staunch opposition than that which we face today. And yet their actions, their art and their words have been immortalized by us. So, for all those vegetarians out there who compassionately ignore those who criticize their food choices, I present some famous quotes by those who have helped shape our civilization.

I do feel that spiritual progress does demand at some stage that we should cease to kill our fellow creatures for the satisfaction of our bodily wants.
- Gandhi

Oh, my fellow men, do not defile your bodies with sinful foods. We have corn, we have apples bending down the branches with their weight, and grapes swelling on the vines. There are sweet-flavored herbs, and vegetables which can be cooked and softened over the fire, nor are you denied milk or thyme-scented honey. The earth affords a lavish supply of riches, of innocent foods, and offers you banquets that involve no bloodshed or slaughter: only beasts satisfy their hunger with flesh, and not even all of those, because horses, cattle, and sheep live on grass.
- Pythagoras

I have no doubt that it is a part of the destiny of the human race, in its gradual improvement, to leave off eating animals.
- Thoreau

I have learned from an early age to abjure the use of meat, and the time will come when men such as I will look upon the murder of animals as they now look upon the murder of men.
- Leonardo da Vinci

Non-violence leads to the highest ethics, which is the goal of all evolution. Until we stop harming all other living beings, we are still savages.
    - Thomas Edison

A human can be healthy without killing animals for food. Therefore, if he eats meat he participates in taking animal life merely for the sake of his appetite.
    - Tolstoy

NANCY CALLAN

Nancy Callan is past-President of EarthSave Canada and now edits the bi-monthly EarthSaver newsletter.

EarthSave Canada is a non-profit, educational organization promoting awareness of the health, environmental, and ethical consequences of our food choices. EarthSave Canada advocates the move towards a plant-based diet for better health, environmental sustainability, and compassion toward nonhuman animals.

Nancy lives in Vancouver and teaches ESL to adult refugees and immigrants. She is also the author of two ESL textbooks, Callan's Jigsaws and Callan's Canada Jigsaws.

CONSCIOUS CONSUMER CHOICES

When I first read the book *Your Money or Your Life*, I became aware of the concept of the monetary value of one hour of your life's energy. The concept is quite simple. In a nutshell, you calculate your income and subtract from it all the expenses that go into earning that income. For a given individual, that might include transportation, a professional wardrobe, even lunches at restaurants and contributions to colleagues' baby showers. Hiring someone to do work you could do yourself but don't have time for because of your job is also included in this calculation. The total is then divided by the number of hours you work to arrive at a realistic calculation of your real hourly wage. The authors, Dominguez and Robin, then encourage the reader to make note of all expenditures, without judgment, for a given time period. As you look back over your record of expenditures, you can then begin to determine, based on how much of your life's energy went into earning the money for that expenditure, whether it is in alignment with your values. That assessment will be completely individual, as values are a very personal thing. My own values centre around enhancing my health and treading lightly on the planet. The book helped to reinforce the path I am on now, to live and spend more consciously.

Living consciously in alignment with our values is a challenge for everyone in our over-processed, fast-paced, consumer-oriented world and I am no exception. I enjoy cooking a wholesome meal with love and attention. But when I'm on the go and get a craving, it can be hard to resist. Those popcorn-like puffed corn snacks can be quite a temptation for me. But when I satisfy a craving by purchasing a tasty snack and then look on the packaging and see that it contains not only little nutrition, but products detrimental to my health, I feel duped by my taste buds and clever marketing. The amount of money I spent on the overpriced, cleverly marketed snack feels wasted, and the gratification of my unhealthy addiction to salt, sugar or oil does not make up for that waste. It's money down the drain and it harms my health. Buying that snack does not fit in with my values.

But food choices are not just about my health or my pocketbook. Where you decide to eat on the food chain affects the health of the planet. For example, we know that water is becoming an increasingly precious resource on Earth. Some say the competition for water could become just as fierce as the current geopolitical struggle over oil. Less water is used to produce food for me for a year as a vegan than is used to produce food for me for a month on a meat-centred diet. Global warming, pollution, habitat destruction and species endangerment are only some of the other consequences linked to a meat-centred diet. Eating lower on the food chain is one of the most significant consumer choices I can make, enabling me to tread more lightly on the planet.

But what if I significantly reduce my meat consumption and eat organic meat where possible? That was my first step on the road to being a vegetarian. I simply cut down. I ate meat when I was out at restaurants or visiting relatives. I didn't buy it for eating at home. And that in itself was a big step. Being a gourmet cook was part of my self-concept. I had meat thermometers and liked to cook roasts to perfection. I knew exactly which herbs were best with which meats. I had lots of meat cookbooks. But while it might have been better for my health and lessened my impact on the environment, eating meat, whether organic or conventional, meant that animals would suffer and be killed. My consumer choices were still not in alignment with my values. Did I want a world where animals are treated as commodities, raised in inhumane conditions on factory farms, and killed in unnecessarily large numbers? No. I can't morally support a food production system that raises chickens in battery cages or removes veal calves from their mothers after birth and raises them in crates where they are unable to turn around. I can't support a system that delivers cows in overcrowded trucks hundreds of miles to slaughterhouses, where they often collapse from heat exhaustion and lack of water.

So, what if I were to hunt and kill, skin and cook the animal myself, I wondered, philosophically. Then, the animal could live a natural existence, out in the wilderness, until the moment I hunted it down. But unless I were starving and had no other food choices, I would not choose to kill an animal for my dinner. Why then, would I pay someone else to do this for me? It just didn't seem any less abhorrent if someone else did it and I didn't have to think about it. So, I stopped eating meat completely. Now I'm at the point where it's not appetizing for me to have flesh on my plate. That transition did not occur overnight, though. It was a slow process of learning other things to eat and ways of making traditional recipes with alternative ingredients.

We all have to draw the line somewhere when it comes to killing. Some killing is inevitable, inadvertent and unintended. We unknowingly kill insects merely by walking and breathing. Mechanical plows and harvesting machines take a huge toll on wildlife. Commercially grown rice is one of the crops responsible for the greatest number of deaths of higher animals, particularly amphibians. Should I avoid rice? Bananas? Coffee? The list goes on. The fact is that we live in a society based on the wasteful exploitation of the natural world. It is very challenging to live lives consistent with peaceful stewardship of the planet. But while I can't live a completely cruelty-free life, I can easily limit the amount of suffering and killing I inflict on the planet. I can choose to live a more compassionate, peaceful existence.

One of the most effective and direct ways to influence the world around me is through my consumer choices. These choices are not about restrictions, but about empowerment. The more I align my consumer choices with my values, the more aware I become of my own agency, within society and in my own life. In other words, this is the concept of *voting with your dollars*. This personal empowerment, furthermore, has far-reaching impact on my own sense of well-being and on those around me. But it is not about living up to puritanical standards and it's not about conforming to a label, such as *vegan*. I don't judge others who choose, for various reasons, to include some animal products in their diet. We all have our own path to walk in this life, and I don't deny that all food choices carry an impact. But through my work with EarthSave, I encourage others to consider their consumer choices and to make choices that enhance their health, reduce the toll on the environment, and lessen unnecessary animal suffering. In my opinion, they are choices that enhance our lives.

For more information about EarthSave Canada, visit their website at www.earthsave.bc.ca .

This project has been blessed by its contributors. They have consistently encouraged me and reminded me of the importance of what we're creating. I've had both the self-imposed pressure of living up to their expectations and the incredible gift of their support and wisdom. These are people who have had the courage to follow their hearts and I have found strength and nourishment not only from their essays but also from their phone calls, emails and letters. With encouragement and compassion, they have kept me going.

And none more so than my next contributor. He has delved deep into the workings of the human mind and heart. He has a wealth of experience and knowledge and his consistent support of Softly On This Earth has been both insightful and inspirational.

DR. STEPHEN E. LINN

Stephen E. Linn, Ph.D., leads a variety of seminars and workshops through Em*power*ing People, in Vancouver, BC. He has presented his ideas to numerous audiences in the United States and Canada. His seminars and workshops include Making Sense of Feeling, Getting Beyond You vs. Me, Why Relationships Succeed or Fail, The Real Rules in Relationships, and Em*power*ing Parents. He has written two books, *I Am What I Am*-Volume 1-Essays on Being Human and Volume 2-On Relationships.

Em*power*ing People offers seminars and workshops to help participants achieve effectiveness and satisfaction in their relationships and in their work worlds through increased awareness, esteem and interpersonal skills.

STRANGER IN A STRANGE LAND

From time to time, my mother would scornfully say to me, e*veryone's out of step but Johnny!* I imagine she would have called it chutzpah for me to even imagine that I might have something to say about life that could be of value to someone. I doubt that her judgment would have been any different had I been awarded a Nobel Prize.

My father was similarly critical. By age eight, I was sure I wanted to be an industrial designer. Around 1945, I designed an automobile windshield washer. It was primitive, given my young age, but also ahead of its time, since none existed. I showed it to him, hoping that he'd be impressed and would guide me in getting it patented, as was urged by patent attorneys' advertisements in magazines like Popular Science. Instead, he impatiently replied that if such a thing was possible, the automobile companies would already be making it, and that I should stop wasting my time on such useless undertakings. About a year later, the first cars with windshield washers came on the market. (I never challenged him on it – I was afraid to.) His response was also underwhelming when, at age 50, I earned my Ph.D. I don't think he even shook my hand. There certainly were no "wows," smiles, or slaps on my back.

For most of my life I succumbed to my parents' somber judgments; unable to understand why they were so critical, I concluded that I was flawed somehow. Although I put on a brave front, I was quaking and reserved behind it. For instance, I had several businesses in my late twenties and early thirties, including freelance design, a tutoring service and swim instruction. But I undertook them with trepidation. My hidden belief was that I wasn't very competent and was somehow "illegitimate," that I didn't really "belong," and hadn't a right to be doing what I was doing. As a result, I did little more than dabble in these businesses.

So, for a kid who saw himself as the plainest of the plain and the least significant of the insignificant, it's been quite a journey, one that grows more illuminating and exciting as time goes on. I've reached a point in my healing, growth, and experience at which I realize that my journey and the discoveries I've made along the way can provide meaningful insight and hope to others.

From as far back as I can remember, everything about relationships was a puzzle to me. I was a "stranger in a strange land." I tried to make sense of what was happening around me, struggled to distinguish true from false, but was confused by all the contradictory and misleading information. I tried to understand relationships: How were we supposed to be with each other? What did it mean to love? More recently, I wondered why people so often treated each other unkindly and destructively. My ongoing effort to answer such questions is a thread that runs through my life, both personally and professionally. At this point, I believe I've acquired a clear and accurate picture of how things are and how they've come to be this way, as well as how we can move beyond this perilous moment in our personal and cultural evolution, so as to genuinely arrive at the caring, co-operative, ethical and non-violent future for which so many of us yearn.

Some people might claim I was destined to arrive where I am, as though it was meant to be. Obviously, the possibility was there, but the bricks that can be used to create a path can also be used to block up a doorway. There were so many unexpected possibilities that came my way, so many unexpected turns as my path unfolded, that the destinations I arrived at were very often different from the ones I had set out for.

Three experiences that have profoundly affected my life exemplify this. They are my studies in *existential-phenomenology*, my training in and teaching of *Parent Effectiveness Training* (PET) and *Teacher Effectiveness Training* (TET), and my training in and practice of Organic Process Therapy (OPT), a unique form of *primal therapy*.

1. Existential-phenomenology was the orientation of the psychology department at Duquesne University, where I studied for my Ph.D. in clinical psychology. Until my studies there, I had very little knowledge and understanding of existential-phenomenology. I had decided to apply there primarily because the program seemed humanistic, in contrast to the cognitive-behavioural programs offered almost everywhere else. But I was completely mistaken. In fact, on one of my first days there, to my dismay, the chairman of the department declared that the existential-phenomenological orientation was definitely not humanistic psychology.

2. During my early years at Duquesne, in order to fend off poverty, I sought some sort of training that would enable me to earn extra money. Of the possibilities available, I chose the only one I could afford: Dr. Thomas Gordon's Effectiveness Training (PET and TET). I hadn't a clue as to how profoundly this would affect me, both personally and professionally.

3. My involvement with OPT is a similar story. In the autumn of 1976, I drove halfway across Pennsylvania to attend a conference not related to therapy. I happened to meet a woman there who was also a therapist. She waxed enthusiastically about the "great work" that the psychologist, Daniel Miller, was doing in primal therapy. I had previously been involved as a client in a different form of primal therapy for more than four years, unfortunately with negligible results. So when she told me about Dan's great work and urged me to come and meet him, I was extremely skeptical, to say the least.

    Nevertheless, just before Christmas, I drove some 250 miles to meet him. When we finally met, I experienced no "electricity." Moreover, I quickly realized that he and I had extremely different theoretical orientations. I certainly had no sense that *this is what I've been looking for.* Even so, I registered to attend the weekend OPT workshop that he was offering there three months later. That workshop changed my life. The experience was so immediately life-altering for me that I invited Dan to come to my Center to lead another OPT workshop. It, too, was a profound experience. So I enquired about and quickly registered for OPT training, which I subsequently practiced for 25 years.

The three of these together – my existential-phenomenological studies at Duquesne, the Effectiveness Training and OPT – have profoundly influenced my understanding of *what it means to be human*, as well as of how to *become* and *be* human. This has enabled me to grow more human, as well as to illuminate the path for others. Without my involvement in all three, I might never have become conscious enough to even be aware of this issue.

In each case, I reached for one thing and found something entirely different. I realize now that this has happened often in my life, that I've really stumbled blindly into those experiences that have most altered and enhanced my life. I see now that how they've affected my life was not only unforeseen, but unforeseeable.

I've discovered that life is a courageous and continuing adventure. It's a journey upon which we embark without ever being able to foresee where our efforts will lead us. Even so, we're each existentially responsible for determining and traveling along our own particular path. I've learned that John Lennon was right, life really is what happens while we're busy making other plans. But I've also learned that those "other plans" and efforts are not wasted; that they're just as important in determining where our paths will lead us.

So, where *has* my path led me? During more than 25 years as an existential-phenomenologically-oriented Organic Process psychotherapist, I've come to see that much of what we do with each other is violent, abusive, wounding and disempowering.

When I say violent, I mean more than just physically violent. In my view, any deceitful or coercive words or deeds are violent.

By this measure, not only are battery, rape and war violent, but so are spanking, lying (including "white lies," lies of omission and exaggeration) and cheating; so are blaming, shaming, "guilting," urging, demanding, criticizing, name-calling, ridiculing, bullying, threatening, punishing, daring someone, teasing, bad-mouthing and making fun of someone; so, too, are boasting, putting oneself down and playing the victim. Although it may not be immediately apparent, so is telling someone not to cry, worry or be afraid. Even if said in a compassionate voice, these statements urge the other person to stifle who he or she is. Nevertheless, society actually encourages many of these behaviours.

I now realize that being *adversarial* (characterized by competition, in which there are winners and losers) is ubiquitous on our planet and frequently praised. It's commonplace in such endeavours as advertising, sales, politics, jurisprudence, sports, education, finance and personal relationships. But we rarely realize that it leaves "winners" in fear of losing their status and "losers" ashamed and self-deprecating. So competition, too, is inherently violent, abusive, wounding and disempowering. Moreover, it encourages reciprocal and often clandestine violence, such as deception, cheating, coercion, the use of force against those less powerful, and disconnection from and diminished concern about others. Being adversarial ultimately destroys trust, distorts perception, and shifts everyone's focus from self-fulfillment to self-protection and self-aggrandizement.

Several years ago, I read *Influence: The Psychology of Persuasion*, by Robert B. Cialdini. I know we commonly view persuasion as perfectly normal. But after reading the book I began to realize that attempts to persuade are essentially efforts to manipulate (for example, "Do it for me?" "Pretty please?" "For a limited time only!" "Trust me!"). As such, no matter how subdued, they are also violent. (I'm sure this was not the message Cialdini intended.)

In my view, then, none of us has the right to try to persuade anyone. But we always do have the right and responsibility to honestly inform: to tell others what we want and don't want, like and don't like. We also have the right and responsibility, to ask for what we want, and to express how important it is to us, as well as to refuse what we don't want. What matters here is our intention; is it to inform or is it to manipulate?

From my OPT experience, as well as from many conversations with students, clients, colleagues, friends and acquaintances, I've come to the conclusion that most childhoods are full of violence, perpetrated not only by parents, but also by siblings, relatives, playmates, neighbours, teachers, and clergy. (for example, spanking, rewards and punishment; also, "Don't you ever talk back to me!" "No dessert until you've eaten your vegetables!" "You're grounded!" "What's wrong with you?" "What did I tell you?" "I'm ashamed of you." "Because I said so!" "How could you do that?" "Chill out!" "Hey, Fatso!")

The majority of wounds from such violence remain unhealed for almost all of us. OPT has taught me that the degree to which we fail to heal these wounds is the degree to which we will make violent attempts to achieve what we want. It's also the degree to which we will respond violently to the violence of others. In the process, we will have little understanding of why we're acting this way, or of the disturbance we are creating and perpetuating. Many argue that such behaviour is an intrinsic part of human nature, inherited from our animal past. I agree that it's inevitable that a species without language will be adversarial. But what's scarcely recognized is that language makes possible a radically different stance. Language gives us the ability and the means to richly articulate and enact care. It also enables us to be co-operative and caring when there's conflict: to genuinely seek mutually satisfying solutions together, and to not be fully satisfied until everyone is satisfied. I suggest, then, that it's language that makes it possible for us to live peacefully and co-operatively with one another. Nevertheless, in spite of what language avails us, it seems clear that much of our effort tends to be in the service of adversarial intentions that would be appropriate and inevitable only if we were still without language.

In other words, I'm asserting that our not-yet-fully-acknowledged woundedness, our "unfinished business," is what interferes with our carrying out the mandate and responsibility bestowed by language. This inevitably results in disturbed and disturbing relationships – personal, commercial and political. Until this is widely appreciated and acted upon, I see no hope for ending the violence that has characterized and plagued Homo sapiens for all these thousands of years.

I've also come to the conclusion that every act of violence is an "instead-of." An instead-of is what I am or am not doing or saying in order to avoid genuinely acknowledging, expressing and experiencing my distress and concern. For example, when you forget my birthday, I may smile at you and tell you that it's okay, instead of telling you that I was hurt. However, there are no free lunches; whatever doesn't get "lived-out," gets "acted-out." So I might subsequently act coldly towards you, or purposely forget your birthday to show you what it feels like.

Further, every "instead-of" is an addictive act. For example, rather than tell you that I was hurt by what you've said or done, I might badmouth you to someone else, drink some alcohol, or eat some "comfort food," in an effort to salve my wounds. But OPT has taught me that whatever I try to choke down inexorably continues to strive for expression. Consequently, every such effort to flee from frightening feeling and expression can seem to succeed only temporarily, at best. Thus, as the appearance of success wanes, I will be driven to continue engaging in "instead-ofs" with ever-increasing vigour and frequency.

Whenever I withhold my truth from you, I am positing you as an adversary. This all but precludes any possibility of resolution and connection, just when I need it most. Since I can only pretend to be who I'm not, I am also engaged in a fight against myself. This is a struggle I can never win. OPT has taught me that the degree to which I choose to choke down such expression is the degree to which I am opting for short-term gains (e.g., momentarily reduced anxiety or fear), but at the always greater price of long-term losses (e.g., a lonely, banal, haunted, addicted existence).

I've concluded that when we don't heal our wounds, we are condemned to repeat our history. To heal our wounds, there are three things we need to do:
  Get accurate information about living life
  Finish our "unfinished business"
  Learn and practice and use the dialoguing (interpersonal
  communication) skills.

I say that we need to get accurate information because I've discovered that much of the information by which we've been urged to navigate our lives is erroneous. Perhaps the most disturbing of these errors is the claim that we can choose how we feel. Virtually all the "gurus" claim this is so. According to them, for example, if I feel scared, all I have to do is "reframe" or think happy thoughts or simply smile (for example, "Cheer up! Things'll get better!" "Look at the bright side." "Just don't worry about it!"). Such ideas have often been espoused in popular movies and songs. Do you remember the song, "Don't Worry, Be Happy"? As preposterous as I know its prescription is, this song won a Grammy award for "Song of the Year" in 1989. Or, consider "Gray skies are going to clear up, put on a happy face," from the 1960 Broadway Musical, *Bye Bye Birdie.* Or "Smile though your heart is aching" (words by John Turner and Geoffrey Parsons with music by Charlie Chaplin).

Consider another example:
Just let a smile be your umbrella on a rainy day.
And, if your sweetie cries, just tell her
That a smile will always pay.
(from the 1948 movie, Give My Regards to Broadway)

Existential-phenomenology and OPT have both taught me that such attempts to escape distress are patently futile. We can't choose how we feel. If we really could, surely nearly all of us would already have chosen to be happy, which is not the case by any stretch of the imagination. I also suggest that we can't choose what we want, can't choose our attitudes, and can't choose to forgive or to trust, either. We can't, for very long, even choose what we think. These are all addictive acts, involving a fruitless and disturbing struggle against our selves. In the short run we might believe we've found relief, but in the long run we will, instead, be haunted by precisely what we're trying to evade.

I've come to see that how we feel is not merely a physiological or biological reaction; that, first and foremost, how we feel at any moment is our spontaneous "evaluation" of the success or failure of our efforts, and what that means to us. Fully embodying how we feel, then, vividly illuminates and thematizes for us what we're trying to achieve, whether and how well we're succeeding, and how important it is to us that we achieve it. Thus, how we feel is our "navigational instrument," our "compass," rather than something to squelch. If, for example, I want to pay my bills on time and expect to receive the money to do so in the mail, I might feel disappointed, frustrated, angry, and/or scared when I discover that the money hasn't arrived as I had hoped. (I suspect that we've all had this experience.) The more important paying my bills on time is to me, the more intensely distressed I will feel.

There is no "wrong" or "negative" or inappropriate feeling. And feeling distressed is not a sign that I am weak or inadequate. Furthermore, we are *always* feeling, always being affected. Sometimes we're *thematically* aware of it –focused on it – and sometimes we're not. Unless our bodies are already damaged in some way (through heart disease for example), we are fully capable of genuinely acknowledging, experiencing and expressing all that we feel.

Shortly after 9/11, New York City Mayor Rudolph Guiliani cried in public in the face of such great loss. He then stated, *I try very hard not to cry in public, but I just couldn't help it.* His statement is instructive. It illuminates that virtually all of us have been infected with the almost universal injunction to choke back and hide our pain.

Guiliani couldn't help it because, as I've said, how we feel "yearns" to be expressed. Whenever we try to choke it down, it continuously "strives" for expression. For me, one of the most significant lessons of OPT is that *the way out is through*. It's clear to me now that this spontaneous expression of feeling and desire is precisely what heals our wounds. It's also clear to me that this is what enables us to recognize our genuine intentions, our true worth, and our mutual connectedness. It seems incredibly ironic to me that, at the very moment when someone is most *whole*, as when Guiliani was crying, we typically say that he or she has *broken down*.

Guiliani's tears were a form of "real-talk" (from Dr. Leslie Farber, The Ways of the Will). When I engage in real-talk, I am "speaking my truth," I am dialoguing. I'm convinced that dialoguing is the basis for healing our wounds, and competent relating. I've discovered, for instance, that even though I may feel hurt and angry and disappointed when the other person does not treat me with respect, if I "finish" my end of the dialogue with this person. That is, if I tell that person that the way he or she treated me has hurt me – I will come away with my "ego" intact. I've also discovered that what holds me back from doing so is my fear of being negatively judged and consequently of being harmed or abandoned if I acknowledge how I feel, for example, if I admit that I feel hurt or ashamed or afraid of looking foolish.

I've also found that a feeling we've choked down because we were afraid or ashamed to express it, doesn't simply disappear. We literally choke it down. We clamp our jaws shut, control our breathing and tighten muscles throughout our bodies, trying to keep from feeling our pain. But, there are no "free lunches"; doing so significantly and negatively affects our postures, our voices, our understanding and attitudes, our possibilities.

I've learned that the key to healing our wounds is the completion of choked-back emotional expression. Rather than trying to stop ourselves from feeling down, hurt, sad, guilty, scared, or angry, or trying to start forgiving or trusting, or wanting what we don't want, we need to acknowledge ourselves fully – our distresses as well as our pleasures. Rather than choke down what discomforts us, we need to fully "embrace" it. Rather than try to "get somewhere else," as we're commonly urged to do, we need to embody "where we are." The degree to which we don't do so is the degree to which we misconstrue our reality, fail to recognize genuine care, and either fearfully draw back from reaching out for what we really want or continue to reach out for what we don't want.

It will always be frightening to begin to express whatever we've choked down, since we did so from a deep fear of harm or abandonment. For this reason, such wounds can generally be healed only in the presence of genuine care. This calls for a competent "guide" and "witness," someone who truly acknowledges who the other person is, who genuinely trusts that person's "body-self" to know what it must do next to heal. This could be a capable friend, but it's more likely to be a competent therapist.

Nearly 70 years on this Earth have taught me that we have become who we are through our relationships with others, and that our relationships are the most significant undertakings in our lives. I suggest that the most important of these are the parent-child and mating relationships. A major responsibility of parents is to help their children to be empowered, or, as one poster described it, to give them roots and wings. We are empowered when we know what we want, feel free to reach out passionately for it, and are able to take pleasure in achieving it or to embrace our distress when we fail to do so.

In general, relationships are "nourishing" only to the degree that the participants are empowered and empowering. Therefore, a major responsibility of mates is to help each other to be empowered. Relationships, in general, are "nourishing" only to the degree that the participants are empowered and empowering. To be empowered and empowering requires competence. The most important skills for attaining this competence are the dialoguing skills. In spite of this significance, extremely few mates or parents have ever received any training in these skills. The fact that few of us have had competent role models further exacerbates this problem.

Moreover, what has been and is still commonly considered to be good parenting actually systematically disempowers children. Many parents are likely to see their children as wild animals needing to be civilized and trained, as malleable objects in need of shaping, as vulnerable beings who need to be toughened, and/or as empty containers needing to be filled. Consequently, they interact with their children through strategies, such as "time-outs," derogatory statements (for example, "children should be seen and not heard," "spare the rod, spoil the child"), and punishment.

I've come to realize that the predominant parenting strategy is control, and that it is innately violent. It is carried out primarily by means of threats of harm or abandonment, such as scaring, shaming and guilting the child, should the parent's demands not be obeyed. This is so common that few people would bat an eyelash if they witnessed this behaviour. Most people consider it normal for a parent to exclaim, *If you don't come right now, I'm not going to take you*! or *Don't you ever talk back to your mother!* or *I don't want to have to tell you one more time, young man!* or *Stop acting like a child!*

Such parenting strategies are so common that we tend to see them as normal and necessary, and to view alternative approaches as unrealistic, even immoral. We even rationalize such wounding as valuable 'character builders.' What we miss is the damage done to the child.

Parents, then, are likely to focus on controlling their children's behavior, rather than on connecting with them. This renders the children hypersensitive to their parents' and others' judgments of them. As a result, our planet is full of people fearfully concerned about what others will think of them. They are more concerned about manipulating those judgments than about how their actions will benefit or harm themselves and others.

These parents fail to understand that from the very beginning their children are separate and unique individuals who need to be recognized as equal in value to adults. Children are persons. They have a right to be protected and to be respected for who they are and are becoming. They have a right to reach for what they want, and need to be supported and guided in their pursuits. They need to be genuinely listened to, acknowledged and validated whether they're distressed or pleased, and they have a right to protest when displeased with how they're being treated. Ironically, when parents fail to understand this, their children are likely to become or do precisely what the parents were striving to prevent.

In the '60s, comedian Dick Gregory used to cry out, *Wake up America!* He was trying to get people to realize that something was terribly wrong in the US with regard to civil rights and the Vietnam War. Today, I'm compelled to cry out, *Wake up World!* with regard to how badly we treat our children under the designation of "good parenting."

Back then, we began to realize that peace, love and co-operation were essential to being human. But I've come to realize that we were wrong in thinking that we could achieve and maintain them using the same adversarial strategies used by the people we were protesting against. It seems clear to me that the degree to which people fail to heal their wounds is the degree to which they will continue to be less-than-competent mates, parents and change agents. It's also the degree to which they will fail to achieve what I believe is made possible and mandated by language.

Given the many gains that were achieved in the '60s, such as the end of the Vietnam War and the Equal Rights Amendment and other civil rights, it seemed like the genie was out of the bottle and could not be put back in. I sadly realize now that this was an inappropriate metaphor. It now seems to me that a more accurate metaphor is that of a pendulum which, over the centuries, has swung back and forth, from a concern for human rights, connection and care to that of hierarchy, right and wrong, good and evil, punishment and vengeance.

The following table briefly contrasts these two perspectives:

Human	Homo sapiens
Inclusive	Exclusive
Others as potential friends; kin	Others as potential injurers, rivals
Openness, empathy, trust	Opponents, co-conspirators.
Cooperation, love, peace	Competition, winners and losers
Negotiate differences in search of mutually satisfying solutions	Negotiate to win; pre-emptive attack for self- protection
Ethical: the ends don't justify the means	Self-centered; the ends justify the means
Choose short-term losses in order to achieve long-term gains	Opt for short-term gains, even though it may lead to long-term losses
Don't polarize; see many hues, many shades	Polarize; see blacks and whites
many shades	right and wrong, good and evil, good and bad
Clarify	Mystify
Respect for self and others, no matter how disturbed	Critical of self and/or others

or disturbing they may seem
to be

Attempt to do no harm   Fail to see the harm
                                         they may do

      No matter how life came about, and as painful as it sometimes is, I've come to see it as an extraordinary and precious "gift." I've also come to recognize that everyone and everything is in it together, that we are all kin, all related, all interrelated. This is what I understood, so many years ago, when the Beatles intoned, "I am the walrus (I'm advised that this is not at all what the Beatles meant, but this is what it meant to me then and it does so even more today.)

      I believe that we owe it to ourselves, each another, and life itself, to make every effort to heal and to keep from further harming ourselves, each other and our planet. But at this point, given our widespread failure to grasp this, and the immense destructive power we now possess, I'm very scared that unless we take heed, we'll be compelled and I would say doomed to continue on the destructive path we're on; that we're in imminent peril of losing all that we have. I believe it's worth every effort to prevent that from happening. I believe that we can still make real the non adversarial future that language avails us and that many of us ardently hope for.

      In my view, we can succeed only if we set about to heal our wounds, and learn to take the very best care of ourselves, each other and the world that sustains life. I'm convinced that OPT and congruent practices are the means to genuinely heal our wounds and that, together with the dialoguing skills, they can provide us with the means to become competent humans and enable us to live peaceful, loving, ethical and co-operative lives. This is what keeps me striving to share this view and to help people learn how to heal and become competent mates, parents and friends.

Empowering People is located in Vancouver, BC, Canada. You can learn a great deal more about Empowering People and its mission by visiting its website at www.empoweringpeople.net .

SOFT FOOTSTEPS

We've reached the end of this collection of thoughts. In doing so, we've opened up the possibility of an infinite number of further dialogues. Infinite because a collective conscience is unfolding around us. Like the ripples spreading outward from a stone cast onto water, our efforts are reaching farther and farther. This expansion, this growth, began way before *Softly On This Earth* was born in my heart. Softly is but another ripple on the water.

Since the first keystroke of this project began bringing these wonderful souls together, I have dialogued with many people and feel a great sense of hope for our future. This collection of essays could go on much farther and perhaps it will but, for now, this feels right. This feels like a good place to pause, collect all these messages together, and send them out into the world.

All of the contributors to *Softly On This Earth* bring hope to the lives of others, and have been doing so, consistently and consciously, for a long time. I invite you to read beyond the essays they have written for this book. Each essay has been followed by a website and there you will find a great deal more information about each individual and about the work they are doing. This is important. When we read something, hear something or see something that really moves us, we are well advised to pursue it further, to find the inspiration behind the emotion. It is then that we begin to grow. And it is then that we might just start spreading a little hope of our own.

If we have cast a little hope into the lives of our readers, we have succeeded. If we have shaken the perception of the way things have always been done, wonderful. If we have inspired thoughts, words and actions that overcome cruelty and promote loving attention, we have succeeded magnificently.

Please do not fear the activist inside of you. Please do not fear your own beating heart that wants to burst forth from your chest and sing out your most glorious songs. Sing freely and loudly and when you are told to be silent, when you are told *Don't quit your day job*, sing even louder and truer. Because your own true song is beautiful and the world needs to hear it. Now, maybe more than ever before, the world needs to hear your song. Ignore the skeptics. They have their reasons for needing control but that doesn't involve you. Their issues are none of your business. Unless they are. Then you can love them, accept them and just keep right on singing. And, if it's not something that makes your heart sing, I urge you strongly, *quit your day job*. Walk away from complacence. Walk away from fear and into the arms of courage. You'll find you're in good company.

If your efforts, your best intentions, seem insignificant to you, think again. It's time we North Americans shed our delusions of insignificance and became accountable for our actions. Because we are, by far, the heaviest consumers on Earth. Every action and every word does have consequences that affect the collective conscience. Whether or not it is clear to you, not only are you significant, you are an integral part of what's going on around you. You are having an effect on somebody and something right now. It's time we started to live that way.

With that in mind, I offer this list of simple steps everyone can take right now and every day to walk more softly on this Earth.

Soft Foot Steps

Consume less. We North Americans are consuming the rest of the world's resources. We must stop that. The first step is to stop consuming what we don't need. Ask yourself *Will I be happy about this purchase one week from now?*

Reuse everything. Share what you no longer want with others, give it away or find other uses for it. Millions of tons of someone else's treasure wind up in North American landfills every year.

Educate yourself. Make friends with your library. Take out books on health, social ethics and the environment. Study the websites listed after every essay in this book and follow the links to other related sites. Go to workshops and lectures.

Be skeptical. Every time you think you've learned something, get at least two more views on it and then let your heart create your own truth. Even then, be skeptical and continue to learn. There are a lot of false prophets out there, some of whom are well intentioned and some not.

Stop ingesting toxins. You are the food you eat. Sugar, caffeine, nicotine, animal fats, alcohol and pesticides are not food. They are toxins. Stop consuming them now and live a healthier, happier, longer life. Incidentally, it takes the human body at least 90 days to truly adjust to a new way of eating so be patient with yourself. It takes a while to start feeling the difference.

Move from an animal-based diet to a plant-based diet. It takes ten times as much land to grow beef as it does to grow food crops. We North Americans could feed all of the world's hungry many times over by reducing our beef consumption by just 10 percent. Plus we would ease the suffering of animals in slaughterhouses everywhere and enhance our own health dramatically. Get informed about this. Our hospitals are full of people whose diets are built upon animal products. Obesity is a product of animal products. A well-balanced vegan diet cannot produce obesity. There are so many reasons to stop eating meat.

Make friends with a recycling centre. There are recycling centres almost everywhere and their efforts can greatly reduce our footprint on this Earth. Paper, cardboard, glass, metal, plastic, batteries – they can all be made into something else. This reduces our landfills, reduces our need to pillage the world's natural resources and provides employment for people. If there isn't a recycling centre near you, start one.

Compost. There is no need to let your waste food scraps (and garbage bags) wind up in a landfill. All vegetable matter can be composted easily. It provides nourishment for new life. If you don't have a garden, give your compost to someone who does. Better yet, plant your own garden.

Buy locally. Promote your local economy and save the world's environment from the enormous burden of transportation by cargo planes, trains, trucks and ships. Your local producers will thank you and the Earth will thank you. It's as easy as checking the labels or asking the produce clerk.

Spend time in nature every day. Allow yourself the grace and silence of the natural world. Let the wind caress your face and breathe deeply. Resting, or exercising, in the embrace of a forest provides us with essential energy for life.

Be gentle with yourself and others. We live in a world that seems to be growing more hectic and careless all the time. It's time to change that. Make eye contact with everybody, make eye contact with deer and robins, make eye contact with cows, make eye contact with homeless people, make eye contact with God – whatever you perceive that to be. And then reach inside your heart and smile at them. All of them. Eye contact followed by your radiant, loving smile.

Slow down. There are no ordinary moments in life. Every moment is potentially beautiful and deserves your attention. And you deserve its beauty. For every moment lived to its greatest potential, another moment of potential greatness will present itself. Unless you rush right by it.

Let go of needing a Meaning of Life. There is no meaning of life. Life is an opportunity to create meaning. So stop beating yourself up trying to figure it all out. You create the world you want to live in. You have free will. You do get to make this all up as you go along. Unless you give that freedom away, which almost everyone does every minute of every day. We can create up to about 90 percent of what happens to us. And even with the 10 percent of crap that will still blindside us, we can choose how we react to it.

Forgive. Forgive the actions of others. Forgive yourself. Forgive life for not being what you expected. Through forgiveness, we find acceptance and then we really start to live. Through forgiveness, we create ourselves anew. Through forgiveness, we leave easier footsteps for others to follow.

Now, I request of all of you, don't let it stop here. You, too, are a messenger. All of your words and all of your actions are vastly more powerful than you know. Please make your words count. Please make your actions count. Embrace the world; embrace the wonderful souls all around you. This is a beautiful life we have and it deserves our attention and our care. It yearns for our soft footsteps.

I invite you to delve deeply into the information contained within the web sites listed after every essay in this book. There is a wealth of research, hard work and incredible inspiration contained within each site.

I also strongly recommend reading some or all of the following books. The words of these authors have helped transform many lives, including mine.

The Food Revolution, *How your diet can help save your life and the world* – John Robbins (Conari Press)

The Official Earth Day Guide to Planet Repair – Denis Hayes (Island Press)

Stormy Weather, *101 solutions to global climate change* – Guy Dauncey & Patrick Mazza (New Society Publishers)

Navigating the Tides of Change – David La Chapelle (New Society Publishers)

Vegan, *The new ethics of eating* – Erik Marcus (McBooks Press)

Radical Acts of Love, *How compassion is transforming our world* – Susan Skog (Hazelden)

Friendship With God, *An uncommon dialogue* – Neale Donald Walsch (Putnam)

One Makes The Difference, *Inspiring actions that change our world* – Julia Butterfly Hill (Harper San Francisco)

It could be argued that, in the past, a lack of information was the cause of a widespread lack of awareness. That is no longer the case. Information is everywhere. It needs only to be tapped into. I believe that, today, apathy is the cause of a widespread lack of awareness. And apathy, my friends, is a choice, not an affliction.

Apathy is not in the vocabulary of the authors listed above. Nor is it for the 32 contributors to this book. And apathy is no longer tolerable in my life. My greatest hope is that through our work, and choices of your own, apathy is also no longer tolerable to you. Because apathy is a choice – a bit of a cop-out really – and one with dire consequences for precious souls everywhere. But a little courage erases apathy and then we evolve into a different society altogether. And all together.

It's as simple as taking your own mug to the coffee shop in the morning instead of using their paper cups. You won't be hurting their business by bringing your own mug – they're not making any money off of those take-out cups.

It's as simple as picking up a few items for the food bank the next time you're shopping for groceries. Many markets make it easy for you and have food bank drops right in the store. If they don't, ask them to.

It's as simple as starting a car pool. Or better yet, leaving your car at home. Or, even better, selling your car and ridding the roads of one more driver.

It's as simple as buying a sandwich for the homeless person on the corner instead of avoiding eye contact.

You don't have enough money to be charitable? Well, perhaps you could consider saving a little money by avoiding alcohol, cigarettes, restaurant meals and all-terrain vehicles in favour of a more simple, satisfying and caring life. You might even find you have more money left over than you know what to do with.

Those are the simple things. Beyond them, you can get courageous. Start a web site to inspire others. Write an article for the newspaper or a magazine you like. They thrive on articles from their readers. If yours is well written, there's a good chance you'll get published. Write a whole book. Conduct an interview with a person who inspires you and contact a local radio or TV station to air the interview.

Send emails and phone calls to your elected representatives to express both your concerns and your compliments. Don't be afraid to do this – it's the only way these people will know what we want. There are a lot of really powerful lobby groups who are giving them a lot of money to make choices for them. How will they know any other opinions if we don't contact them? It is, in fact, your civic duty to express yourself. And if your opinions feel very worthy and important to you, run for office yourself. We need you.

Even more important than contacting your elected officials is contacting corporations. Tell them what you think of their products and the way they treat the world they're living off. Express your concerns and your comments loudly and clearly. Vote with your wallet. Don't buy what you don't believe in and let them know about it. Buy what you do believe in and let the others know about it. Vote with your wallet. It has immense power. And the most powerful choice is not to use your wallet at all. We can cripple even the biggest corporations if we all just stay out of our wallets.

We have choices to make. There's no reason to run from them. Leaping into choices can be great fun and very rewarding. And the more courageous choosing you do, the easier it becomes. So, smile at the skeptics and walk on by, down your own beautiful path, leaving only soft footprints behind you.

I wish you well on your path and I thank you for joining me on mine. Live well.

Namaste

Ethan Smith
Pender Island, BC, Canada
Summer 2004

ISBN 1-41204127-9